Politics and Society
in Southeast Asia

Politics and Society in Southeast Asia

PETER A. POOLE

McFarland & Company, Inc., Publishers

Jefferson, North Carolina, and London

LIBRARY OF CONGRESS CATALOGUING-IN-PUBLICATION DATA

Poole, Peter A.
Politics and society in Southeast Asia / Peter A. Poole.
p.   cm.
Includes bibliographical references and index.

ISBN 978-0-7864-4545-5
softcover : 50# alkaline paper ∞

1. Southeast Asia — Politics and government — 1945–
2. Southeast Asia — Economic conditions— 21st century.
3. Southeast Asia — Economic policy.   I. Title.
JQ750.A58P68   2009   320.959 — dc22   2009033421

British Library cataloguing data are available

Cover image ©2009 Shutterstock

Manufactured in the United States of America

*McFarland & Company, Inc., Publishers
Box 611, Jefferson, North Carolina 28640
www.mcfarlandpub.com*

TABLE OF CONTENTS

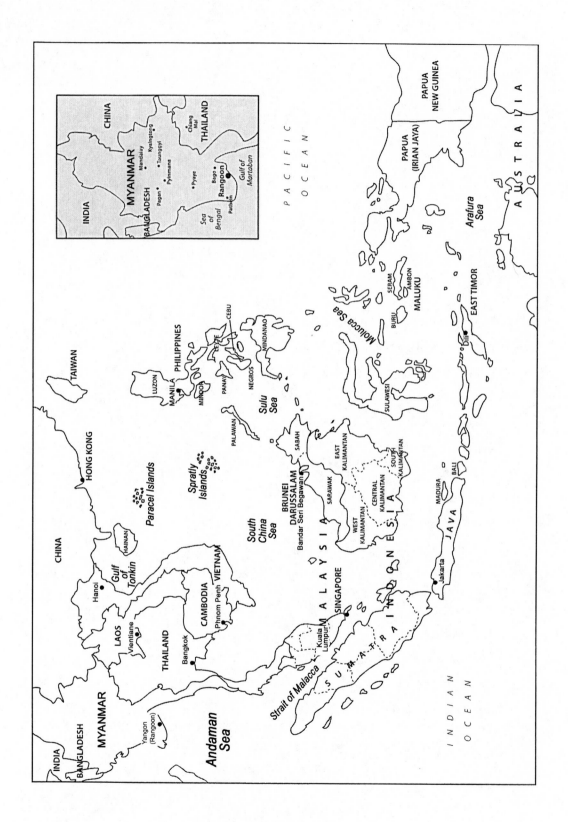

Indonesia and surrounding countries.

PREFACE

This book is designed for the use of college students and others who may be interested in how the people of Southeast Asia are trying to develop their political, economic and social systems. After the 1997 Asian financial crisis caused severe hardship in Southeast Asia, many of the governments tightened their regulation of banks and other financial institutions and adopted conservative fiscal policies. They also formed closer trade and investment ties with their Asian neighbors to make themselves less vulnerable to fluctuations in Western markets.

But by early 2009, it was clear that the Asian countries had failed to "decouple" their economies from the West. Forecasts of economic growth in Southeast Asia for 2009 were drastically reduced, but a modest recovery was forecast for 2010.. Unemployment was on the rise, and many manufacturing firms were forced into bankruptcy. However, it still seemed possible that developing Asian countries might not suffer as much as they did during the last crisis in 1997 because of the reforms they had instituted since then. They may even have some lessons to teach the rest of the world about how we should manage our political and economic affairs.

The political systems of Southeast Asian countries cover a broad spectrum, from military dictatorship and absolute monarchy to democratic and "semi-democratic" states. Singapore and Malaysia are also much wealthier than the others. While the similarities among these ten countries (such as the need to cope with ethnic and religious diversity) may be less obvious, they may help to explain why these are among the more successful developing countries in the world. To facilitate comparisons, the chapters follow the same outline. The index is also designed to encourage comparisons of political, economic, social, and historical concepts.

I was drawn to the field of Asian studies initially by scholars like Bernard Fall, one of the most insightful writers on Indochina. He and his wife Dorothy spent several months in Cambodia while I was serving in the U.S. embassy there in the early sixties. His energy and enthusiasm were contagious. The last time I saw him was in 1965 when I was preparing to do research in Thailand for my dissertation. "Get out in the field!" he said, almost propelling me out the door. "That's the only way to find out what's happening." Tragically, he died shortly after that when he stepped on a grenade in Vietnam.

Since then, a great many people have helped me learn what's happening in this rapidly changing part of the world, and often I gained the most from those who disagreed with my interpretation. Special thanks are owed to those who took the time to read one or more of these chapters and make suggestions: Maureen Aung-Thwin, MacAlister

1

Brown, Pek Koon Heng, William Liddle, Walter Pullar, Frederick Shaffer, David I. Steinberg, Lewis Stern, and Joseph Zasloff.

Others who provided insights about the recent (post-independence) history of these ten countries include: Ambassador Prok and MR Pimsai Amranand, Alex Barrasso, Frederick Z. Brown, Ambassador Chan Heng Chee, Nayan Chanda, David Chandler, Kavi Chongkittavong, Ambassador John Gunther Dean, Stanley Karnow, Amy Kazmin, Kenneth Landon, Milton Osborne, Ambassador Anand Panyarachun, Harry Slifer, and Rex and Caroline Stevenson.

Of course, the responsibility for errors that remain in the text is mine alone.

I am grateful to the reference librarians at Dartmouth College, George Mason University, and American University for their kind assistance.

This book is dedicated to my wife, Rosemary Poole, whose love and support and sound judgment have kept me going.

INTRODUCTION

Most of Southeast Asia's 600 million people live in what the World Bank defines as "middle-income" countries.[1] Their economic goal, as articulated by their political leaders, is to join the ranks of the world's advanced countries as soon as possible. But this will be extremely difficult, not least because of the wide range of political systems in the region, as noted in Table I.1. Making the leap from "middle-income" to "advanced" status will be much harder than rising from low- to middle-income status, the World Bank warned. It will require improved governance, a major upgrade of the countries' educational and financial systems, and the training or recruitment of large numbers of highly qualified managers.[2]

Table I.1
Founding Members of ASEAN Compared with Newer Members

	2008 Population (in millions)	2005 Longevity (in years)	2005 GDP per Capita (U.S. $)	Political System*
Founders of ASEAN				
Singapore	4.6	78.7	27,490	Semi-Democratic
Malaysia	27.0	73.2	4,960	Semi-Democratic
Thailand	67.0	70.0	2,750	Semi-Democratic
Philippines	90.5	70.4	1,300	Democratic
Indonesia	245.0	66.8	1,280	Democratic
New ASEAN Members				
Brunei	0.4	76.4	24,100	Absolute Monarch
Vietnam	85.2	70.5	620	Communist
Cambodia	15.0	56.2	380	Semi-Democratic
Laos	6.5	54.7	440	Communist
Myanmar	57.6	60.2	200	Military Junta
Total:	599.6			

Source: World Bank and national governments.

*The reasons for describing the political systems of four of these countries as "semi-democratic" are explained in the text.

As Table I.1 suggests, the five founding members of the Association of Southeast Asian Nations (ASEAN) have much in common. They are economically more advanced than the newer members of ASEAN, and their political institutions are stronger and more democratic than those of the five newer members. In the past, relations between neighboring states in Southeast Asia were often marked by hostility, and there was little basis for economic cooperation because they competed as exporters of similar products to the same markets. They are now part of a more closely integrated Asian economic community, which may at some point evolve into a political union to compete with the European Union and North America, as discussed in chapter 11. To maximize their influence in such a union, the founding members of ASEAN will have to use every means at their disposal to help the newer members raise their political and economic standards.

The semi-democratic form of government in Malaysia and Singapore is a system of one-party rule in which elections are held at regular intervals and opposition parties are allowed to participate within fairly tight constraints, but have no real possibility of winning.[3] The media are largely government-controlled, but information circulates more or less freely on the Internet. Leaders of countries such as China, Thailand, and Cambodia have expressed interest in this system because it enables a dominant party to hold power indefinitely while satisfying some popular demands for democratic participation.[4]

A variation of this system exists in Cambodia, and some form of semi-democratic government could conceivably emerge in one or more of the other new countries in ASEAN (i.e., Vietnam, Laos, Myanmar, or Brunei).[5] But existing regimes are usually afraid that any political concessions can quickly get out of control, as happened when the Burmese military junta organized elections in 1990 and pro-democracy forces defeated the junta's party. In Thailand, where people are used to having more political freedom, moving back to a semi-democratic form of government after the 2006 military coup was seen by many as a serious obstacle to their goal of joining the ranks of advanced countries.[6]

The chapters that follow discuss in detail how each of the Southeast Asian countries is grappling with these goals. But first we need to summarize Southeast Asia's early post-colonial experience in which the development of ASEAN played a central role.

Association of Southeast Asian Nations (ASEAN)

The foreign ministers of Thailand, Singapore, Malaysia, Indonesia, and the Philippines took the lead in organizing ASEAN in 1967.[7] Thailand, which alone had never been colonized, played a key role in setting the agenda for ASEAN under the leadership of Foreign Minister Thanat Khoman, who naturally made sure that Thailand's interests were addressed.

At the time ASEAN was formed, the member states were all extremely weak and threatened by insurgent forces within their borders. Economic growth depended on commodity exports and was either slow or stagnant. Poverty was common and helped breed political conflict. The leaders agreed that national survival was their chief concern, so they made peace with each other, strengthened their state institutions, and sought new ways to promote economic growth. ASEAN's five members all had close ties with the West, but they did not form a military alliance. Their aim was to "create an 'entente cordiale' or informal coalition of like-minded states that would cooperate to minimize Great Power interference in their affairs and maximize their leverage vis-à-vis these powers by speaking with one voice."[8]

The ASEAN states' primary goal was thus to end a situation in which their weakness and instability made them prime targets for cold war rivalry between China, the United States, and the USSR. But they first demonstrated their ability to influence events in their region by taking a united stand against Vietnam's 1978 invasion and subsequent occupation of Cambodia.[9] Vietnam was supported by Moscow until the Soviet Union collapsed in the late 1980s–early 1990s. China was intermittently at war with Vietnam in the same period, and China supported the Khmer Rouge forces that resisted Vietnam's occupation of Cambodia. The United States supported non-communist Cambodian guerrilla forces that opposed Vietnam's occupation of Cambodia and along with many other governments provided aid to Cambodian refugees camped on the Thai border. ASEAN members did not see eye-to-eye on the challenge posed by Vietnam's invasion of Cambodia. The Thai saw Vietnam as a threat to their northeast region, so they helped the Chinese government provide aid to Pol Pot's forces. The Indonesian and Malaysian governments favored a conciliatory policy toward Vietnam, because they were suspicious of China's long-term goals in Southeast Asia.[10]

Nevertheless, resisting Vietnam's hold on Cambodia became the first major test of ASEAN's ability to influence events in their region, and throughout the 1980s, ASEAN prevented the pro–Vietnamese regime in Cambodia from occupying Cambodia's UN seat. When the global cold war began to wind down in the late 1980s, Indonesia took the lead among ASEAN states in helping to broker the Paris Peace Conference that ended the Cambodian phase of the Indochina war.[11]

Even more than ASEAN's diplomatic success, its members' spectacular economic growth contributed to their organization's prestige. Beginning in the late 1960s, they opened their countries to foreign capital and technology, developed new industries, and began to export manufactured goods. They also enlisted the entrepreneurial skills of their Chinese minorities, who had often been regarded with deep distrust. By the early 1990s, the ASEAN states were viewed as "miracle economies" that seemed destined to replicate the success of South Korea and Taiwan.[12]

ASEAN enlarged itself during the 1990s by taking in Vietnam, Laos, Myanmar, and Cambodia. Critics warned that the growing diversity of the organization might make achieving agreement on important issues impossible. But the mixture of comparatively rich and poor countries created new opportunities for intra-regional trade and investment where few had existed before, and the ASEAN Free Trade Area (AFTA) was created to stimulate trade and investment in the region. A growing middle class of consumers contributed to the region's growth by purchasing locally assembled cars, trucks, and appliances. Yet when Southeast Asia was rocked by the 1997 financial crisis, ASEAN leaders failed to adopt common measures to cope with it, and the prestige of the organization suffered a blow.

Thailand, Malaysia, Indonesia, and the Philippines were hardest hit by the crisis, and these countries entered a period of political turbulence. In Thailand, Thaksin Shinawatra, a billionaire businessman who had entered politics in the mid–1990s, gained massive popular support especially among the poor rural Thais, but he was overthrown by the Thai military in 2006. In Malaysia, Prime Minister Mahathir's rule ended after he fought with his reform-minded deputy, Anwar Ibrahim. In Indonesia, President Suharto's thirty-two year reign was ended by the financial crisis, but democratic reforms were instituted by his successors. And in the Philippines, a "People Power" revolution brought President Gloria Arroyo Macapagal to power.

The ten country chapters that follow are arranged in such a way as to facilitate comparisons between countries. Each chapter is divided into five sections: People and Cultures; Historical Background; Political System; Economic Development; and Foreign Relations.

People and Cultures

Because of the ethnic complexity of the Southeast Asian countries, each chapter begins by asking the following kinds of questions: Which ethnic group is politically dominant? Are some ethnic groups given special rights and privileges because they are considered "indigenous"? How have ethnic politics been influenced by policies of the previous colonial regime? What is the social status of women? How much political influence do women have? How do living standards vary in urban and rural areas?

Table I.2 shows that Islam is the main religion in the island states while Buddhism predominates on the mainland. How much religious freedom is allowed in these countries? What role does religion play as a political force?

Table I.2
Religious Affiliations in Southeast Asian Countries, by Percent

	Muslim	Buddhist	Christian
Island Countries			
Malaysia	60	19.2	9.1
Indonesia	88	1	8
Philippines	5	1	94
Singapore	20	50	10
Brunei	67	10	10
Mainland Countries			
Thailand	4	88	8
Laos	1	65	1.3
Myanmar	4	87	4.5
Cambodia	3	95	2
Vietnam	0.7	50	10

Source: Europa World Year Book 2008, based on figures compiled by the national governments.

Historical Background

As Table I.2 suggests, many Southeast Asian countries trace their history back to the great Hindu-Buddhist empires that arose in the first millennium, including the Angkorian empire on the mainland and Srivijaya, which was based on Sumatra. In Thailand, Myanmar, Laos, and Cambodia, the earlier form of Buddhism (Mahayana) was gradually replaced by Theravada Buddhism, which was brought to Southeast Asia by missionaries from Sri Lanka beginning around the year 500. Buddhists in Vietnam (the only country in the region that was colonized by China), mainly practice a more Sinicized form of Buddhism.

Before the arrival of the first European colonists in the early 1500s, Islam was introduced in the island countries of Southeast Asia by Arab traders and missionaries, and its influence gradually spread from west to east, making Islam the dominant religion in Indonesia, Malaysia, Brunei, and the southern Philippines. This hastened the collapse of Hindu-Buddhist empires in the islands, but Islam did not entirely displace the older belief systems. Instead, Islam added another strand of religious belief. In the sixteenth century, Catholic missionaries began to introduce Christianity in the Philippines, the eastern islands of Indonesia, and Vietnam. Protestant missionaries followed in the nineteenth and twentieth centuries. In Indonesia, Vietnam, and Singapore, Christians have more influence today than their numbers would suggest.

The issues covered in the historical section also include the role of colonial powers in shaping and modernizing the state institutions of these countries. How did the colonial powers prepare their colonies (or fail to prepare them) for independence? Which policies of the colonial powers have been adopted, changed, or abandoned by the independent governments that succeeded them? What role does a monarchy (or the leftover symbols of a monarchy) play in legitimizing these governments?

Political Systems

How have the political and social systems of the Southeast Asian countries evolved since independence? Have they adopted some form of multi-party democracy? If one political party has dominated the government, how much freedom has it allowed other parties? What political role do the armed forces play in these countries? Does political power change hands as a result of elections or by some other means, such as military coups? How effective are these governments at protecting the rights of their citizens and the rule of law? How effective are they at managing their economies? In countries with one-party rule, how is the monopoly of power maintained? In countries with multi-party systems of government, are the governing coalitions of parties strong enough to carry out effective policies? Are the people free to form nongovernmental organizations that can set their own political or social agendas? How much control does the state exercise over the media?

Economic Development

As Table I.3 shows, the financial crisis that struck Southeast Asia in 1997 was a watershed event. It revealed a pattern of weaknesses that existed in most Southeast Asian countries. This included a system of "crony capitalism" in which government leaders provided contracts and subsidies to government-linked corporations in return for their political support. The managers of these corporations often lacked the competence to keep their companies going without government subsidies. Financial institutions tended to be corrupt and held high percentages of non-performing loans, as Table I.3 shows. Thailand, Malaysia, Indonesia and the Philippines all had negative growth in 1998. The other ASEAN states were also hit by the crisis, but only indirectly because of their economic dependence on the worst-affected countries.

Table I.3
Impact of the 1997 Financial Crisis (Percentages Are for 1998)

	Non-performing loans*	GDP growth (%)	Inflation (%)
Indonesia	48.6	-15	75
Thailand	45.0	-8	8
Malaysia	10.6	-6	5
Philippines	10.4	-0.2	8
Singapore	N/A	1	2
Vietnam	N/A	5.8	10
Laos	N/A	4.0	142
Cambodia	N/A	1.0	12.6
Brunei	N/A	1.0	0
Myanmar	N/A	5.7	36.9

Source: World Bank, *East Asia Update*, November 2005, Washington, D.C., p. 59.
*As of December 1998.

Yet by 2005 economic reforms had been put in place, and growth in most of the Southeast Asian countries had recovered to an average level of 5.5 percent a year, as shown in Table I.4.

Table I.4
Economic Growth (by Percent GDP) of Southeast Asian States, 2005–10

	2005	2006	2007	2008	2009	2010
Mainland States						
Thailand	4.5	5.1	4.9	2.6	-4.4	1.4
Vietnam	8.4	8.2	4.9	6.2	1.6	2
Cambodia	6	10.8	10.2	5	3	2.2
Laos	7	8.3	7.5	7.5	3	2.2
Myanmar	5.2	3.9	0.9	0.9	0.3	1.2
Island States						
Malaysia	5.3	5.9	6.3	4.6	-3	1.1
Singapore	5.3	8.2	7.8	1.1	-8.8	0.9
Indonesia	5.6	5.5	6.3	6.1	-1.4	0.5
Brunei	0.4	5	0.5	2	2	1
Philippines	5.1	5.4	7.2	4.6	-1.9	1.4

Sources: International Monetary Fund and Economist Intelligence Unit, April 2008. Figures for 2009 and 2010 are EIU forecasts.

The country chapters that follow analyze the causes and the political consequences of the 1997 financial crisis in more detail. They also examine the new economic development strategies that the ASEAN states have adopted because of intense competition with China for export markets and foreign direct investment. Are export industries still the driving force behind economic growth in these countries? Or is personal consumption by a growing middle class becoming a more important factor? What role does the service sector (including tourism, financial services, and call centers) play? To what degree are the Southeast Asian countries becoming integrated into an Asian economic community?

Foreign Relations

Southeast Asian diplomats often say that ASEAN is the "cornerstone" of their countries' foreign relations. What exactly do they mean by this? And is it true of both the older ASEAN states and the newer ones? Generally, the most difficult problems the ASEAN countries face are with their immediate neighbors, so an obvious question is whether they have been able to improve relations. How effective are the ASEAN states in dealing with important transnational issues that affect their region, such as organized crime and terrorism, and trafficking in arms, drugs, and persons? How well are they coping with regional environmental problems? Why is membership in the World Trade Organization so important to these countries, and how does it affect their trade policies and relations with other states? What role does religion play in the foreign policy of the predominately Muslim nations (Indonesia, Malaysia, and Brunei)? How important is the Non-aligned Movement to these and other Southeast Asian countries? What does each Southeast Asian country hope to achieve through its relations with the United States and China?

The concluding chapter looks at the role Southeast Asia has begun to play in an increasingly integrated Asian region. The countries of Asia are becoming closely linked economically, but they remain very cautious about political integration. This raises some interesting and important questions about the future of Southeast Asia which sees itself as dependant on good relations with Japan, China, India, Australia and the United States, which has traditionally maintained the balance of power in the Asia-Pacific region.

– 1 –

THAILAND

Democracy Challenged

As the map in Figure 1.1 shows, Thailand occupies a central and potentially dominant position on the Southeast Asian mainland.

The 2006 military coup, Thailand's first since 1991, was unexpected because Thailand has generally been ahead of its neighbors in creating democratic institutions. Only a few days before the coup, analysts in Bangkok were saying they believed an election would be held before the end of 2006 and Prime Minister Thaksin Shinawatra would win a solid vote of confidence because of his strong support among rural voters. Very few people knew that King Bhumibol's closest advisors had decided Thaksin must be removed because he was building a support network in the army and police and polarizing the country.[1]

On September 19, 2006, while Thaksin was attending the UN General Assembly in New York, the Thai military overthrew his government, suspended the constitution, and promised to write a new one in time to hold elections by late 2007. At first, the coup was supported by many people in Bangkok, where Thaksin's autocratic style had made him highly unpopular. But when the interim government (composed of senior bureaucrats) seemed unable to manage the economy effectively, they began to lose the support of Thailand's political elite, a class that includes politicians, journalists, academics, business leaders, and heads of nongovernmental organizations.[2]

A new constitution which was drafted under the coup group's direction was approved in a 2007 referendum because most of the Thai people probably believed it was the only way to end the political crisis and return to civilian government. But Thai and foreign analysts feared the new constitution would weaken democratic institutions, restore the army's political influence, and discourage foreign investors by imposing new nationalistic limits on their holdings. Analysts argued that what was needed to achieve increased economic growth was a strong, democratically elected government with a clear mandate to make tough political decisions.[3] The government that was formed after the December 2007 election was a coalition of six pro–Thaksin parties that were wary of provoking another military coup. A year later, that coalition was replaced by a rival group of parties led by Prime Minister Abhisit Vejjajiva and the Democrat Party.

Abhisit was undoubtedly sincere in wanting to restore political stability to Thailand and revive the economy, which was hard hit by the 2009 global recession. But the party

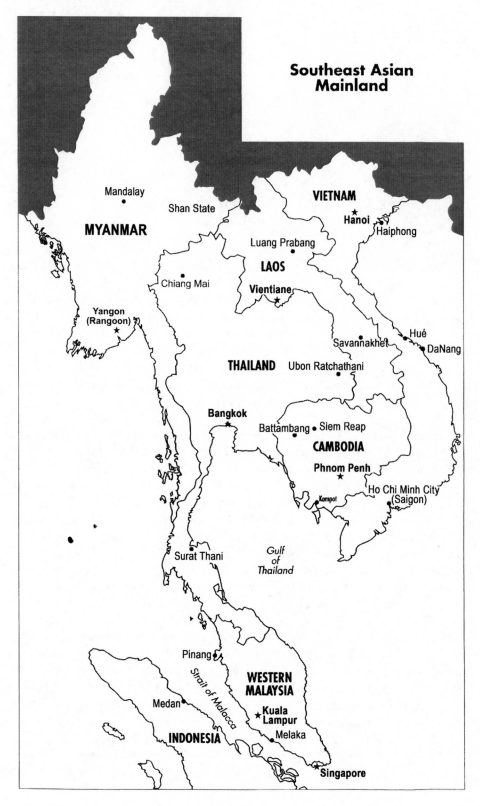

Figure 1.1.

composed of Thaksin's supporters was the strongest party in parliament as of 2009, and it could regain power if it managed to win back some of the smaller parties that defected to Abhisit's coalition in December 2008. Abhisit had the support of Thailand's revered King Bhumibol as well as the military and civilian bureaucracy. But the king was old and in poor health, and the military had lost prestige through their 2006 coup and their poor management of the government during 2007.

People and Cultures

Thailand is a middle-income country with a population of 67 million people and a tradition of openness to foreign ideas. Two-thirds of the people live in rural areas, but most of the modern economy is centered in Bangkok. Ninety-five percent of the people are Buddhists, and the Chinese are the largest minority group, as indicated in Table 1.1. While relations between ethnic groups have generally been good, a Muslim separatist movement flared up in the south in 2004 and has become a serious problem.

Thailand is divided into four main regions: Central, Northeastern, Northern, and Southern. Each region has its own dialect of the Thai language, and each has one or more ethnic minority groups that play an important role in Thailand's relations with neighboring states. In the 2001 and 2005 elections, Thaksin's support was strong in all four regions except the South, where support for the Democrat party was concentrated.[4]

Central Region

About 22 million people live either in Bangkok or on the central plain that is drained by the Chao Phraya River. They speak the Thai dialect which is taught in schools and used in government. Bangkok dominates the political, economic, and cultural life of the nation, creating a sharp urban-rural divide in Thai society. Until the 1960s, higher education was only available in Bangkok, but many schools and universities have since sprung up in the provinces. Even so, Bangkok is still where ambitious young people go to begin their careers. It is where half the gross national product is created and most of the government's budget for infrastructure projects is spent.

"OVERSEAS CHINESE" MINORITY

People whose families came from southern China over the last 200 years are heavily concentrated in Bangkok. But they also play a major role in the economic life of provincial towns and cities throughout Thailand. During the first half of the twentieth century, the Thai government tried to limit their economic influence and force them to abandon their culture. But in the 1960s, Thai leaders realized they needed the support of Chinese businessmen to achieve their economic goals. Since then, many middle and upper class Thai and Chinese families have been linked by marriage, thus combining their political and economic influence. Since the 1980s, people of Chinese descent have reached the highest political offices.[5]

Northeastern Region

The 22.5 million Northeastern Thai (known as Isan) speak a dialect that is closely akin to the language spoken by the Lao people on the eastern side of the Mekong River,

Table 1.1
Thailand: Demographic Overview

Population (2008 estimate): 67 million (66% rural)

Ethnic Groups (2008): Tai 75%, Chinese 15%, Lao, Malay, Khmer, Vietnamese, Karen, and hill tribes small percentages

Undocumented Aliens (2007 estimate): 1 million (mostly Burmese)

Religious Affiliations (2008): Buddhist 95%, Muslim 4 to 5%, Christian, Hindu, and animist small percentages

Literacy (2007): females 93.9%, males 97.1%

Income per Capita (2008): U.S. $2,750 ($8, 266 purchasing power parity)

UN Human Development Index Ranking (2003): 73 (out of 177)

Government Expenditure on Education (2007): 19% of budget

College and University Graduates (1999): 3.3 million

Life Expectancy (2006): females 75 years, males 68 years

Infant Mortality Rate (2006): 19.5 per 1,000 live births

HIV/AIDs (2003): 1.5% of persons aged 15 to 49

Personal Computers (2004): 3,716,000

Internet Users (2004): 6,872,000

Passenger Cars (2004): 2.3 million

Vans and Pickup Trucks (2004): 3.3 million

Sources: Royal Thai Embassy, Washington, D.C.; *Europa World Year Book*; Economist Intelligence Unit; U.S. Department of State, "Background Notes: Thailand," October 2007.

but the Central Thai and Northeastern Thai dialects are mutually intelligible. The arid northeastern plain has long been the least developed region in the country. With a third of the Thai population and land area, it produces only about an eighth of the gross national product, and per capita income is by far the lowest in the country. The reasons for this include drought, lack of investment, and the migration of many farm workers to Bangkok and other cities.[6] Thaksin gained strong political support from Northeastern voters in the 2001 and 2005 elections, and 63 percent of the Northeasterners who voted in the 2007 referendum opposed the new constitution, indicating that support for Thaksin remained high in the region.[7]

During the cold war, Thai leaders in Bangkok tended to view the Isan as backward and politically unreliable, with strong leanings toward communism. In the 1960s, there were also about 75,000 Vietnamese living in Thailand, many of them in the Northeast, and a somewhat larger number of Cambodians. Some Thai officials were concerned about the subversive potential of these people, but there was little evidence that they were pro-communist. Most came to Thailand as political refugees or to find jobs.[8]

Northern Region

The 12.3 million Northern Thai are proud of their region's past greatness when it was the center of a large empire. Chiang Mai, the leading city in the region, is the second most important city in Thailand. (As a native of Chiang Mai, Thaksin had strong support in the North.) Karen and other Burmese refugees and migrants make up a large percentage of the roughly one million illegal workers in Thailand. In addition, about 120,000 Karens have lived for years in refugee camps in Northern Thailand. The question of how to deal with migrants and refugees from Myanmar is a major issue in Thai-

Myanmar relations and was a source of conflict between Prime Minister Thaksin and the military.

TRIBAL GROUPS

Hill tribes in Northern Thailand, including the Hmong and Mein, numbered about 800,000 in 2006. Most of these people lack Thai citizenship, and many do not have legal title to their traditional lands and hunting grounds. They are the least assimilated minorities in Thailand and are sometimes abused by Thai officials. Government and private development projects often encroach on their traditional territory. However, they have made some progress in protecting their rights, often with the aid of Thai nongovernmental organizations.

Southern Thailand

MUSLIM SEPARATIST MOVEMENT

Around half of the 8.7 million people in Southern Thailand are Muslims, including about 2 million who speak Malay as their first language. In 2004, a Muslim separatist movement, which had been dormant for many years, flared up in the south, probably as a result of radical religious teachings in the private Muslim schools in the area. The Thai government imposed martial law, executed a heavy-handed security crackdown in Muslim schools, and authorized the police to use lethal force against suspected terrorists. Instead of suppressing the uprising, however, these tactics provoked more violent clashes in which 792 people were killed during 2007, bringing the total number of deaths from four years of insurgency to 2,776, according to a Prince of Songkhla University research group.[9]

After the anti–Thaksin coup, the army's first Muslim commander, General Sonthi, announced a more conciliatory policy toward the separatists, and King Bhumibol made it clear that he wanted to avert a religious conflict between Muslims and Buddhists. But more than 300 schools in southern Thailand were closed indefinitely after attacks by Muslim insurgents, and several arson attacks against schools in Northern Thailand raised fears that the southern violence might be spreading northward. In July 2007, General Sonthi conceded that the insurgency had intensified, and Thai analysts said the army had failed to implement General Sonthi's conciliatory approach.[10]

Status of Women

Thai women have traditionally enjoyed much higher social and economic status than women in China and India. A major reason for this was that until very recently the Southeast Asian mainland was underpopulated, and human labor was highly valued. Parents usually passed on equal shares of their property to their sons and daughters.[11]

By the late twentieth century, the number of Thais enrolled in secondary and higher education had increased dramatically, with male and female students enrolled in almost equal numbers. Women are now well represented on university faculties, and women students outnumber men in many university programs. Women are also well represented in the upper levels of the bureaucracy and corporations, but very few women are active in politics.

The Middle Class

Urbanization and rapid economic growth have led to the rise of a middle class composed of businessmen, academics, government bureaucrats and other professionals. They comprise approximately 10 percent of the population and are heavily concentrated in Bangkok, but they play an active role in the life of provincial towns and cities as well.[12]

Members of the middle class tend to be well informed about political and social issues, and many have traveled or studied abroad. As discussed in a later section on Thai civil society, middle class Thais have developed a wide range of nongovernmental organizations that work to further social and political causes such as rural development, women's rights, and environmentalism. Thus, the middle class has played a major role in the growth of Thai democracy. Because they are concentrated in Bangkok, they probably have more influence than their numbers warrant, while the great majority of Thais who live in rural areas have little or no political influence.[13]

Religion

Buddhism

Although Thai culture emphasizes hierarchy, Buddhism is one aspect of their culture that most of the Thai people experience in the same way regardless of their social class or the region where they live. Because Buddhism encourages nonviolence and humility, it has been emphasized by King Bhumibol as a means of easing relations between Buddhists and Muslims in Southern Thailand. However, Buddhism has also been used at times by right-wing politicians to try to impose the idea that peasants and workers should meekly accept their social status and not try to better themselves.

In the early 1960s, when Buddhists were engaging in political activism in Vietnam, Prime Minister Sarit Thanarat gave the highly conservative Department of Religious Affairs responsibility for controlling the Thai Buddhist clergy. But reform-minded Buddhist monks, such as Buddhadasa Bhikku and Phra Phimonthan, attracted a large following in Sarit's time by preaching that the individual could pursue enlightenment without necessarily following the teachings of the Buddhist hierarchy or the state.[14]

Historical Background

Thailand is the only Southeast Asian country that has never been colonized by western powers, but some Thai leaders have been remarkably successful at borrowing foreign ideas to strengthen their state. King Mongkut, who reigned from 1851 to 1868, transformed the monarch's role from that of a Hindu god-king engaged in mainly ceremonial functions to the more human and Buddhistic role of a statesman involved in running the government.[15] His son, King Chulalongkorn, reigned from 1868 to 1910 and reorganized the Siamese bureaucracy along western lines, making it an instrument for modernizing the country. The Thai people's willingness to open their country to foreigners was reflected in the fact that a million Chinese immigrants were absorbed during the reigns of King Mongkut and King Chulalongkorn.

In 1932, the Thai military seized power in the first of many coups, and the Thai army, allied with civilian bureaucrats, became the dominant force in Thai politics for the next sixty years.[16] In 1946, King Bhumibol Adulyadej ascended the throne, and he reinvented the king's role as a constitutional monarch who legitimized military-bureaucratic rule.[17] During his long reign, King Bhumibol has presided over the gradual emergence of democratic institutions while keeping political conflict from leading to civil war (see Table 1.2). The king worked closely with Sarit Thanarat, who was prime minister from 1957 to 1963, because their interests in economic development and political stability coincided.[18]

Table 1.2
Events in Thai History

1351	First great Siamese empire founded at Ayudhya.
1781	Founding of the present (Chakri) dynasty in Bangkok.
1851–68	King Mongkut adopts role of a Buddhist statesman.
1868–1910	King Chulalongkorn continues Mongkut's reform agenda.
1932	Bloodless coup begins long period of military rule.
1938–44	Phibun Songkram allies Thailand with Japan.
1944–47	Civilian government resumes ties with the West.
1946	King Bhumibol Adulyadej ascends throne.
1958–63	General Sarit Thanarat launches rapid economic growth.
1973–76	Student uprising and brief democratic interlude.
1976–80	Gen. Kriangsak's coup installs right-wing government.
1980–88	Gen. Prem Tinsulanond heads semi-democratic government.
1988–91	P.M. Chatichai Choonhavan supports peace with Vietnam.
1991–93	Coup crisis is resolved by king and Anand Panyarachun.
1993–2001	Chuan Leekpai alternates in power with conservatives.
1997	Major financial crisis; democratic constitution adopted.
2001	Election of wealthy populist Thaksin Shinawatra as P.M.
2004	Muslim secessionist struggle begins in Southern Thailand.
2005	Second election victory of Thaksin. Thai economy falters.
2006	Yearlong political crisis leads to anti–Thaksin coup.
2007	New military-dictated constitution approved in referendum, and pro–Thaksin civilian coalition government formed after December 2007 election.
2008	Abhisit Vejjajiva becomes prime minister after a vote of Parliament.

In 1973, when student demonstrators took to the streets of Bangkok to demand reform, King Bhumibol intervened to stop the military from firing on them. A brief period of democratic government followed, and the ruling elite expanded to include political party leaders and Sino-Thai businessmen. But the king supported a military coup in 1976 when Thais were worried that communist victories in Indochina would spread to Thailand.[19] During the 1980s, General Prem Tinsulanond led a government composed mainly of elected politicians, although he himself did not compete for a seat in parliament. He suppressed a number of coup attempts by junior officers and presided over a period of rapid economic growth based on mainly Japanese investment in Thai export industries. After leaving office, Prem remained an influential political figure behind the scenes, serving as head of the Privy Council and as one of King Bhumibol's closest advisors.[20]

1991 Coup

When the cold war ended, Prime Minister Chatichai Choonhavan planned to normalize relations with the communist governments in Indochina. For this reason and because he also challenged the army's political and economic interests, the military overthrew him. Anand Panyarachun, a highly respected diplomat, was chosen to head an interim government. Anand was close to the king, and he instituted economic reforms that were popular with Bangkok business leaders. But when the army chief of staff tried to take over the prime ministership, protestors filled the streets of Bangkok, and at least fifty civilians were killed in clashes with the military. King Bhumibol intervened and told the army chief to step down. He then appointed Anand to head another interim government and organize elections.[21]

During the 1990s, Chuan Leekpai, the mild-mannered leader of the Democrat party, was twice elected to lead coalition governments that opposed military intervention in politics. The army, under reformist leaders, pledged to stay out of politics. Between Chuan's two administrations, a conservative coalition of mainly provincial politicians held power from 1995 to 1997, when they were overwhelmed by the sudden collapse of the Thai currency.

The 1997 Asian financial crisis began in Thailand and quickly spread havoc throughout the region. In the worst affected countries, it shook the confidence of the ruling class and paved the way for significant political reforms. In Thailand, former prime minister Anand Panyarachun was already serving as head of a committee charged with drafting a new constitution. The committee quickly produced a document that was more democratic than previous Thai constitutions and no longer provided a political role for the military. The constitution was designed to make the elected government stronger and less corrupt by reducing the number of small provincial parties in parliament and by giving new powers to the Commission on Elections and other watchdog bodies.[22]

The Thaksin Phenomenon

The winner of the first elections held under the new constitution was Thaksin Shinawatra. A billionaire businessman and former police official from a Chinese family in Chiang Mai, he had played an unimpressive role in the conservative governments of the mid–1990s. The Democrat party lost the 2001 election because it was identified with highly unpopular belt-tightening measures required by the International Monetary Fund in return for emergency financial aid.

Thaksin won a landslide victory by promising rural Thai voters that he would provide small loans for development projects and social services such as medical clinics. In the past, surprisingly few Thai politicians had paid much attention to rural voters' needs, and Thaksin's enormous wealth caused many people to believe his promises. He also gained the support of many Thai business leaders by promising them debt relief and by attacking foreign investors for taking advantage of the financial crisis to buy up Thai commercial assets at fire sale prices.[23]

The economy recovered during Thaksin's first term in office, and he built a powerful network of supporters, including politicians, corporate leaders, and military chiefs. But he made no secret of his aim to turn Thailand into a one-party state like Lee Kuan Yew's Singapore. He soon polarized the country with the brutal tactics he used to deal with Thailand's drug problem and a Muslim separatist movement that broke out in southern Thailand. On Thaksin's orders, the police used lethal force indiscriminately against alleged drug dealers, and in one particularly bad incident in the southern insurgency, seventy-eight Muslim detainees were smothered in a police truck.[24]

Nevertheless, with strong rural support in Northern and Northeast Thailand, Thaksin won another sweeping victory in the 2005 election, but then his troubles started. The economy began to go sour, and the southern insurgency took a turn for the worse. On several occasions, the king publicly rebuked Thaksin for using strong-arm tactics instead of diplomacy in dealing with the Muslim separatists.[25] In January 2006, Thaksin angered the Bangkok elite by selling his communications company to the Singapore government's investment firm for a tax-free $1.9 billion. Forced on the defensive, Thaksin called a snap election, which he won, but the result was annulled after the king cited undemocratic procedures.[26] Even so, Thaksin remained popular with rural Thais, and he was expected to win another election scheduled for October 2006. So the army took advantage of his absence from the country and overthrew his government on September 19, 2006. He was convicted of corrupt practices and sentenced to two years in prison, but he fled Thailand and was living abroad as of 2009.

Political System

After the 2006 coup, Thailand was governed by a military-appointed government operating under an interim constitution. In August 2007, the voters approved a new constitution drafted according to the wishes of the coup group. Half of the members of the Senate (upper house of parliament) would be appointed by a select committee that included judges and heads of regulatory agencies. The electoral system for the lower house of parliament would go back to a system of large, multi-member parliamentary constituencies instead of the smaller, single-member districts introduced in 1997. The 2007 charter also prescribed a wide range of policies that must be followed. The military must receive "adequate" amounts of "modern" weapons, and the king's concept of a "sufficiency economy" would emphasize moderation rather than rapid economic growth. Most analysts saw the new constitution as a step backward to the era of weak coalition governments with the military and civilian bureaucracies retaining strong political influence.[27]

The 1997 Constitution

Unlike previous Thai constitutions, the 1997 constitution did not assign a political role to the military. It was drafted under the leadership of Anand Panyarachun at the height of the 1997 financial crisis, and it sought to strengthen the government to cope with such crises in the future. Thus, the electoral process was revamped in ways that made it easier for wealthy parties dominated by corporate leaders and technocrats to gain power. Small provincial parties, which were seen by the drafters as corrupt and incompetent, found that the new rules worked against them. For example, a party had to win at least 5 percent of the vote to be asked to join a governing coalition, and to be eligible to run for parliament, a person had to have at least a B.A. degree.[28]

To reduce corruption in the electoral system, the 1997 constitution sought to reinforce the powers of the existing National Counter Corruption Commission (NCCC). Responsibility for running elections was assigned to a new Election Commission instead of the Ministry of Interior. A Constitutional Court was created with broad powers of judicial review. The practice of vote-buying was made illegal, and candidates who broke the new electoral laws could be barred from politics for five years. The equally common practice of paying large bribes to well-known politicians to switch parties was discouraged by requiring politicians to belong to a party for ninety days before they could represent it in an election.[29]

By favoring well-funded parties over small provincial ones, many of these reforms helped Thaksin put together a landslide victory in the 2001 election. He also ignored any constitutional provisions that stood in his way, and after he was elected he packed the various regulatory bodies with his loyal supporters. In the midst of the 2001 election, Thaksin was indicted for failing to report some of his income while serving in a previous administration, but he refused to step down, and the Constitutional Court eventually cleared him.[30]

The Monarchy

As King Bhumibol reached his sixtieth year on the throne in June 2006, the question of who would succeed him was a matter of concern to his people. After his eldest daughter chose to live abroad and remove herself from the succession, the king gave his second daughter, Princess Sirindhorn, the title of Maha Chakri (Crown Princess), making her eligible to succeed to the throne. Princess Sirindhorn was extremely popular with the Thai people because she dedicated herself to the same national interests that occupied her father.

Her brother, Crown Prince Vachiralongkorn, was sometimes criticized for a lack of discipline and commitment. But Thailand has never had a reigning Queen, and the Crown Prince was apparently being groomed to succeed his father, who was eighty in 2008. An unpopular succession could deprive Thailand of an immensely valuable focal point of national unity, and it might allow undemocratic forces that had been held in check by King Bhumibol to reassert themselves.

Office of the Prime Minister

Sarit Thanarat reorganized the OPM during his premiership (1958–63), and it has controlled many of the strings of power ever since. It includes the Budget Bureau, the National Economic and Social Development Board, the National Security Council, the Council of State, the National Intelligence Agency, and the Public Relations Department. Of course, the power and influence of each Prime Minister varies depending on his character and the circumstances in which he governs. In the 1990s, Chuan Leekpai was quite effective in his dealings with the military, but he was overwhelmed by the financial crisis. Thaksin had tight control over parliament and wide influence in the corporate world, but his effort to gain control over the military was probably the main factor that led to his downfall.

The Bureaucracy

As noted earlier, the country's central administration was modernized by King Chulalongkorn in the 1890s along the lines of the British colonial administration in Malaya.

Civilian and military bureaucrats ran the country until the early 1970's's, when the influence of businessmen and political party leaders began to be felt. By the 1990s, civilian and military bureaucrats were retreating into the background, but the 2006 military coup brought them to the fore again, and they comprised most of the interim government. Critics of the new draft constitution in 2007 argued that it would restore the power of civilian and military bureaucrats at the expense of elected political leaders.

The civilian bureaucracy, including the police and teachers in state-run schools and universities, number well over a million. Personal contacts play a key role in staffing many, perhaps most, of these positions. As in most Southeast Asian countries, these "patron-client relations" play a major role in launching successful bureaucratic careers and in the advancement of civilian and military bureaucrats to more senior positions.

The Military

As already noted, the Thai armed forces (particularly the army) dominated Thai politics from 1932 to 1992 and reasserted themselves in 2006. Like other branches of the Thai political elite, they are highly factionalized.[31] Some of the factions consist of officers of the same class of a military academy. For example, Chulachomklao Military Academy Class 5 officers were behind the 1991 military coup, while another military faction known as the "Young Turks" opposed it. Like the Indonesian army, the Thai armed forces have traditionally claimed the role of protectors of Thai values. They have justified their frequent coups against civilian governments on the grounds that they have higher standards of patriotism and honesty, but in reality the military is no less corrupt than civilian bureaucrats and politicians. Although they did avoid the political limelight during the 1990s, Thaksin felt he needed their support and re-politicized them for his own purposes.[32] At the time of writing, the leaders of the 2006 coup had not fully revealed the role they foresaw for the military after the restoration of civilian government.

The Police

Thaksin Shinawatra was the first career police officer in half a century to become a major political figure in Thailand. He began his business career by selling computers and other communications equipment to the government. He placed many of his relatives and former classmates at the Armed Forces Academies Preparatory School in positions of command, and he built a network of senior police and military contacts that was second only to that of army General Prem Tinsulanond.[33] Corruption and links to organized crime have limited the effectiveness of the Thai police in dealing with the country's serious problems of drug trafficking, child prostitution, and Islamic terrorism.[34]

The 2000–2001 Elections

The 1997 constitution was first tested in the 2000 election for the Senate and 2001 election for the lower house of the legislature. The Senate was directly elected for the first time, and candidates were not supposed to belong to a political party. But this rule was not strictly enforced, and many senators were linked to old party machines. The election was marred by considerable vote-buying and other irregularities, and the Election Commission ordered reruns in many constituencies.

As Table 1.3 shows, Thaksin came close to winning an absolute majority in the lower house election in 2001.

He prepared for the election by organizing a new party called Thai Rak Thai ("Thais Love Thais"). Using his vast personal fortune, he paid scores of politicians who were proven vote-getters to join his party before the constitutional ban on party-switching went into effect. Through alliances with the Chart Thai and New Aspiration parties, Thaksin soon had a large majority in the lower house.[35]

The 2005 and 2006 Elections

Thaksin's broad public support lasted until 2003, because the economy righted itself in the first two years of his administration. But he began to lose the support of middle class voters in 2003 when his anti-drug dealer campaign led to more than 2,000 extrajudicial killings by the police. The king reprimanded Thaksin for this, and their relations grew even cooler after Thaksin responded to the outbreak of Muslim dissidence with heavy-handed military repression instead of the gentler methods favored by King Bhumibol. Thaksin also showed his contempt for the Constitutional Court, the National Counter-Corruption Commission, and political reformers in general.[36] Yet in the 2005 election, his majority of 377 out of 500 seats was substantially higher than his 2001 victory, because his rural supporters remained loyal.

Table 1.3
2001 Thai National Assembly Election

Party		Region		Center &		
	North	Northeast	South	Bangkok	Party List	Total
Thai Rak Thai	54	69	1	76	48	248
Democrat	16	6	48	27	31	127
Chat Thai	3	11	—	21	6	43
Chat Patthana	2	16	—	4	7	28
New Aspiration	1	19	5	3	8	36
Seritham	—	14	—	—	—	14
Social Action	—	1	—	—	—	1
Ratsadon	—	1	—	—	—	2
Thin Thai	—	1	—	—	—	1

Sources: Results as announced by Thai national Election Commission on February 2, 2001. *Note:* The number of seats won by some parties in the four regions of the country do not equal the "Total" column on the right.

In 2006, Thaksin's sale of his Shin Corporation to the Singapore government's holding company for a tax free $1.9 billion gave his political opponents the issue they needed to put him on the defensive, because he had claimed he was opposed to foreigners gaining control of Thai assets during the long and deep recession that followed the 1997 financial crisis.

Thaksin's opponents held a series of large public rallies in Bangkok, and he was compelled to call a special election in April 2006. Because the opposition boycotted it, the king called the election undemocratic. When it was learned that Thaksin paid people to run against his party to give the impression of a contested election, the Supreme Court ruled that the election was invalid.[37] Thaksin was reduced to the status of a caretaker prime minister, but when it appeared that an election would be held before the end of 2006 and Thaksin would win, the military staged their coup while he was at the UN in New York.

Political Parties

Pro-Thaksin Parties

After seizing power in 2006, the coup group banned political party activity. But in June 2007, the ban was lifted on all parties except Thaksin's Thai Rak Thai (TRT), which was dissolved by court order. Thaksin was among the 111 TRT members who were barred from politics for five years, but many of his other supporters joined the already existing People's Power Party and sought to gain the support of Thaksin loyalists in rural areas. Although he remained abroad during 2007, Thaksin chose Samak Sundaravej, a controversial right-wing politician, to lead the People's Power Party, which won 235 seats in the 2007 parliamentary election. Samak then formed a coalition with five other parties. Although he was not well liked by many of his coalition partners, Samak became prime minister of the new government, which was sworn in January 2008.[38]

The five smaller parties that joined the People's Power Party in the coalition were: Chart Thai (with thirty-four seats), Puea Pandin (twenty-two seats), Matchimathipataya (eleven seats), Ruam Jai Thai Chart Pattana (nine seats), and Pracharaj (five seats). The leader of Chart Thai, Banharn Silapa-archa, served as head of a notoriously corrupt government in 1995, earning the nickname "Mr. ATM" because of all the bribes he handed out. Banharn was succeeded as prime minister by retired army general Chavalit Yongchaiyudh. Like Thaksin, Chavalit was popular with rural voters, especially those in the Northeast whom he courted with economic development projects.[39]

The Democrat Party

When it was in power in the 1990s, the Democrat Party worked closely with the army on military reform, and the party initially saw the military overthrow of Thaksin as justified. But the Democrats soon became critical of the coup group's management of the government and economy, and they argued that the 1997 reform constitution should be amended but not replaced. In the 2007 election, the Democrats won 164 seats and became the official parliamentary opposition. After losing the 2001 and 2005 elections, the party's leadership passed to Abhisit Vejjajiva, who tried to change the party's elitist image, which was a liability in rural areas.[40] In December 2008, Abhisit was elected prime minister by a majority of the members of Parliament, some of whom were persuaded by the military to vote for him.

The Cabinet

In 2006, the coup group chose a cabinet which was composed of technocrats, bureaucrats, and military officers, much like the interim government led by Anand Panyarachun after the 1991 coup. In Thai cabinets, the most important ministers are usually the economic team, which is led by the finance minister and includes the ministers of economics, commerce, and industry. They hold a weekly meeting that generally includes the prime minister and is more likely to produce important decisions than the weekly meeting of the full cabinet, which mainly serves to keep ministers informed.

The economic team appointed by the 2006 coup leaders was politically inept to a surprising degree. For many months, they failed to maintain the flow of funds, which Thaksin had used to build his support among rural voters. They also stressed the need to tighten restrictions in the Foreign Business Act, in spite of Thailand's urgent need for foreign investment. The new government led by the People's Power Party was considered unlikely to restrict foreign investment, but it might limit opportunities for foreign retail operations to expand in Thailand.[41]

The Judiciary

Thai courts have often failed to hold powerful and influential people accountable for criminal offenses, so the 1997 constitution sought to strengthen the existing court system, and it also created a new Administrative Court in which people could bring suits against the government. Muslims in Southern Thailand were given the right to apply to provincial Islamic Committees in cases involving family disputes, marriage, divorce, probate, and related matters. The new Constitutional Court was given broad powers to rule on the constitutionality of laws and enforce reform measures in the 1997 constitution. But its first major act was to clear Thaksin of violating the law while serving in a previous administration. The 2007 military-dictated constitution gave members of the judiciary a role in choosing half of the members of the upper house of parliament.

Civil Society

Thailand's nongovernmental organizations (NGO's) trace their origins back to traditional village self-help groups. In recent decades, hundreds of modern NGO's have been set up, mainly by middle and upper class Thais who are concerned with rural development, the rights of women and minorities, and social problems such as drug addiction, prostitution, and HIV/AIDs.

Thailand's first economic development NGO was the Thailand Rural Reconstruction Foundation, which Dr. Puey Ungphakorn created in 1969. He was the preeminent technocrat of his day and became Governor of the Bank of Thailand. His son, Jon Ungphakorn, carried on his work through the Thai Volunteer Service organization.[42]

Many people who became active in civil society out of religious conviction in the 1960s and seventies were inspired by Buddhadasa Bhikku. His meditation center in Southern Thailand attracted large numbers of Thai intellectuals and professionals. Buddhadasa's ideas about free will and the individual's duty to work for a better society conflicted with the conservative views of Field Marshal Sarit Thanarat and other Thai dictators that Buddhists should accept their predetermined role in society.[43] The environmental impact of large plantations and commercial fishing operations often undermined the livelihood of rural Thai, and in the 1990s, these people began to organize to protect their way of life. The Northern Farmers Network, made up of Karens and other forest-dwellers, was organized to protect traditional land rights. Small boat fisherman attempted to limit the impact of large trawling operations. Many campaigns were organized, some successfully and some not, against the building of dams on the Mekong and other rivers that required the relocation of large numbers of rural people.

Anand Panyarachun, the diplomat and business leader whose views often reflected those of the king, urged Thai bureaucrats to recognize the contribution which NGO's could make rather than resenting their initiatives. When Anand presided over the drafting of the 1997 constitution, he asked NGO leaders to contribute ideas, which were included in the final document. Two of the most prominent campaigners were Meechai Viravaidya, who led a highly publicized campaign for AIDS prevention and Bamrong Kayota, a leader of the Assembly for the Poor.[44]

The Media

Beginning in the 1980s, controls on the print media were gradually lifted, and during the 1990s, the Thai and English-language newspapers were as free to criticize the government and campaign for reforms as any newspapers in the region. Two excellent English-language dailies are the *Bangkok Post* and *The Nation,* which can be read online at www.bangkokpost.com and www.nationmultimedia.com.

After he came to power in 2001, Thaksin tried to stop newspapers from criticizing his policies by threatening them with a loss of advertising or by suing them for defamation. In 2004, he forced the editor of the *Bangkok Post* to resign, but the newspaper continued to criticize his administration. In 2005, one of Thaksin's cronies announced that he planned to buy a controlling interest in the *Bangkok Post* and the influential Thai-language daily *Matichon,* which had also been critical of Thaksin. But he was forced to scale back his plans because of the resulting public outcry. Then another media tycoon, Sondhi Limthongkul, began holding weekly anti–Thaksin rallies that attracted huge Bangkok crowds.[45]

The coup group that seized power in 2006 placed new restrictions on both the print and electronic media. Restrictions on print media were gradually relaxed as the coup group prepared to hand over power to an elected government, but the military was likely to continue to monitor TV broadcasts. During 2007, coup opponents began to use the Internet to rally public opinion. One of their favorite themes was to claim that the real leader of the coup was General Prem Tinsulanond, the head of the king's Privy Council. In April 2007, the coup group briefly closed Thailand's most popular Internet chat room because of anti-coup postings that indirectly implied the king was behind the coup.[46]

Thailand has five VHF-TV networks, and satellite and cable TV are widely available along with the Internet. TV and radio have always been dominated by the military and the government, and TV news has always been much more tightly controlled than the print media. An independent commercial channel (ITV) was opened in 1996, but the financial crisis made it difficult to get adequate financing. Reformers inserted a clause in the 1997 constitution guaranteeing media freedom and an independent broadcasting commission to manage frequencies. But the military extended the lease period on its main TV channel and packed the broadcasting commission with nominees.

Economic Development

Beginning in the late 1950s, Thailand had four decades of rapid economic growth, averaging 7.8 percent a year. The growth rate was highest from the late 1980s to the mid–1990s, powered by high levels of investment in industries that manufactured goods for export. Income from the tourist industry also rose sharply during this period, while income from agricultural exports (which still play an important role in the economy) rose slowly and unevenly, depending on the weather and world demand.

Financial Crisis

The bubble began to burst in 1996, when Thai exports declined because of a sudden drop in worldwide demand. There was also a very poor rice harvest in the same year. In 1997, these factors led currency speculators to launch an attack on the Thai currency, which soon lost much of its value along with the Bangkok stock market. Thus, the Thai economy registered 10.8 percent *negative* growth in 1998, and millions of people lost their jobs and savings. A slow recovery began in 1999, but growth did not reach the extraordinary level of the previous decade because of the global recession in 2001 and increased competition from China and other countries.[47]

During Thaksin's first term in office (2001–2004), the economic growth rate improved, reaching 7 percent in 2003. But shortly after he was reelected in 2005, the growth rate sagged below 4 percent because of another bad harvest plus the impact on tourism of the 2004 tsunami and the avian flu problem. Thaksin tried to encourage consumer spending by increasing the salaries of government officials, raising the minimum wage, and providing debt relief for people with large credit card debts.[48] He also tried to privatize some state-owned companies, but his plans met resistance from unionized employees and failed to attract many investors. Thaksin's main infrastructure project, a new airport, ran into delays but opened after he was deposed in 2006.[49]

Self-Sufficiency

The head of the interim government that replaced Thaksin said he planned to pursue an economic policy of "self-sufficiency," based on a concept developed by the king. He noted that the king and the coup group were concerned about the gap between rich and poor people, and "self-sufficiency" meant moving away from a policy of maximizing GNP growth and adopting a new approach to ensure that everyone had the basic necessities of life.[50]

The interim government shocked the foreign business community in Thailand by initiating a series of measures that seemed contrary to Thailand's traditional openness to foreign investment. These included controls on foreign investment (which were partially rescinded), nonrecognition of foreign drug patents, and talk of tightening the country's deliberately ambiguous laws on foreign investment and land ownership. In 2008, Thailand, the world's largest exporter of rice, responded to the worldwide food shortage by proposing a plan to stabilize rice prices in the ASEAN region, but analysts disagreed on how effective such a localized plan would be.[51]

Table 1.4
Thailand's Economy, 2007–10
(figures are percentages unless otherwise indicated)

	2007	2008	2009	2010
GDP Growth	4.9	2.6	-4.4	1.4
Agricultural Production Growth	1.8	5.1	2.0	3.0
Unemployment	1.4	1.4	4.1	4.4
Inflation	2.2	5.5	-1.2	2.7
Government Budget Balance	-2.4	-1.1	-4.7	-4.4
Exports (U.S. $M)	150.0	174.7	141.8	147.4
Imports (U.S. $M)	-124.5	-157.3	-118.5	-123.7

Source: Economist Intelligence Unit, "Thailand, Country Report," April 2009. Figures for 2009 and 2010 are EIU forecasts.

As Table 1.4 shows, Thailand's economic growth slowed in 2008 and was negative (-4.4 percent) in 2009, but was expected to recover slightly in 2010. Data in Table 1.4 suggests that the country's economic performance under the interim government in 2007 was not substantially worse than in previous years. But since recovering from the 1997 economic crisis, Thailand's growth has been somewhat below the Southeast Asian average of 5.5 percent and well below Thailand's average growth rate from 1985 to 1995, when real per capita GDP more than doubled.

Foreign Relations

To magnify its influence on regional and global issues, Thailand relies on a network of international organizations, including ASEAN, the Asian Development Bank, various Mekong River basin development schemes, and the United Nations family of organizations. The city of Bangkok hosts the UN's regional Southeast Asian headquarters, and Thailand played a major role in supporting the UN-brokered transition in Cambodia (1991–93) and the UN peacekeeping operation in East Timor in 1999. Thailand also belongs to the broader regional grouping known as APEC (Asia-Pacific Economic Cooperation), which held its annual summit in Bangkok in 2003.

Thailand and ASEAN

The Thai foreign minister, Thanat Khoman, played a leading role in the formation of ASEAN in 1967, even though Thailand was the only member state located on the Southeast Asian mainland. Thailand also took the lead in shaping ASEAN's opposition to giving Cambodia's UN seat to the Vietnam-dominated government in Cambodia in the 1980s. But Thailand's anti–Vietnamese alliance with China was opposed by Indonesia's President Suharto, who opened a dialogue with Hanoi to show he had no intention of being reduced to the role of a mere follower of Thai policy.

With the end of the cold war, Thailand favored ASEAN membership for Vietnam, Laos, Cambodia, and Myanmar because forming close ties with these four neighboring countries would expand its markets and increase its influence in ASEAN.[52]

Despite their policy of nonintervention in each other's affairs, the ASEAN states have adopted a policy of "constructive engagement" with the Burmese generals in Myanmar, and have tried to persuade them to allow more political freedom. Malaysia has led this initiative. Thaksin's brand of constructive engagement seemed primarily aimed at opening the Burmese market for his company's telecom services.[53]

Most ASEAN governments expressed concern about the Thai coup and called for a restoration of democracy. Indonesia's civilian defense minister drew the lesson that politicians must "get their act together" and provide better governance or the military would step into the vacuum. Philippine President Arroyo was probably concerned that the Thai example might encourage a coup in Manila. Thai relations with Singapore were clouded by doubts that the coup group cast on the legality of Singapore's purchase of Thaksin's company.[54]

Thaksin's heavy-handed approach to the Thai-Malay secessionist movement soured Thailand's normally good relations with Malaysia, and the coup group failed to implement a more conciliatory approach to the insurgency. However, the Thai coup did not impede cooperation among the ASEAN states in the area of foreign and security policy. A few weeks after the Thai coup, the ten ASEAN states reached agreement in principle on a new antiterrorism pact.

Thailand and the United States

The U.S.-Thai security alliance dates from the 1954 Manila Pact and a communique signed by Secretary of State Dean Rusk and Thai Foreign Minister Thanat Khoman in 1962. During the Vietnam War, the Thais allowed the United States to mount bombing raids in Laos and Vietnam from Thai air bases. But when the war ended in 1975, the U.S. military presence in the region was sharply reduced.[55]

Since then, U.S. leaders have tended to show less interest in Thailand and Southeast Asia, although President Bush designated Thailand a "major non–NATO ally" in 2003 because of Thaksin's vocal support for his antiterrorism policy. Before the 2006 coup, the two countries were trying to negotiate a free trade agreement, but the talks were put on hold after the Thai Parliament was dissolved in 2006 and the army overthrew the government.

Thai leaders almost certainly value the presence of the U.S. Seventh Fleet in the western Pacific, where it helps to discourage China and other powers from making destabilizing moves. The once extensive U.S. military mission in Bangkok is now quite small, but the United States still provides training and equipment to the Thai armed forces. The United States and Thailand also conduct joint training operations and cooperate closely on counterterrorism and drug-trafficking in the region. The U.S. aid program focuses on the HIV/AIDS problem, refugee assistance, and efforts to control trafficking in persons.[56]

Thai Relations with China

Sino-Thai relations have improved markedly since the cold war era when China sometimes supported communist forces in Northeast Thailand and Indochina. More Thai students now study in Chinese universities than in the United States, and China has supported the development of new universities in Thailand. Shortly before he was overthrown by the Thai military, Thaksin told Chinese leaders that he welcomed a "strategic partnership" with China, and Premier Wen Jiabao used the same term to describe China's relationship with ASEAN a few weeks later.[57] Trade between Thailand and China has increased steadily, but the Thais were not altogether happy with the initial results of their bilateral free trade agreement with China. They accused the Chinese of "dumping" low cost products on Thai markets and failing to allow easy access for Thai products in China. Nevertheless, the ASEAN states and China have agreed to negotiate a free trade agreement by 2010.[58]

Conclusions

In the 1960s, when Thai Foreign Minister Thanat Khoman allied his country militarily with the United States and took the lead in forming ASEAN, democracy was a distant goal at best for Thailand and seemed an all but impossible dream for many of its newly independent neighbors. Thanat believed that building strong state institutions was the key to survival and mutual support must replace the impulse of Southeast Asian leaders to wage self-destructive wars among themselves. The Thai government, like other ASEAN members, gave priority to economic development rather than the creation of democracy, but after decades of economic growth and the creation of an urban middle class, pressure for democratic reform increased.

During the 1990s, many people believed that the Thai military had permanently retreated from politics, and democratic institutions were firmly entrenched. But the military still regarded themselves as an important stabilizing force in Thai society. The 2006 coup caught many people by surprise, but above all it demonstrated the army's surprising incompetence at managing a country as advanced as Thailand is becoming. The interim government imposed a reactionary constitution that will more than likely be amended. The coup leaders also failed to establish that Thaksin and his government were corrupt, and the Thai people firmly repudiated the interim government's efforts in the December 2007 election.

What future political role will the Thai military seek to retain? Do they plan to make themselves the stabilizing force in Thai society when King Bhumibol eventually leaves the scene? Will they be willing to stay in the background and let the leaders of political parties, business firms, and other professions get Thailand back on track toward rapid economic and political development? For better or worse, Thailand's political drama will be closely watched by neighboring states, and the way in which these questions are answered will have important consequences for the rest of the region.

Further Reading

Chantavanich, Supang. "From Siamese-Chinese to Chinese-Thai: Political Conditions and Identity Shifts Among the Chinese in Thailand." In Leo Suryadinata, ed., *Ethnic Chinese as Southeast Asians* (Singapore and New York: Institute of Southeast Asian Studies and St. Martin's Press, 1977) pp. 232–59.

Connors, Michael Kelly. *Democracy and National Identity in Thailand.* New York and London: RoutledgeCurzon, 2003.

Keyes, Charles F. "Buddhism and National Integration in Thailand," *Journal of Asian Studies*, 30(3), 1971.

_____. *Thailand: Buddhist Kingdom as Modern Nation-State.* Bangkok: Duang Kamol, 1989.

McCargo, Duncan, and Ukrist Pathmanand. *The Thaksinization of Thailand.* Copenhagen: Nordic Institute of Asian Studies, 2005.

Morell, David, and Chai-Anan Samudavanija. *Political Conflict in Thailand: Reform, Reaction, Revolution.* Cambridge, MA: Oelgeschlager, Gunn and Hain, 1981.

Phongpaichit, Pasuk, and Chris Baker. *Thailand, Economy and Politics.* Oxford: Oxford University Press, 2002.

_____, and _____. *Thaksin and the Business of Politics in Thailand.* Chiang Mai: Silkworm Press, 2004.

Skinner, William G. *Chinese Society in Thailand: An Analytical History.* Ithaca: Cornell University Press, 1957.

Wyatt, David K. *Thailand: A Short History.* New Haven: Yale University Press, 1984.

– 2 –

VIETNAM

Still a Long March Ahead

In 1986, Vietnam was at war with China and isolated from most of the world because its forces were occupying Cambodia. The Soviet Union was beginning to collapse and could no longer pay for the occupation or to prop up Vietnam's stagnant economy. Faced with these multiple crises, Hanoi's leaders adopted the policy they called *doi moi* (renewal), which led to a dramatic improvement in the country's economic performance. This enabled communist party leaders to regain the political initiative which they had been losing.

Since the early 1990s, Vietnam has achieved one of the highest growth rates of any developing country in the world and reduced by half the number of people living in poverty.[1] The Vietnamese Communist Party (VCP) still controls the political system, but the standards of governance and the rule of law have improved slowly. Having joined ASEAN in 1995, Vietnam now has good relations with all its neighbors and all the major powers. It joined the World Trade Organization in 2007, and it attracts more foreign investment than any ASEAN state except Singapore.

But Vietnam still has a long way to go to achieve the goal of becoming a modern developed country. Government decision-making is slow and far from transparent. Corruption at all levels of the ruling party and government remains a major problem despite serious efforts to root it out. The media and higher education are stifled by political controls, and the rule of law has not been fully implemented.[2] As in many other countries, the gap between rich and poor and between rural and urban dwellers is growing rapidly. But as discussed in the Economic Development section of this chapter, Vietnam continued to have economic growth during the 2009 global recession. Aided by a large government stimulus program, more than half a million new jobs were created in the first half of 2009 while inflation eased substantially. Vietnam's exports declined only slightly from their high level in 2008.

People and Cultures

Vietnam is one of the most ethnically homogeneous countries in Asia, with Vietnamese comprising from 85 to 90 percent of the population, as Table 2.1 shows. Their original homeland spanned the border between what is now southern China and north Vietnam. As the Vietnamese people gradually migrated down to the Mekong River delta, regional differences developed. The people of north, central, and south Vietnam still tend to identify with their regions despite much intermarriage between the three groups.

Table 2.1
Vietnam: Demographic Overview

Population (2007): 85.2 million
Annual Growth Rate of Population (2007): 1.004%
Ethnic Vietnamese (2007): 85–90% of total population
Ethnic Groups (2007): Chinese 3%, Khmer Krom, Tai, Chams, and hill tribes small percentages
Religious Affiliations (2007): Buddhist 50%, Christian 10%, Cao Dai 1.5 to 3%, Hoa Hao 1.5 to 4%, Muslim 0.7%
Literacy (2006): 90% (females 91.4%, males 95.5%)
Primary School Students (2001): 94%
Secondary School Students (2001): females 64%, males 70%
Colleges and Universities (2003–04): 187
Enrollment in Higher Education (2003–04): 993,900
Government Expenditure on Education (2002): 11.3% of budget
Infant Mortality Rate (2007): 17.4 per 1,000 live births
Life Expectancy (2007): 70.8 years
Income per Capita (2006): U.S. $726 ($2,490 purchasing power parity)
People Living on $2 per Day (2007): 28.2 million
Human Development Index Rating (2004): 112 out of 177 countries

Sources: United Nations, *Demographic Yearbook*; *Europa World Year Book*; Vietnamese government statistics; U.S. Department of State, "Background Notes: Vietnam"; World Bank, Washington, D.C.

Ethnic Groups

CHINESE

As in most Southeast Asian countries, the Chinese play an important economic role in Vietnam. They are mostly concentrated in south Vietnam, where they engage in rice trading, milling, real estate, and banking. After the sharp deterioration in relations between Vietnam and China in 1978–79, an estimated 450,000 Chinese fled south Vietnam by boat or were expelled across the northern border into China. But many have since returned to Vietnam, and they were becoming more integrated into Vietnamese society. Their ties with other Chinese communities in East and Southeast Asia attract a substantial amount of foreign investment to Vietnam.[3]

HILL TRIBES

There are some fifty tribal groups in Vietnam ranging in size from over a million to less than 100,000.[4] Most of these people live in the central highlands or the mountains of northern Vietnam. Some are converts to Protestant Christian denominations, and many are related to similar groups in Laos, Cambodia, Thailand, and China. Relations have long been tense between these mountain people and the Vietnamese government, especially when their ancestral lands were taken over by the government for economic development.

In 2001, Nong Duc Manh became Secretary-General of the Communist Party of Vietnam. His mother was an ethnic Tai and a servant of Ho Chi Minh, who was rumored to be Nong Duc Manh's father.[5] One of Manh's first acts after taking office was to visit the central highlands, where tribesman had demonstrated to protest corrupt practices by local officials, religious persecution, and encroachment on their ancestral lands by ethnic Vietnamese. Manh ordered local officials to work closely with tribal leaders, and he promised to help the tribal people gain better access to schools and government jobs.[6]

Khmer Krom

An estimated 600,000 to a million ethnic Khmers (Cambodians), known as Khmer Krom, live in south Vietnam near the Cambodian border and in the Mekong delta area. They have largely avoided assimilation by the Vietnamese, and they still practice the Theravada form of Buddhism. Their treatment by the Vietnamese has long been a source of conflict between the Cambodian and Vietnamese governments, with Cambodia accusing Vietnam of mistreating the Khmer Krom and violating their rights, particularly their right to practice their religion.[7]

Chams

The Cham people (descendants of the people of Champa) live along the southern coastal plain of Vietnam and in eastern Cambodia. According to a leading specialist on Southeast Asian Muslims, they now number "fewer than 900,000," but earlier reports put their numbers much lower.[8] They are mostly Sunni Muslims, although many of them have married Vietnamese and become at least partially assimilated to Vietnamese culture. The Vietnamese government has reportedly restored some of the ancient buildings of Champa as tourist sites. The Muslim Association of Vietnam organizes annual pilgrimages to Mecca.

Health and Education

One of the main reasons for Vietnam's rapid economic growth has been the government's investment in human capital. But the elimination of rural collectives in the 1980s meant that many Vietnamese lost access to free schools and medical facilities, and this caused serious unrest in rural areas. In recent years, the government has responded by increasing its investment in rural health and education facilities, especially in the poorest provinces where the hill tribes are concentrated.[9] But anything beyond the most basic forms of health care are available only to people who can afford to pay for these services.[10]

Status of Women

Vietnamese women have a very high rate of literacy (91.4 percent) for such a poor country. They often make the key decisions in their households, but they are expected to defer to their husbands in public. Vietnamese women hold very few senior positions in the communist party or cabinet level positions in the government, but they occupy many senior positions in the bureaucracy. Also, many of Vietnam's bravest reform advocates and leaders of nongovernmental organizations have been women.[11]

The Middle Class

The free market reforms adopted since 1986 have hastened the development of an urban business class in Vietnam that has a lifestyle similar to the middle class in Thailand or Malaysia, but they constitute a much smaller percentage of Vietnam's total population, perhaps 5 percent as opposed to about 10 percent in Thailand and Malaysia. They operate a considerable number of nongovernmental organizations, as discussed in a later section of this chapter, but they have not been allowed to organize politically. Economically, they are highly motivated to achieve financial success. This is accepted by the communist party and viewed as contributing to Vietnam's economic growth.[12]

Religion

Many Vietnamese families maintain altars in their homes that are dedicated to their ancestors, but they may also practice one of the world religions. The communist party keeps a close watch on religious organizations to make certain they do not challenge its authority. There was some easing of restrictions on religious groups in 2006 while Hanoi needed U.S. support for admission to the World Trade Organization. But after Vietnam joined the WTO in 2007, a number of religious dissidents were imprisoned.

BUDDHISM

Over the centuries, Vietnamese Buddhism has been heavily influenced by contact with Chinese Buddhism, making it distinct from the Theravada Buddhism of Thailand and Cambodia. Although Buddhist clergy have sometimes been a dissident force in Vietnamese politics, the religion has never played the central role in Vietnamese society that Theravada Buddhism has in Cambodia, Laos, and Thailand. In 1982, most of the Buddhist sects in Vietnam were formed into the state-approved Viet Nam Buddhist Church. The dissident Unified Buddhist Church of Viet Nam was banned in the early 1980s, and its leader, Thich Huyen Quang, has been under house arrest ever since.

CHRISTIANITY

Roman Catholicism was first brought to Vietnam by French missionaries in the seventeenth century, while Protestant missionaries arrived much later. Catholic Vietnamese are concentrated in south Vietnam, because there was a massive movement of Catholic families from north to south Vietnam after the country was divided in 1954. Many of the Protestants are members of tribal groups in the central highlands. Religious groups are not allowed to carry out social programs without official approval, presumably because they might be seen as evidence that government programs are inadequate.[13]

HOA HAO AND CAO DAI SECTS

Several million Vietnamese belong to the Hoa Hao, Cao Dai, and other sects that draw upon a mixture of eastern and western ideas found in various religions and philosophical writings. These sects, which are concentrated in south Vietnam, are also carefully watched by Vietnamese authorities for any signs of political intrigue. Members of these sects have been imprisoned for protesting the harassment of their followers and for trying to contact the UN Special Rapporteur on Religious Intolerance.[14]

Historical Background

Vietnam is the only country in Southeast Asia that has ever been occupied and colonized by the Chinese. During the Chinese occupation from 111 B.C. to 939 A.D., Vietnamese culture became thoroughly Sinicized, but the Vietnamese have fought many battles against Chinese invaders and won some notable victories.

The March South

In 1471, the Vietnamese conquered the kingdom of Champa which lay to their south, and they began to migrate down the eastern coast of mainland Southeast Asia. As landless Vietnamese peasants steadily occupied territory to the south, Vietnam's rulers incorporated these areas into their kingdom. All Vietnamese know the proverb, "The laws of the emperor stop at the village gate." Villagers have traditionally had some autonomy in running their own purely local affairs. The state was mainly responsible for the improvement of agriculture and (in the north) maintaining an elaborate system of dikes, while the village was required to pay taxes, provide military recruits, and maintain internal order.[15]

Table 2.2
Events in Vietnamese History

111 B.C.–A.D. 939	Chinese occupy kingdom of Nam-Viet.
1200s	Vietnamese successfully resist Mongol invasions.
1400s	Chinese effort to reabsorb Vietnam fails.
1859–84	French gain control over all of Vietnam.
1930	Ho Chi Minh launches Indochinese Communist Party.
1942–45	Vichy French allied with Japanese conquerors.
1945	Ho "dissolves" Communist Party; declares independence.
1946–54	War with France ends at Dien Bien Phu. Vietnam partitioned at 17th parallel; U.S. becomes involved in Vietnam.
1968	Tet offensive undermines U.S. people's support for war.
1973	Under a truce agreement, U.S. forces leave Vietnam.
1975	Vietnamese communist forces occupy Saigon.
1979	Vietnam occupies Cambodia; battles with China begin.
1986	Sixth Party Congress announces *doi moi* policy.
1989	Vietnam withdraws troops from Cambodia; cold war ends.
1995	Vietnam and U.S. resume relations; Vietnam joins ASEAN
2000	U.S. and Vietnam sign Bilateral Trade Agreement.
2001	Unrest in Vietnamese highlands; Nong Duc Manh is named Vietnamese Communist Party leader at Ninth Party Congress.
2006	Nong Duc Manh reelected at Tenth Party Congress. U.S. and Vietnam sign another major trade agreement.
2007	Vietnam joins World Trade Organization. U.S. provides $400,000 to clean up contamination from Agent Orange defoliant.

In the 1700s, Vietnamese migrants reached the Mekong River delta, an area of exceptionally rich farmland which had been part of Cambodia for centuries. Although it was sparsely settled by Khmers and Chams when the Vietnamese arrived there, the Vietnamese met with little resistance in the Mekong delta. However, when they tried to colonize the rest of Cambodia and impose Vietnamese culture on the Khmer people, they met with strong resistance and were forced to abandon the effort, as described in chapter 3.

French Colonialism

During the nineteenth century, France occupied Vietnam, Laos, and Cambodia and set up a colonial administration under a French governor-general. By recruiting Vietnamese to work in Cambodia and Laos, the French laid the groundwork for future ethnic conflict in those two countries.

French control over Vietnam lasted less than a century, but its influence was profound. French missionaries introduced Vietnam to Catholicism, and French scholars studied Vietnamese history and helped preserve the culture. But the colonial administration was deliberately exploitative, and its opium monopoly created millions of addicts. The French also did their best to prevent the rise of a Vietnamese nationalist movement and did little to prepare the country for independence.[16]

The Vietnamese scholar gentry responded to French domination of their country in different ways. Some radicals, like Phan Boi Chau, thought foreign support was necessary to oust the French. More moderate leaders like Phan Chu Trinh believed that Vietnam could be modernized and democratized by collaborating with the French and building schools throughout Vietnam. One of Trinh's students was Ho Chi Minh, who later founded the Indochina Communist Party and literally sold Phan Boi Chau to the French to raise money for his political activities.[17]

Vietnam's Struggle for Independence

During World War II, Japan's occupation of Vietnam gave Ho Chi Minh a chance to organize the Viet Minh, a coalition of anticolonial groups. On September 2, 1945, he proclaimed the independence of the Democratic Republic of Vietnam. The French fought an eight-year war to regain control of the country, but they were defeated in the battle of Dien Bien Phu in May 1954.

At a meeting in Geneva of all the parties with an interest in Indochina, French and Vietnamese representatives agreed to a temporary division of the country at the 17th parallel, with a provisional communist government in the north and a provisional noncommunist government in the south. Elections to unify the country were to be held in 1956, but the south Vietnamese government refused to allow this and declared itself the Republic of Vietnam in 1955. The United States, which had backed the French war effort, began providing economic and military aid to the Saigon regime in the hope of preventing communist forces from unifying the country.[18]

The United States Enters the War

In 1961, President Kennedy sent thousands of U.S. military advisors to south Vietnam in what soon led to direct U.S. involvement in the war. But massive U.S. military and economic aid failed to shore up President Ngo Dinh Diem's government, and Diem was assassinated by his own generals in 1963 shortly before the assassination of President Kennedy. Under President Johnson, the United States steadily increased its ground forces in the south and mounted air attacks against north Vietnam.

Congress and the United States public initially accepted Johnson's claim that U.S. ships had been attacked in the Tonkin Gulf and that U.S. interests would be seriously harmed by communist victory in Vietnam. But after the communist Tet offensive in 1968, American public opinion turned against a war that seemed both pointless and unwinnable.[19] After President Nixon succeeded Johnson in 1969, he accepted a truce and withdrew U.S. forces in 1973. Although the U.S. continued to provide limited military aid, Saigon fell to the communists in April 1975, and Vietnam was unified under communist rule.

A Disappointing Peace

Vietnam's leaders hoped their victory would win them acceptance by the rest of the world. But their invasion of Cambodia in 1979 and their alliance with the Soviet Union led to war on two fronts—with the Chinese army when it invaded Vietnam and with Khmer Rouge guerrillas in Cambodia. Thailand and China supported the Khmer Rouge while the United States supported non-communist guerrillas.[20]

In south Vietnam, communist economic and political controls created enormous suffering. Hundreds of thousands of former officials were herded into "reeducation" camps. A disastrous currency reform followed by the expulsion of Chinese residents from north Vietnam and the flight of many more from the south brought economic chaos. Under the communist system of agriculture, farmers could not even cover their costs of production with what the government paid for their crops. As food production fell, serious shortages plagued a country that had once been a major rice exporter. Hundreds of thousands of Vietnamese fled the country and sought refuge abroad.

1986, the Turning Point

In 1986, after years of experimenting with partial reforms, the Sixth Party Congress of the Vietnamese Communist Party (VCP) recognized the need for fundamental changes of economic and foreign policy. The VCP had little choice because the failure of Soviet-style policies had created massive dissatisfaction with communist rule. Nguyen Van Linh was chosen as Secretary-General of the party, and under his leadership many top officials were replaced. Under the new policy of *doi moi* (renewal), certain free market economic reforms were adopted, beginning with the agricultural sector.

Vietnam also made a much more determined effort than it previously had to broaden its diplomatic and economic ties with all countries, especially China, ASEAN, and the United States. Since these countries strongly opposed Vietnam's occupation of Cambodia, and Moscow could no longer afford to pay for it, the VCP Politburo decided to begin withdrawing its forces from Cambodia and Laos and reduce the size of its standing army.[21] During 1987 and 1988, the communist party allowed much more open debate on its policies, but the outpouring of criticism by communist and noncommunist intellectuals caused the party to reimpose controls.[22]

Since the early 1990s, Vietnam has had one of the highest economic growth rates in the world as the reforms begun by Linh attracted foreign and domestic investment. The Asian financial crisis in 1997 produced a temporary reduction in Vietnam's growth rate because Vietnam's trading partners were badly hit by the crisis. Conservative elements in the VCP seized their chance to push back against the reformers and institute more repressive policies against those whom they considered dissidents. But after Nong Duc Manh became party leader in 2001, the VCP resumed its policy of slowly implementing economic and political reforms.[23] Manh was reelected to a second five-year term as leader of the VCP at the Tenth Party Congress in 2006.

Political System

The constitution, which was approved in 1992, reaffirmed the leading role of the Vietnamese Communist Party, although it implied that the party's power should be limited by the rule of law. It strengthened the powers of the prime minister and president by giving them the necessary staff to manage day-to-day functions of the government. The constitution also described the National Assembly as the highest representative body of the people and the only organization with legislative powers.

These executive and legislative institutions have in fact become more powerful since the constitution was proclaimed, but the communist party still chooses the president and prime minister and approves all National Assembly candidates. Thus, the constitution was clearly designed to legitimize the VCP's leading role while imposing very few limits on its power. Yet by endorsing the policy of *doi moi*, the constitution suggests that economic development has replaced "building socialism" as the top priority of the state.

The constitution makes clear that the most powerful person in Vietnam is the secretary-general of the communist party, who takes the lead in shaping policy. He is followed by the prime minister who manages the government. The third-ranking figure is the president who chairs the National Defense and Security Council and nominally heads the armed forces. Naturally, the relative importance of these three leaders depends to some degree on their personal abilities and the circumstances in which they serve.

Secretary-General Nong Duc Manh was born in 1940 to a Tai ethnic minority family in north Vietnam, and he is the first member of a minority group to head the VCP. He has neither affirmed nor denied the rumor that he is Ho Chi Minh's son. He studied forestry at a college in Hanoi and then continued his studies in Leningrad from 1966 to 1971. Returning to Vietnam two years after Ho Chi Minh's death in 1969, he worked in the field of forestry until 1980 and then began serving in a series of high level political positions.[24]

As president of the National Assembly from 1997 to 2001, Manh raised the legislature's profile by televising their debates, and he made a number of official trips abroad, further enhancing his own leadership credentials. He was chosen by the party hierarchy to be secretary-general of the VCP in 2001, succeeding Le Kha Phieu, who was accused of using military intelligence against party members and slowing the pace of reforms.[25] The Chinese government strongly urged the 9th Party Congress to reappoint Le Kha Phieu, but Manh was chosen instead, and economic ties with China have been strengthened during his tenure.[26] Manh is known as a consensus-builder. He has emphasized the fight against official corruption and the need to address the problems of ethnic minorities who live in the poorest provinces.[27]

Prime Minister Nguyen Tan Dung was born in south Vietnam in 1949 and has a law degree. He had a career as a political officer in the army before becoming deputy minister of Home Affairs and a member of the Central Police Party Committee. He has also been governor of the State Bank of Vietnam and chairman of the National Financial and Monetary Committee. In 2006, he succeeded Phan Van Khai as prime minister, and some analysts question whether Dung is as committed to reform as Phan Van Khai was.

President Nguyen Minh Triet was born in 1942 in south Vietnam and has a degree in mathematics. He spent his early career as a leader of the communist youth movement and became head of the party committee that runs Ho Chi Minh City. Like others who have held that position, he has gained a reputation as a political and economic reformer.

The Vietnamese Communist Party (VCP)

The secretary general of the VCP heads the fifteen-member Politburo, which is the country's highest policy-making body. It is assisted by the 150-member Central Committee, which meets twice a year. Although in theory the government and communist party are now separate, all senior positions in the government are still occupied by leading party officials. The party congress meets for a few days every five years to ratify decisions that have been worked out in advance in closed meetings of the Central Committee and the Politburo. Recent scholarship based on archives opened since the end of the cold war indicates that the party has always been less monolithic than its propaganda claimed and more of a coalition of ideological factions.[28]

Ho Chi Minh, who served as president of the Democratic Republic of Vietnam from 1954 until his death in 1969, was of a middle class background. Although he was trained in Moscow as a Comintern agent, he tried during 1940s to build a broad coalition of leftist forces. Ho spent most of the 1930s in Moscow and China but returned to Vietnam at the outbreak of World War II. There he formed the Viet Minh, which was communist-dominated but included many anticolonial groups.[29]

Ho's "clan" or faction within the party included General Vo Nguyen Giap (victor in the battle of Dien Bien Phu) and Pham Van Dong, prime minister of north Vietnam from 1954 to 1987. A more radical faction that favored class struggle and the early imposition of Soviet-style industry and collective agriculture throughout Vietnam was led by Truong Chinh, who was party leader from 1941 to 1956 and briefly in 1986. He sometimes criticized Ho Chi Minh's "bourgeois" background and his failure to "crush counter-revolutionary elements." Ho Chi Minh is now the focus of a personality cult created by the VCP to reinforce its own diminished prestige.[30]

The Vietnam Peoples Army (VPA)

The army is subordinate to the Vietnamese Communist Party, and it supports the party's political aims. The VPA is probably more highly regarded by the Vietnamese people than the VCP, because the VPA liberated Vietnam from colonial rule, unified the country, and defended it in clashes with Chinese forces between 1979 and the late eighties. Vietnam's armed forces numbered 1.3 million in 1987, but they were reduced to 484,000 by 2005, at which point the defense budget was estimated at $3.5 billion.[31]

Senior officers in the VPA are usually members of the communist party and strongly support its monopoly of political power. But several retired generals have spoken out against corruption in the party and in favor of democratic reforms. The army does not share the party's reputation for corruption, but like the military in Thailand, Indonesia, and Myanmar, the VPA controls an extensive network of economic interests. These include weapons manufacturers and companies that produce goods for sale to the civilian population.

The Police

Like the military, the Vietnamese police support the communist party's monopoly of political power, and they help maintain internal security, but this is primarily an army responsibility. In urban areas, the police perform normal police functions, but in rural areas they deal with sensitive political matters under the VCP's direction. There is also a paramilitary unit called the People's Armed Security Force, which deals with armed uprisings by dissident groups. The police are supposed to play a key role in the party's efforts to curb corruption, but there is a serious problem of corruption in the police services themselves.[32]

The National Assembly

Although the constitution says the National Assembly as the highest representative body of the people, it primarily serves to legitimize continued one-party rule by the VCP. The communist party decides who can run for election to the National Assembly and what parties can participate. Most people who are chosen are VCP members. The party must also approve any significant legislative initiative, although some laws proposed by party leaders have been rejected by the National Assembly, and its debates help to air the conflicting interests of different regions of the country. Nong Duc Manh raised the profile of the National Assembly when he was head of it, and his successor followed the same policy.[33]

Elections for the National Assembly are held every five years, and the body meets twice a year for seven to ten weeks. But a standing committee meets every month, and a number of functional committees also meet regularly. In the 2002 election, 759 candidates (including 13 independents) ran for 498 seats. Members of parties other than the communists won 51 seats, and independents won 2 seats, but the other 445 seats were won by VCP members.[34] The 2007 election produced a similar result.

Since most of the deputies (members) belong to the communist party, it is highly unusual for any of them to break ranks with the party leaders on an important issue. A rare instance of this occurred in 1988 when mismanagement during a food shortage led to famine in parts of north Vietnam. Members of the National Assembly supported by a group of military veterans called for the resignation of the Minister of Agriculture.[35]

Corruption is a problem in most Southeast Asian countries, but Vietnam lacks any true opposition parties that might help to expose it. Singapore has found that paying government officials a generous wage is the best way to reduce corruption, but Vietnam is too poor to do this. Like Indonesia, it has had to rely on making an example of high-level offenders. In 2005, the National Assembly ratified a long-awaited anticorruption law, which required all officials and their close relatives to disclose their assets. In the same month, the deputy head of the State Inspectorate's department of economic inspection was arrested on charges of bribery and corruption.[36]

The Judiciary

The rule of law is gradually being established in Vietnam, in large part to serve the goal of economic development by encouraging foreign and domestic investors. The 1992 constitution states that the communist party operates within the framework of the law and the constitution. But the country is still in transition from a system in which the communist party decided what was legal and what was not.

The judicial system includes the Supreme People's Court, local courts, and military tribunals. The presiding judge of the Supreme People's Court and the chief prosecutor are both chosen by VCP leaders and confirmed by the National Assembly for a five-year term that coincides with that of the National Assembly. In 1997, a judge of the Supreme People's Court became the first of many members of the judiciary to be convicted of corruption.[37]

Civil Society

Although Vietnam's communist leaders are firmly opposed to political pluralism or anything that smacks of political competition with the VCP, hundreds of nongovernmental organizations (NGOs) were allowed to set up shop after the *doi moi* policy was adopted in 1986. The NGOs can make policy recommendations or perform services like helping people with AIDs, as long as they do not explicitly or implicitly criticize the party's effectiveness. On policy issues, the NGOs generally support the aims of the VCP and state institutions.[38]

The NGOs in Hanoi are mostly staffed by retired government officials, and they are generally involved in research and efforts to influence government policy on a range of social and economic issues. These groups include the Center for Education Promotion and Empowerment, the Rural Development Services Center, the Center for Research on Energy and Environment, and the Center for the Fight Against AIDS.[39]

In Ho Chi Minh City, the NGOs are more likely to be engaged in social work and direct action to help vulnerable groups in the population. These NGOs include the Center for Social Work with Children, the Club for Saigon Train Station Kids, the Thao Dan Street Children Care Program, and the Buddhist Bo De Free Kitchen. A few of the organizations in Ho Chi Minh City were in existence before *doi moi* and may have been influenced by the work of U.S. and French NGOs in the 1960s and 1970s.

Most of the southern, social work-oriented organizations are very small with only a handful of members and a very limited budget. As long as they operate on a small scale and without political fanfare, the government does not interfere with their work. But the communist party tends to view religious organizations as a threat if they have a large membership and clergy who command greater respect than VCP cadres. When they engage in large-scale social programs such as flood relief, the government sees them as implicitly criticizing its failure to provide adequate relief.[40]

Another source of conflict between the government and NGOs is the fact that NGOs compete for funding from foreign aid programs and international NGOs, which adds to the concern of conservative officials about the growth of foreign influence in Vietnam. The NGOs in Hanoi and in Ho Chi Minh City receive about a quarter of their funding from foreign sources.[41]

The Media

The Culture and Information Ministry supervises the activities of all electronic and print media in Vietnam. Recently, newspapers have been allowed to expose certain examples of corruption and other failures of the system that the VCP is trying to correct. For example, in 2005, reporters for the *Thanh Nien* newspaper were allowed to gather and publish evidence that rules designed to halt the spread of avian flu were not being properly enforced.[42] But a 2005 decree banned public gatherings that had not been approved by the VCP, and a 2002 decree authorized the police to destroy publications that the party had not approved.[43]

In Hanoi, the main daily newspaper is *Nhan Dan*, the official VCP organ, with a circulation of 180,000. In Ho Chi Minh City, *Sai Gon Gia Phong* is the leading daily paper and VCP organ with a circulation of 100,000. The officially sanctioned English-language newspapers are *Viet Nam News* in Hanoi (www.vietnamnews.vnagency.com.vn) and *Saigon Times* in Ho Chi Minh City (www.saigontimesweekly.saigonnet.vn). The website of the Voice of Vietnam, the government's radio station is www.vov.org.vn).

By 2001, there were 800,000 personal computers in use in Vietnam and 400,000 Internet users.[44] This allowed a small percentage of the population to keep in touch with each other and share news of current developments. But a special police unit seeks to monitor and control the Internet.

Most Vietnamese in rural areas get their news through radio, television, or the Internet. Access to such media has greatly increased during the past decade, but the content is closely supervised by government ministries and the VCP. According to one study of a village in Hoa Binh province, the VCP cadre determined who was allowed access to newspapers that reached the village. When twelve color TV sets were provided to the village, VCP cadre kept one in a building where everyone could use it and appropriated the rest for their personal use.[45]

People in Vietnam's urban areas have better access to information than those who live in rural areas. But Vietnam cannot hope to develop a knowledge-based economy capable of competing with more advanced countries like Japan, South Korea, and Taiwan unless the party and state stop trying to control the flow of information.

Economic Development

From 1946 to 1975, Vietnam's economic growth was greatly handicapped by nearly constant warfare. For a decade after the communist victory in 1975, the country's growth was further stifled by the imposition of Soviet-style economic institutions and by a two-front war with China and Pol Pot's forces in Cambodia. By 1986, when Vietnam's leaders adopted the policy of *doi moi*, the country was in a severe economic crisis.

The new policy was aimed at transforming Vietnam's economy from a centrally planned system to one in which market forces operated alongside a substantial state sector and the communist party retained a monopoly of political power. Some basic measures such as land reform and price stabilization were implemented quickly, but other reforms like privatizing state enterprises were handled with extreme caution, because the VCP was unwilling to concede that communism had failed. They were also afraid that privatizing the large state companies and making them more efficient would lead to massive unemployment.[46]

The period 1989–1992 was a crucial period in which Vietnam's main source of foreign aid in the Soviet bloc disappeared while the United States maintained its embargo against aid to Vietnam by the World Bank and International Monetary Fund. Forced to rely on its own resources, the Vietnamese government instituted macroeconomic controls that brought the country's triple-digit inflation down below 20 percent by 1992. While Russia and east European states suffered declining growth in their first years of reform, Vietnam's growth rose from 4.7 percent in 1989 to 8.1 percent in 1992.[47]

Agricultural output surged when farmers gained long-term leases to the land they tilled, which they could either sell or transfer to their children. From a net importer of food in the 1980s, Vietnam soon became a major exporter of rice and other foodstuffs. Nutrition levels improved, rural incomes rose, and agricultural exports earned badly needed foreign exchange. According to the World Bank, Vietnam's economic growth averaged 7.4 percent a year in the decade ending 2003, and the number of people living in poverty was reduced by half—from 58 percent of the population to 28 percent.[48]

From 1993 through 2007, Vietnam's economy grew by more than 7 percent a year, powered by an industrious work force, very high levels of investment, and strong markets for the country's exports. Domestic consumption also played an increasing role toward the end of this period, and growth rose above 8 percent. But by 2008, Vietnam's economy began to suffer once again from rising inflation. The causes included weak macroeconomic management by the government, which was obsessed with the goal of higher growth and ill-equipped to handle the flood of foreign investment and remittances which poured in from abroad. Although Vietnam was an important exporter of rice, it struggled to control soaring food prices, which created severe hardship for Vietnam's urban workers. Fearing strikes and uprisings by suddenly impoverished workers, the government banned rice exports and vowed to make fighting inflation its top priority.[49]

Table 2.3 shows the economic outlook as of April 2009. The main reason that lower growth was expected in 2009 was the reduced demand for Vietnamese exports in the

Table 2.3
Vietnam's Economy, 2007–10

	2007	2008	2009	2010
GDP Growth	8.5	6.2	1.6	2.0
Agricultural Production Growth	3.7	3.8	2.1	3.0
Industrial Production Growth	17.0	14.6	-2.2	0.8
Inflation	8.9	24.4	4.8	3.6
Exports (U.S. $B)	48.6	61.3	45.6	48.3
Imports (U.S. $B)	52.6	77.8	50.2	51.8

Source: Economist Intelligence Unit, "Vietnam, Country Report," April 2009. Figures for 2009 and 2010 are EIU forecasts.

U.S., Europe, and Japan, which were hard hit by recession. A slow recovery of Vietnam's growth rate was expected in 2010 as demand for Vietnamese exports was expected to grow.

Problems of a Fast-Growing Economy

Although Vietnam has some highly skilled technocrats and diplomats, it needs many more to manage its expanding relations with foreign governments, corporations, and international organizations. The education minister has met resistance from conservative VCP colleagues in his effort to upgrade Vietnam's universities and give them more freedom to raise academic standards.[50] Also, the incomes of urban residents have been growing by at least twice the rate of incomes of people in rural areas. More than 25 percent of the population, including many minorities, still live below the poverty line. Government salaries have lagged far behind those in the private sector, and corruption acts as a major drag on development by discouraging investors.[51]

Policy debates within the party have become more open, but the policy-making process and even the identity of key decision-makers is often far from clear. Aid donors and foreign businessmen frequently complain about the slow pace at which reforms have been implemented, particularly the privatization of state enterprises. And by focusing on obtaining foreign direct investment, the Vietnamese government is sometimes accused of neglecting to develop an entrepreneurial class of Vietnamese.

Yet interestingly, in 2004 and 2005, the output of Vietnam's non-state industries that were financed locally grew much faster than the output of the state-owned and foreign-invested sectors.[52]

Foreign Relations

When they joined ASEAN in 1995, Vietnamese leaders made it clear that they supported the traditional ASEAN principle of noninterference in member states' affairs. While hosting an ASEAN summit in December 1997, Vietnamese leaders announced publicly that Cambodia (a close ally of Vietnam) would join ASEAN at an unspecified future date, even though several member states had not yet agreed to this.[53] This bold gesture made some analysts suspect that Vietnam would want to lead a group of new ASEAN members that resisted the older members' support for multiparty democracy. But Hanoi has generally avoided public dissent from ASEAN's policy of "positive engagement" with Myanmar. Vietnamese leaders seem to realize ASEAN can not serve as an effective diplomatic bloc if its members openly disagree about basic principles. This sort of restraint helped Vietnam gain the support of its ASEAN partners for a seat on the UN Security Council.[54]

Relations with China

Rivalry for influence over Cambodia led to war between Vietnam and China in 1979. After Vietnamese forces invaded Cambodia, China attacked Vietnam to "teach it a lesson," as Deng Shao-ping put it. During the 1980s there were sporadic armed clashes between Chinese and Vietnamese forces. But in 1991, Vietnam signed the Paris agreement which brought peace to Cambodia. In the same year, diplomatic relations were restored between Hanoi and Beijing. But in spite of many similarities in their domestic policies, they have not been able to resolve all their differences on territorial issues, including conflicting claims to mineral-rich areas of the South China Sea.[55] More than most ASEAN members, the Vietnamese remain wary of China's potential for economic and military dominance of the region. The Vietnamese have a saying, "With China as a neighbor, one must sleep with one eye open."

Relations with Laos and Cambodia

After Vietnam withdrew its occupation forces from Cambodia and Laos in the late 1980s, those two governments (which Vietnam had played a key role in creating) began to act more independently. When Vietnamese living in Cambodia were attacked by Khmer Rouge gangs, the Cambodian government did not protect them. The Vietnamese government also accused the Cambodians of letting dissident groups from Vietnam take refuge in Cambodia.[56] Unlike Cambodia, Laos still relies on Vietnam for military aid, and Laotian leaders openly express their gratitude for it.[57]

Vietnam and the European Union

The EU restored relations with Vietnam in 1990, five years before the U.S. In 1991, President Francois Mitterrand of France became the first western head of state to visit Vietnam since the country was reunified, and France later formed a consortium of oil companies to develop Vietnam's offshore oil and gas deposits. Other European countries have also been generous aid donors to Vietnam and have provided considerable private investment capital.[58]

Vietnam and the United States

In 1993, the U.S. administration finally ended the economic blockade of Vietnam which Congress had long insisted on maintaining. In the following year, the United States and Vietnam established liaison offices in each others' countries, followed by full diplomatic relations in 1995. In 2000 the U.S. and Vietnam signed a Bilateral Trade Agreement (BTA), which greatly reduced tariffs by both countries. A second U.S.-Vietnam trade agreement in 2006 opened the way for Vietnam's entry into the World Trade Organization. Trade between the two countries reached $9 billion by 2007, and the United States ranks as Vietnam's top provider of private investment capital. Security cooperation between the two countries has also grown steadily, with Vietnam hosting five U.S. naval visits in 2007.[59]

Conclusions

The *doi moi* policy adopted in 1986 produced a dramatic turnaround in what had been Vietnam's failing economic and foreign policies. The country's relations with its neighbors and with all the major powers improved dramatically. But as long as the VCP insists on retaining a monopoly of political power, Vietnam is unlikely to reach its goal of joining the ranks of the most advanced countries. The party's commitment to economic reform also faltered when the Asian financial crisis reduced Vietnam's growth rate, because this helped reactionaries like Le Kha Phieu regain control of the VCP.

Nong Duc Manh's appointment as party leader in 2001 restored momentum for political and economic reform. Instead of a purely repressive response to the complaints of hill tribes and religious groups, Nong Duc Manh and his colleagues tried to offer practical solutions to their problems. But many analysts agree that Vietnam's economy can not continue to grow at its present rate unless more definitive results are achieved in combating corruption, protecting human rights and freedom of expression, and establishing the rule of law. It is hard to see how this can be done without the checks and balances of a multiparty system.

Further Reading

Abuza, Zachary. *Renovating Politics in Contemporary Vietnam*. London and New York: Routledge, 2001.

Brown, Frederick Z. *Second Chance: The United States and Indochina in the 1990s*. New York: Council on Foreign Relations Press, 1989.

Chanda, Nayan. *Brother Enemy: The War After the War*. New York: Harcourt Brace Jovanovich, 1986.

Duiker, William. *Ho Chi Minh*. St. Leonards, Australia: Allen & Unwin, 2000.

Elliott, David W.P. *The Vietnamese War: Revolution and Social Change in the Mekong Delta, 1930–1975*. Armonk, NY: M.E. Sharpe, 2003.

Porter, Gareth. *Vietnam: The Politics of Bureaucratic Socialism*. Ithaca: Cornell University Press, 1993.

Stern, Lewis M. *Renovating the Vietnamese Communist Party, Nguyen Van Linh and the Programme for Organizational Reform, 1987–91*. New York and Singapore: St. Martin's Press and Institute of Southeast Asian Studies, 1993.

Tai, Ta Van. *The Vietnamese Tradition of Human Rights*. Berkeley: Institute of East Asian Studies, University of California, 1988.

Van Chi, Hoang. *From Colonialism to Communism, A Case History of North Vietnam*. New York: Praeger, 1964.

Zasloff, Joseph J., and MacAlister Brown, eds. *Communism in Indochina*. London and Lexington, MA: D.C. Heath, 1975.

– 3 –

CAMBODIA

Between Powerful Neighbors

Cambodia has struggled for centuries to avoid being absorbed by Thailand and Vietnam. While foreign intervention has often been a curse, occasionally it has offered a partial solution to Cambodia's problems.[1] In the nineteenth century, French colonial rule saved Cambodia from being dismembered by its neighbors. In the 1970s, Cambodia was almost totally destroyed by civil war (in which the U.S., China, and the Soviet Union intervened), and Pol Pot's orgy of murder and misrule brought death to at least 1.7 million people.[2] Ironically, Cambodia was saved from extinction by a Vietnamese invasion which Pol Pot himself provoked. The United Nations intervened massively from 1991 to 1993 and managed Cambodia's first free election.

Cambodia now has normal ties with its Asian neighbors and the West, but it lags far behind Thailand and Malaysia in economic development and standards of governance. The country is ruled by a coalition of two parties. The dominant one is Hun Sen's Cambodian People's Party, which was originally put in power by Vietnam. The junior coalition partner is FUNCINPEC, which leans toward Thailand. The recent discovery of large oil reserves could be a blessing or a curse, depending on whether Cambodian leaders use this resource for their own or the country's benefit. If the ruling group no longer needs tax revenues to run the state, they might decide to dispense with the semi-democratic freedoms that are currently allowed. Compared to the Burmese junta, Hun Sen allows more leeway for civil society to function, but in 2009 Hun Sen imprisoned the owner of a newspaper affiliated with an opposition party for allegedly publishing articles that could affect political stability.[3]

In some respects, the situation in Cambodia is similar to that in Myanmar, which is also rich in oil and gas. Official corruption is pervasive in both countries. The rule of law is shaky in Cambodia and almost nonexistent in Myanmar. But Hun Sen allows more leeway for civil society to function, provided it does not threaten his own or his party's dominant position.[4]

People and Cultures

As Table 3.1 shows, the Khmer people form 90 percent of Cambodia's population. Most of them live in rural villages and engage in rice farming, and their language, culture, and Theravada Buddhism give them a strong sense of common identity. However,

Table 3.1
Cambodia: Demographic Overview

Population (2008 estimate): 14.9 million (84% rural, 16% urban)

Annual Growth Rate of Population (2008): 1.72%

Ethnic Groups (2008): Khmer 90%, Vietnamese 5%, Chams 2%, Chinese 1%, hill tribes 1%

Religious Affiliations (2008): Most of the Khmer are Theravada Buddhists; there are also Muslims, Christians, and animists

Literacy (2003): females 64.1%, males 84.7%

Income per Capita (2007): U.S. $571 ($2,490 purchasing power parity)

Internet Users (2003): 35,000

Primary School Students (2002): 2,408,109

Secondary School Students (2002): 388,664

Life Expectancy (2007): females 63 years, males 59 years

Infant Mortality Rate (2007): 58 per 1,000 live births

Maternal Mortality Rate (1998): 900 per 100,000 births

HIV/AIDS (2003): 2.6% of persons aged 15 to 49

Percent of Population Living on $2 per Day (2007): 50.3%

Access to Health Services (2007): urban population 80%, rural population 50%

Access to Safe Drinking Water (2007): urban population 61%, rural population 28%

Human Development Index Ranking (2004): 130 out of 177 countries

Sources: Europa World Year Book; Economist Intelligence Unit; Ian Brown, *Cambodia: An Oxfam Country Profile*; United Nations Development Program, *Human Development Report*.

ethnic tension between the Khmer majority and Vietnamese minority plays an important role in Cambodian politics. Many of the people still suffer from the effects of civil war and Khmer Rouge oppression in the 1970s. Land mines have killed thousands of people and left nearly 50,000 with a limb blown off.[5] Moreover, with 60 percent of the population under the age of twenty and large numbers of people unemployed or underemployed, there are major problems of crime, prostitution, and drug abuse.

Ethnic Groups

The four main minority groups in Cambodia are the Vietnamese, the Chinese, the Cham-Malays, and the hill tribes. The tribes are known collectively as the Khmae Loeu (literally "upper Cambodians"). Since Cambodia regained its independence in 1954, the various regimes (except the Khmer Rouge) have regarded the Cham-Malays and Khmae Loeu as assimilable and therefore eligible for Cambodian citizenship. But the Vietnamese and Chinese have not been considered capable of assimilation, so they have not been eligible for Cambodian citizenship. Nor are they guaranteed protection under the 1993 constitution.[6]

THE IMPACT OF KHMER ROUGE GENOCIDE

Scholars including Professors David Chandler and Ben Kiernan have estimated the approximate number of people of different ethnic groups who were living in Cambodia in 1975 when the Khmer Rouge seized control of the country and the number who died during the period (1975–79) when the KR were in power. The population of Cambodia in 1975 was approximately 7,890,000. The three million people who were living in urban areas when the Khmer Rouge seized power (including many who had fled their rural villages to escape the civil war) were driven out of the cities by the KR, who classified them as "new people." The 4.84 million people who were still living in rural areas when the Khmer Rouge seized power in 1975 were classified as "base people" by the Khmer Rouge. The death rate among "new people" (29 percent) was nearly twice as high as among "base people" (15 percent).[7]

Although the exact numbers of the minority groups are not known, it is generally believed that together they form about 10 percent of Cambodia's current population. The Vietnamese, who number about 700,000, are the largest minority group. There are about 150,000 ethnic Chinese, but a considerably larger number of people are of Sino-Cambodian descent. Cham-Malays probably number about 300,000 and the Khmer Loeu hill tribes about 100,000.

THE VIETNAMESE MINORITY

There were almost 400,000 Vietnamese in Cambodia in the early 1960s. They generally lived in their own urban and rural communities and seldom intermarried with Khmers. Under the Lon Nol regime in the early 1970s, thousands of Vietnamese were massacred by government troops (or with their complicity) and many more were forced to flee the country. When Pol Pot seized power in 1975, he was bitterly anti–Vietnamese, and he expelled or murdered most of the remaining members of the Vietnamese community.[8] His frequent guerrilla raids into Vietnam itself provoked the Vietnamese invasion of Cambodia in December 1978.

Vietnamese forces occupied Cambodia from 1979 to 1989 and put a group of pro–Vietnam Cambodians (including Hun Sen) in charge of the People's Republic of Kampuchea (PRK) government. During the 1980s, the number of Vietnamese who reentered Cambodia was perhaps in the range of half a million to a million. The country was occupied by up to 200,000 Vietnamese troops and hundreds of Vietnamese civilian "advisors." Economic conditions were somewhat better in Cambodia than in South Vietnam, especially in the late 1980s when a rebuilding boom in Phnom Penh created a need for construction workers. So large numbers of Vietnamese settled in Cambodia during the 1980s, and many remained there after the Vietnamese troops left. Conditions for the Vietnamese troops were extremely hard. During the eleven-year occupation, 55,300 soldiers died in combat with KR bands or from illness.[9]

During the 1990s, hundreds of Vietnamese were murdered by Khmer Rouge bands, and thousands more were forced to flee the country for their own safety. The Hun Sen regime did not persecute the Vietnamese, but it did not protect them either.[10] One reason for this may have been Hun Sen's desire to rid himself of the stigma of being a "Vietnamese puppet," because he was installed in power by the Vietnamese in the 1980s.

THE CHINESE MINORITY

This group has generally been more welcome in Cambodia than the Vietnamese, and intermarriage between Chinese businessmen and elite Khmer families has been taking place for many generations. As in Thailand, both ethnic groups benefited from such marriages. But during Pol Pot's reign, the Chinese were singled out for brutal treatment, and during the Vietnamese occupation, the Chinese who survived or came to Cambodia in the early 1980s were badly treated by the Vietnamese occupying the country, because Vietnam and China were at war. But after the Vietnamese forces left in 1989, the Chinese were allowed to resume their economic role and to reopen their schools in Cambodia.[11]

The *Chams* are Muslim descendants of fifteenth century refugees from the kingdom of Champa (which was located in present-day Vietnam). Their numbers have been augmented by Muslim immigrants from Malaysia, and they speak the Malay language, so they are often referred to as *Cham-Malays*. They have always lived in separate villages from the Khmer Buddhist majority and have not intermarried with them, but relations between the two communities have been good.[12] Nevertheless, the Khmer Rouge forced the Cham-Malays to abandon their language and religion and killed those who refused.

In the 1980s, Hun Sen gave the surviving Cham-Malays preferential treatment in an attempt to portray his regime as moderate. During the 1990s, the Cham-Malays also received financial support and missionaries from countries such as Pakistan and Saudi Arabia to rebuild their mosques and make the pilgrimage to Mecca.[13]

Cambodia's *Khmae Loeu* hill tribes have generally been regarded by the Khmer people as culturally backward members of their own ethnic group. In the past, the hill tribes have sometimes resisted the government's efforts to assimilate them and develop the northeastern provinces where most of the hill tribes live. During the civil war period, the Khmer Rouge were partially successful in harnessing the grievances of the hill tribes and gaining their support. Today, the Hun Sen regime and Cambodian army are developing the northeastern region for tourism, timber-harvesting, and plantation crops. There have been reports of conflict between the Cambodian government and tribal groups that are similar to the conflicts taking place in Vietnam and Laos between those two states and members the same tribal groups.[14]

Status of Women

As Table 3.1 shows, women in Cambodia have a lower literacy rate than men, because females have less access to education than males. The birth-rate in Cambodia is one of the highest in Asia, and a very large number of women die in child-birth. However, the terrible attrition rate of the civil war period (mid–1960s to mid–1980s) left a population with more female survivors than men. So a large number of women were widowed or never married, and single parent households are much more common now than before the civil war. Rural households (which account for 84 percent of the population) have much less access to medical services and safe drinking water than urban ones, and single women had a difficult time with disputes over land rights after the government abandoned its policy of collective farming in 1989.[15]

As in many Asian societies, Khmer women are severely underrepresented in government, but they run their own households, and they tend to be at least as active as men in village affairs and nongovernmental organizations. During Cambodia's long civil war, women were almost as likely as men to be recruited into the army or guerrilla bands, and some were in positions of command. But after the civil war, Cambodian men expected their wives to behave submissively in public.[16]

Cambodia's extraordinarily young population offers hope for the future, but meeting their basic needs is a major challenge. The number of Cambodian children officially enrolled in primary and secondary schools overstates the number actually attending school, because parents may not be able to afford the necessary clothing or school supplies, or the children may be needed to help with household chores. Moreover, the economy is not growing fast enough to absorb many of the hundreds of thousands of young people trying to enter the workforce each year.

Historical Background

The Angkor empire, which lasted from 802 to 1431, was Cambodia's golden age. Its capital near the town of Siem Reap in northwest Cambodia was one of the largest cities in the world, and its influence extended into Myanmar and Malaya. When Siamese forces overran Angkor, the Cambodians built a new capital at Phnom Penh, which had access to the sea via the Mekong River. Cambodia and Siam fought many wars, but they had much in common, and they influenced each other's cultural development.[17]

Table 3.2
Events in Cambodian History

A.D. 802–1431	The rise and fall of the Angkor empire.
1400s and 1500s	New capital Phnom Penh engages in foreign trade.
1594	Siamese capture Lovek, and Cambodia's long decline begins.
1700s	Vietnamese migrants occupy the Mekong river delta.
1800s	Siam and Vietnam compete for control over Cambodia.
1835–40	Vietnamese occupy Cambodia but fail to "Vietnamize" it.
1863	French protection shields Cambodia from Vietnam and Siam.
1880s	French establish a colonial administration in Cambodia.
1942–45	Japanese allied with the Vichy French occupy Indochina.
1953	France restores Cambodia's independence.
Late 1960s	U.S. bombs and invades Cambodia as civil war begins.
1970	Gen. Lon Nol ousts Sihanouk and seizes power.
1975	KR defeat Lon Nol forces and establish totalitarian state.
1978	Vietnamese invade Cambodia and drive KR out of Phnom Penh.
1991	Paris peace agreement ends the Cambodian civil war.
1991–93	UN Transitional Authority in Cambodia organizes a free election leading to the formation of a coalition government.
1997	Forces loyal to Hun Sen and Ranariddh clash in Phnom Penh.
1999	Cambodia joins ASEAN after Hun Sen holds a free election, as required by the ASEAN foreign ministers.
2004	Cambodia joins the World Trade Organization.
2007	Discovery of large oil and gas reserves in Cambodia.

Cambodia entered a steep decline in the eighteenth century after the Vietnamese colonized the Mekong delta and blocked Phnom Penh's access to the sea. Under pressure from their neighbors, the Khmer ruling class tended to divide into pro–Siamese and pro–Vietnamese factions, further weakening the Cambodian state by their feuding.

French Colonial Rule

France established a protectorate over Cambodia in 1863 and saved the country from being dismembered by Vietnam and Siam. But as the protectorate evolved into a colonial administration, the French did little to prepare Cambodians to govern themselves more effectively. Instead, they brought thousands of Vietnamese to Cambodia and employed them as clerks in the colonial administration, while others were hired to work on plantations. Heavy taxes were imposed by the French and sometimes collected by Vietnamese clerks. Peasant farmers who could not pay the taxes were required to perform up to ninety days a year of unpaid labor on roads and other public works. These aspects of French rule were resented by the Khmer people who staged several major rebellions.[18] However, French rule also helped to preserve the Khmer race and culture by physically protecting the country at an extremely vulnerable stage in its history and by restoring Angkor Wat and other great architectural monuments.

A small elite class of well-connected Cambodians and Sino-Cambodians adopted the French lifestyle and sent their children to school in France. Those who were recruited by the French Communist Party joined the Indochina Communist Party when they returned to Cambodia. Some stayed in Vietnam in 1954 after the first Indochina war and returned to Cambodia when Vietnam invaded in 1978. Others formed the Cambodian communist party (*Pracheachon*), which became virulently anti–Vietnamese under Pol Pot's leadership.

Norodom Sihanouk

In 1941, the French chose nineteen-year-old Prince Norodom Sihanouk as ceremonial king, believing him to be pliant and willing to support their policies. They learned otherwise when he launched a successful campaign for independence, which was granted in 1953. There was little trust between Sihanouk and the Khmer ruling class in Phnom Penh, but he got on well with the rural peasantry who liked his populist style.[19]

In foreign affairs, Sihanouk verbally attacked the west and leaned toward communist China, but he counted on U.S. support to protect Cambodia from the forces of north and south Vietnam. In domestic politics, he tried to keep both the right and left factions of the Cambodian elite off balance. To avoid arrest, the leaders of the communist *Pracheachon* fled to the jungle and organized a guerrilla force which Sihanouk dubbed the "Khmer Rouge" (KR).

Civil War

Against Hanoi's wishes, the KR launched a civil war in the late 1960s to take over Cambodia.[20] For the next twenty-five years, they fought a series of opponents in a struggle that cost nearly 2 million lives and almost destroyed the Cambodian state and culture. Table 3.3 shows who the main combatants were and which cold war antagonists supported them. In 1969, the U.S. began bombing communist base areas in Cambodia, and in 1970, U.S. and South Vietnamese forces launched a ground offensive in Cambodia.[21] Some Cambodians supported the Khmer Rouge, but many others fled to Phnom Penh and Battambang where the Cambodian army provided some protection from the warring parties.

Lon Nol's Republic, 1970–75

In March 1970, Sihanouk was overthrown by General Lon Nol, the head of the Cambodian army, who was as anti–Vietnamese as the Khmer Rouge. His troops killed thousands

Table 3.3
The Cambodian Civil War, 1969–1993

Cambodian Government	*Combatants*	*Foreign Supporters*
Lon Nol's Republic 1970–75	Khmer Rouge Lon Nol's army	China United States
KR's "Democratic Kampuchea" 1975–78	Khmer Rouge Vietnamese Communists	China Soviet Union
People's Republic of Kampuchea, 1979–89 State of Cambodia, 1989–91	Khmer Rouge Non-Communist Khmers PRK & Vietnamese forces	China & Thailand U.S. and ASEAN Vietnam & USSR
UN Transition 1991–93	Khmer Rouge UN peacekeepers	China UN members

of unarmed Vietnamese civilians and drove many others out of the country. But in spite of $1.68 billion worth of U.S. military aid and food supplies, Lon Nol's forces lost ground steadily to the Khmer Rouge guerrillas until he controlled only Phnom Penh and Battambang and a few small towns. These enclaves became crowded with refugees from the countryside and totally dependent on U.S. food and military supplies which were airlifted in or convoyed up the Mekong river by boat.

On April 12, 1975, U.S. Ambassador John Gunther Dean ordered the evacuation of the remaining 82 U.S. personnel plus 159 Cambodians and 35 other nationals who had been employed by the U.S. embassy. While Lon Nol was evacuated, several prominent leaders, including Prime Minister Long Boret and Prince Sirik Matak, stayed behind in the hope that they could play some role in national reconciliation, but they were killed by the KR.[22] There were no clamoring mobs, as in Vietnam, seeking places on U.S. helicopters. Although rumors of the KR's brutality had reached Phnom Penh, most Cambodians awaited their arrival stoically. On April 17, 1975, the KR, dressed in black peasant garb, marched into Phnom Penh. To show their independence of Vietnam, they timed their victory two weeks before north Vietnamese forces entered Saigon.

Democratic Kampuchea, 1975–79

The Khmer Rouge believed they could create a purer form of communism than either the Chinese or the Soviets had. They forced everyone living in towns and cities to move to the countryside to help clear the jungle and plant rice. Many people starved to death or died of illness and overwork before a crop was harvested. The Khmer Rouge tried to kill all educated people and all who supported the previous regime. Members of the Chinese and Cham minorities were killed if they were caught speaking any language but Cambodian. Nearly all members of the Vietnamese minority who had survived Lon Nol's pogroms were either killed or forced to flee into South Vietnam. Pol Pot even ordered the execution of his closest associates if he thought they were connected with Vietnam.[23]

The Khmer Rouge reign of terror lasted from April 1975 to December 1978. Pol Pot launched frequent raids into Vietnam, and these attacks finally provoked the Vietnamese to retaliate. They invaded Cambodia and drove the Khmer Rouge into the mountains near the Thai border. To punish the Vietnamese for invading Cambodia, China attacked Vietnam in January 1979, and fighting between China and Vietnam continued through the 1980s.[24]

The PRK Regime

Vietnamese forces supported by Moscow occupied Cambodia and set up a pro–Hanoi government called the Peoples Republic of Kampuchea (PRK), which had hundreds of Vietnamese "advisors" guiding its actions at every level. Although the PRK let the Cambodian people rebuild their homes and temples, the regime was resented because it imposed tight political controls and allowed a large influx of Vietnamese migrants into the country. Also, during the PRK period, fighting continued between KR and Vietnamese occupation forces. The PRK regime was made up of recent Khmer Rouge defectors to Vietnam plus veteran Cambodian communists who had lived in Vietnam since the 1950s. One of the Khmer Rouge defectors, Hun Sen, became prime minister of the PRK regime in 1985 at the age of thirty-five, and he was still head of Cambodia's government in 2009 after winning the 2008 election.[25]

Clouded Memories of the KR

A number of Cambodians have published accounts of the lives they lived during the Pol Pot era. But at least two-thirds of all Cambodians living today were born after the 1970s and know little of the Pol Pot era except what their families have told them. When Vietnam controlled Cambodia in the 1980s, children were taught in schools that the KR resembled supernatural demons, and Vietnam "liberated" the country. From the early 1990s, Cambodian schools have taught very little about the KR period, because Hun Sen and other government leaders were once members of the KR. For the same reason, efforts to organize a trial for the remaining KR leaders moved slowly. In 2007, the first Cambodian high school textbook to deal with the KR period was published, but a review panel ruled it could only be used as supplementary reading and as a basis for an Education Ministry textbook.[26]

The UN Transition, 1991–93

In 1991, a peace agreement was reached by the Cambodian factions, the ASEAN states, Vietnam, and the permanent members of the UN Security Council. The agreement called for a UN peace-keeping force, disarmament of the Cambodian factions, resettlement of Cambodian refugees, and UN-supervised elections to create a constituent assembly to draft a new constitution and approve a new government.[27]

The carefully prepared and monitored election was the main achievement of the UN mission, which ended in 1993. Despite the KR's efforts to disrupt the election, ninety percent of Cambodia's eligible voters participated. The winner with 45.5 percent of the vote was Prince Ranariddh's royalist party known as FUNCINPEC. Ranariddh's supporters hoped he would be a strong nationalist leader like Sihanouk, his father. Hun Sen and the

Cambodian People's Party received only 42.5 percent, probably because voters were concerned about his ties to Vietnam.

Coalition Government

Rather than accept the result of the election, Hun Sen's party threatened to create chaos by starting a secessionist movement. To break the impasse, a makeshift coalition government was formed with Ranariddh as First Prime Minister and Hun Sen as Second Prime Minister. Although their two parties nominally shared power, the Hun Sen's CPP controlled the army and the bureaucracy.[28] Nevertheless, the coalition provided the country with some political stability, because the two main parties each had more to gain by staying together than by breaking up.

Hun Sen's 1997 "Coup"

In July 1997, forces loyal to Hun Sen and Ranariddh clashed in Phnom Penh. The battle lasted for two days with many casualties. Hun Sen's forces won, and he was accused of carrying out a coup d'etat. But Ranariddh had been negotiating with Khmer Rouge leaders for their support in the upcoming election, and he had secretly imported several tons of weapons into Cambodia to strengthen his private army. Major aid donors and members of ASEAN responded to the clash by threatening to withhold aid, delaying Cambodia's membership in ASEAN, and declaring Cambodia's UN seat vacant. The same countries also insisted that Hun Sen allow elections to be held in 1998 with Ranariddh and his party taking part.[29]

The CPP was able to win the 1998 election without resorting to wholesale cheating, because its tight control of the state enabled it to reward or punish members of the electorate.[30] After the election, the coalition with FUNCINPEC was reestablished, with Hun Sen serving as Prime Minister and Ranariddh accepting the reduced status of president of the National Assembly. Most foreign aid donors resumed providing aid, and Cambodia was admitted to ASEAN while its representatives regained their seat in the UN General Assembly.

Political System

Cambodia's constitution was drafted by the constituent assembly which was elected in 1993 in the country's first democratic election. The document called for a parliamentary form of government with a king as ceremonial head of state and a prime minister chosen by a popularly elected National Assembly. Once the constitution was adopted, the constituent assembly became the National Assembly.

Members of the National Assembly traveled to Beijing where Prince Sihanouk was living and offered him his old title of king, which he accepted despite the limited political powers that went with it. Sihanouk was seventy-one years old and probably in poor health.[31] He had lost touch with his people while living abroad most of the time since he was ousted by Lon Nol in 1970, and he had angered many Cambodians by supporting the Pol Pot regime while it was in power. After becoming king, Sihanouk continued to reside abroad much of the time until 2004, when he abdicated in favor of his son Prince Norodom Sihamoni, a former ballet dancer and choreographer with no experience in government. Sihamoni promised to remain neutral on political issues.[32]

Hun Sen, the "Strong Man"

Prime Minister Hun Sen joined the Khmer Rouge as a teenager in 1970, rose to the rank of deputy commander of the eastern zone, and lost one eye in combat before defecting to Vietnam in 1977. He became foreign minister of the PRK regime in 1979 and prime minister in 1985 at the age of thirty-five. He often described himself as Cambodia's "strong man," and those who had seen him in action described him as intelligent, tough, intimidating, and bombastic.

In the 1990s, he began learning English and he sought to attract western aid and investment to expand the economy. He sent his sons to study in France and in the United States (one was at West Point). But it was typical of his stormy temperament that he railed at the French and U.S. ambassadors when they criticized his sentencing of former Foreign Minister Sirivuddh, and he threatened to mount massive public demonstrations against the U.S. and French embassies.[33]

The National Assembly

Hun Sen's CPP controls the legislative branch, which now consists of the National Assembly (lower house) and a Senate (upper house). The Senate was added in 1999 to provide a prestigious office for Chea Sim, who heads the CPP. Neither the National Assembly nor the Senate plays any independent political role in spite of the impressive list of duties assigned to them in the constitution. The two bodies meet for just a few days a year and rarely initiate legislation or debate measures proposed by the government before approving them.[34]

One contentious issue that did receive some debate in the National Assembly (before being approved on a party-line vote) was a law that would bar all members of the government and National Assembly from holding citizenship in another country. Since many leading members of FUNCINPEC held citizenship in countries to which they had fled in the 1970s (particularly France and the U.S.), this law was designed to benefit the CPP.[35]

Sam Rainsy, Opposition Leader

In 1994, Sam Rainsy, a highly regarded champion of economic and political reform (and son of a former deputy prime minister), was removed from his post as Finance Minister by Prince Ranariddh, who also had him expelled from FUNCINPEC and the National Assembly because Ranariddh was jealous of his popularity. Rainsy formed his own political party, called the Sam Rainsy Party (SRP), and campaigned for economic reform in Cambodia and in foreign countries that provided aid to Cambodia.[36] In the 2003 election, Hun Sen's CPP won seventy-three seats in the National Assembly and its coalition partner FUNCINPEC won twenty-six seats. Rainsy's party won twenty-four seats, so it became the official opposition party.[37]

Cambodian People's Party (CPP)

During the Vietnamese occupation of Cambodia in the 1980s, the CPP was known as the Khmer People's Revolutionary Party (KPRP), and it was an avowedly communist party made up of Khmer Rouge defectors (including Hun Sen) and Cambodian communists who had lived in Vietnam since 1954.

In October 1991 a few days before the Paris peace agreement was signed, the KPRP officially abandoned Marxism-Leninism, changed its name to Cambodian People's Party, and replaced party secretary Heng Samrin with Chea Sim. The party also claimed to favor a free market economy, separation of powers, "liberal democracy," human rights, and political pluralism.[38] Since 1991, CPP leaders have presented themselves as patriotic Cambodians independent of Vietnam, while opposition groups continued to accuse them of being Vietnamese puppets.

FUNCINPEC

In the 2003 election, popular support for Prince Ranariddh's "National United Front for an Independent, Neutral, Peaceful, and Co-operative Cambodia" fell to 20.8 percent from 31.7 percent in the 1998 election. The decline was attributed to poor leadership by Ranariddh, factionalism, and declining public support for the monarchy, due to King Sihanouk's long absences abroad. In 2006, Ranariddh resigned as president of the National Assembly and was ousted as leader of FUNCINPEC. He announced plans to form another royalist party, but relations between FUNCINPEC and the CPP improved, because FUNCINPEC Secretary-General Nhiek Bun Chhay was a close friend of Hun Sen.[39]

The Judiciary

Like the legislative branch, Cambodia's judiciary has been under the thumb of the executive, as shown by its willingness to sentence opposition journalists and politicians to long prison terms for criticizing the CPP and its leaders. The Minister of Justice, a political figure, has intervened in a number of highly political cases.[40] Hun Sen has promised foreign aid donors he would strengthen the rule of law in order to attract more foreign investment, but he himself has frequently intervened in judicial proceedings.

Khmer Rouge Genocide Trial

In 2003, an agreement was reached between the United Nations and the Cambodian government to create an international tribunal to try Khmer Rouge members for crimes committed when they held power from 1975 to 1979. Even so, the process moved ahead very slowly, partly because Hun Sen and other members of his government were once members of the Khmer Rouge. Pol Pot, whose real name was Saloth Sar, died of natural causes before the tribunal was created. By 2008, five people had been detained and charged by the tribunal with committing war crimes: KR diplomat Ieng Sary and his wife Ieng Thirith; Khieu Samphan (who served as president of Democratic Kampuchea during

1975–78); Kaing Guek Eav ("Duch"), who ran the infamous Tuol Sleng prison; and Nuon Chea, who served as Pol Pot's deputy or "Brother Number Two."[41]

Civil Society

Like most autocrats, Hun Sen has found it hard to accept criticism of his government, but in order to maintain good relations with aid donors, he has allowed some media criticism of his policies, and he tolerates the presence of hundreds of nongovernmental organizations (both foreign and domestic) as long as they do not compete with his government for political influence.

The Media

The explosive growth of new print and electronic media began during the UN transition period. Residents of Phnom Penh have dozens of newspapers and magazines to choose from plus six television channels and at least ten radio stations. Most people living outside the main cities of Phnom Penh and Battambang receive their news via radio or television. All of the media in Cambodia are subject to government censorship, but newspapers have more leeway than TV and radio stations to criticize government policy. Radio and television news is generally restricted to bland reporting of the daily activities of Hun Sen and other government leaders.[42]

During the UN transition period, UNTAC made extensive use of electronic and print media and encouraged the growth of private media in preparation for the 1993 election. But press freedom has been far from complete in the years since 1993. Dozens of journalists, mainly those who opposed the government, have been killed or intimidated while others have been bribed to support government policies. Newspapers are also sometimes deprived of advertising revenues by the government. To escape censorship, some newspapers are printed outside Cambodia and delivered to Phnom Penh by air. Several newspapers have managed, despite government pressures, to maintain high standards of objective reporting on social and political issues. These include the *Phnom Penh Daily* which is published in English and Cambodian and the *Phnom Penh Post* which appears every two weeks in English.[43]

Nongovernmental Organizations

As of 2006, there were more than 200 Cambodian and international NGOs operating in Cambodia. Most of the Cambodian NGO's were organized during or after the UN transition period, and they are usually small organizations with very limited funding. Many of them focus on human rights issues and try to help victims of unlawful arrest and detention, torture, sexual mistreatment, and other abuses by officials. Examples of such organizations include the Cambodian Institute of Human Rights (CIHR) and the Center for Social Development.[44]

Economic Development

Cambodia's long civil war caused enormous loss of life and virtually destroyed the entire infrastructure, turning Cambodia into one of the poorest and most isolated countries in Asia. Some rebuilding took place during the Vietnamese occupation in the 1980s, and the UN transition (1991–93) helped to stabilize the political situation. During the 1990s, the economy began to grow by about 5 percent a year, but this was not fast enough to reduce unemployment, and the country's high birth rate meant that per capita GDP grew very slowly. In 2005, the World Bank estimated that it was only $380 per year, and more than half of the Cambodian people were living on the equivalent of less than $2 per day. As in all Southeast Asian countries, the benefits of economic growth in Cambodia are very unevenly distributed.[45]

Cambodia's garment exports remained strong in 2006 and 2007 in spite of competition with China after the world trade in textiles was liberalized. Tourism and call centers were other important sources of economic growth. As Table 3.4 shows, Cambodia's growth fell sharply in 2008 (compared with 2007), and in 2009 it was -3%. The reduced U.S. market for Cambodian textiles was a major reason for the slowdown. The number of tourist arrivals also fell because of the global recession. A slow recovery was expected to begin in 2010. But the Chevron energy company announced that it did not expect to start pumping oil from offshore Cambodian fields until at least 2013.

Table 3.4
Cambodia's Economy, 2007–10
(figures are percentages unless otherwise indicated)

	2007	2008	2009	2010
GDP Growth	10.2	5.0	-3.0	2.2
Agriculture Production Growth	5.0	2.0	3.0	2.2
Inflation	5.9	2	3	3.3
Government Budget Balance	-2.9	-3.0	-5.7	-5.4
Exports (U.S. $B)	4.1	4.3	3.3	3.5
Imports (U.S. $B)	-5.4	-6.4	-5.4	-5.7

Sources: Economist Intelligence Unit, "Cambodia, Country Report," April 2009. Figures for 2009 and 2010 are EIU forecasts as of April 2009, which roughly coincide with IMF forecasts in April 2009.

The Garment Industry

This industry alone provides employment for 265,000 Cambodians, and 90 percent of Cambodia's garment exports go to the United States and Europe. Under an agreement with the International Labor Organization (ILO), Cambodian garment manufacturers undertook to pay their workers a minimum monthly wage which was higher than wages in China and other competing countries. In 2006, Cambodian garment exports to the United States increased sharply even though the system of quotas known as the Multi Fiber Arrangement, which benefited Cambodian exporters, had expired.[46] Despite a dramatic upsurge of Chinese exports in 2006, U.S. firms continued to buy from Cambodian manufacturers because the ILO agreement appealed to their share-holders and customers.

Potential Oil Wealth

In 2005, exploratory drilling by Chevron and other companies began to discover large reserves of offshore and onshore oil. Used responsibly, oil revenue could be put to work to build health clinics, schools, and other infrastructure in Cambodia's largely neglected rural areas. Prime Minister Hun Sen has said he would use the money for development, but his record of exploiting timber and other resources for personal gain is worrisome. Having enough money to run the government without taxes could make him an even less responsible ruler. Thus, many analysts in Cambodia and abroad feared that oil could be a curse for Cambodia as it has been for countries like Myanmar where it has helped highly undemocratic leaders retain their hold on power.[47]

Corruption

As in most Southeast Asian countries, corruption remains a very serious problem in Cambodia and greatly reduces the effectiveness of foreign aid. Government salaries average only $20 or $30 dollars a month, and it is almost impossible for urban dwellers to live on that amount.[48]

However, the Cambodian economy has performed better than might be expected in recent years, as Table 3.4 shows. Reasons for this probably include a growth in domestic consumption and the lack of government interference in certain sectors of the economy, such as tourism and call centers. Also, since Cambodia joined the World Trade Organization in 2004 it has been compelled to work in compliance with WTO rules.[49]

Foreign Relations

For the first time in many years, Cambodia has good relations with all of its neighbors, including Thailand and Vietnam. It is a member of the United Nations and its specialized agencies and now has diplomatic relations with most countries. It became a member of ASEAN in 1999 and the World Trade Organization in 2004. It is also a member of the World Bank, the International Monetary Fund, and the Asian Development Bank.

Relations with ASEAN

In 1995, the Thai and Vietnamese governments both supported Cambodia for membership in ASEAN, and the country was scheduled to join in August 1997. But the armed clash between forces loyal to Hun Sen and Ranariddh in July 1997 caused the ASEAN foreign ministers to put Cambodia's membership on hold. Hun Sen's first reaction was to angrily reject the foreign ministers' offer to help resolve his country's political crisis, but in late July he asked the foreign ministers to mediate the dispute, and he met with them in early August.[50]

To appease the ASEAN members, Hun Sen formed a coalition government with Ranariddh's FUNCINPEC party, but Thailand, Singapore and the Philippines still opposed Cambodia's admission to ASEAN. In December 1997, Vietnam hosted an ASEAN summit meeting in Hanoi and (on its own initiative) announced that Cambodia had been accepted for membership at an unspecified date. In 1999, Cambodia was finally admitted after Hun Sen allowed Ranariddh to take part in a national election.[51]

Has Cambodia under Hun Sen's leadership been supportive of ASEAN's goals and principles? When Cambodia joined ASEAN, many people viewed it in almost the same light as Myanmar—a potentially failed state that might become a Chinese satellite. So far, however, these fears have turned out to be exaggerated. Cambodia's coalition government is hardly a model democracy, but it has more of the attributes of a "semi-democratic" state (as discussed in the introduction) than Vietnam, Laos, Myanmar, or Brunei, the other new ASEAN members. Elections are held at regular intervals, and opposition parties are allowed to compete (under rules laid down by Hun Sen's government). Nongovernmental organizations are tolerated, and there is a (very limited) degree of press freedom. Cambodia now has normal relations with all its neighbors, and its economic growth rate is one of the highest in the region.

In 2002, Cambodia hosted an ASEAN summit meeting and joined an initiative by the island states to work together on the problem of terrorism. Cambodia has also worked on development projects with Laos and Myanmar in keeping with ASEAN's goal of bringing these countries up to the level of the older ASEAN members. Thousands of tourists from ASEAN countries visit Cambodia each year, making tourism a major industry, and many ASEAN countries have invested in Cambodian hotels, garment factories, cement plants and other ventures. Thus, while Myanmar's junta is an embarassment to ASEAN, they can take pride in the fact that they have helped Cambodia recover from the near fatal trauma of the Pol Pot years.

Relations with Thailand

Thailand is Cambodia's most important trading partner, and large numbers of Cambodians work in Thailand, both legally and illegally. Leaders of the two countries now exchange visits on a regular basis. Although relations are sometimes strained by territorial and other issues, these conflicts have been less bitter than Cambodia's disputes with Vietnam, partly because the Khmer and Thai people share the same religion.

Relations with Vietnam

The official relationship between Cambodia and Vietnam can now be described as normal, a distinct improvement over the recent past when Vietnamese troops occupied Cambodia and Vietnamese "advisors" controlled the PRK government. Although there is little warmth in relations between the Khmer and Vietnamese people, the two governments have managed to resolve a number of issues through negotiation. Hun Sen's government has been trying to shed its image as a Vietnamese puppet, and Hanoi has tried to demonstrate that it has no territorial designs on Cambodia. One unfortunate result is that Vietnamese living in Cambodia are allowed few rights and are given no protection by Hun Sen's government.[52]

Relations with Japan

Japan is the leading provider of foreign aid to Cambodia, and has even increased its support in recent years while reducing its total foreign aid budget. In return, the Cambodian government has supported Japan's bid for a permanent seat on the UN Security Council. Japan has acted as a spokesman for other aid donors in dealing with Cambodia on political issues such as human rights violations. Hun Sen seems to resent Japanese overtures of this sort less than those made by the United States and other Western governments.[53]

Relations with Europe

France and many other European governments have provided generous foreign aid to Cambodia, as has the European Union. However, Hun Sen has shown little patience when European diplomats have lectured him on political issues such as protection of human rights. For example, in 2005 he turned a deaf ear when an EU delegation urged him to restore Sam Rainsy's parliamentary immunity and let one of his colleagues out of prison.[54]

Relations with China

The Chinese supported the Khmer Rouge during the 1970s and eighties, but relations between China and Hun Sen's government improved in the 1990s. As a gesture of defiance toward governments that criticized his clash with Ranariddh in July 1997, Hun Sen announced that he was expelling Taiwan's Economic and Cultural Representative Office and aligning Cambodia with China.[55] Chinese economic aid to Cambodia has increased substantially since then, and in 2000 President Jiang Zemin paid the first official visit to Cambodia by a Chinese head of state in more than thirty-five years. Following in his father's footsteps, King Sihamoni visited China in 2005.

Relations with the United States

Although Hun Sen taught himself English and sent one of his sons to West Point, he nursed considerable bitterness toward the United States for its past support of his opponents.[56] Since the clash between troops loyal to Hun Sen and Ranariddh in 1997, the United States has provided aid to Cambodia mainly through NGOs. This aid supports efforts in Cambodia to build democratic institutions and promote economic development and respect for human rights. Key U.S. concerns include counter-terrorism, reform of the customs service, de-mining and removal of other unexploded ordinance, and accounting for MIAs.[57]

Conclusions

Is the Cambodian state beginning to develop the strength to compete for survival in a global economy? In the 1970s, a brutal civil war almost destroyed Cambodia completely. The country was rescued by the Vietnamese invasion and occupation and later by the United Nations intervention. It is probably too soon to tell how much staying power the new Cambodian state has. Its economy and political institutions are still weak, and it relies heavily on foreign aid, foreign investment, and foreign markets, all of which are beyond its control. Much may depend on whether future oil revenues are used for the good of the people or simply to enrich their leaders.

After decades of war and destruction, Cambodia is reasonably stable and on good terms with its neighbors. The great achievement of the present generation of Cambodian leaders was to save their country from total destruction by Pol Pot's regime. Will the next generation of Cambodians be healthier, better educated, less corrupt and traumatized by war than the present ones? If so, Cambodia may have a brighter future than seemed possible only a few years ago.

Further Reading

Brown, MacAlister, and Joseph J. Zasloff. *Cambodia Confounds the Peacemakers, 1979–1998.* Ithaca: Cornell University Press, 1998.

Chandler, David P. *Brother Number One: A Political Biography of Pol Pot.* New South Wales, Australia: Allen & Unwin, 1993.

Corfield, Justin, and Laura Summers. *Historical Dictionary of Cambodia.* Lanham, MD: Scarecrow Press, 2003.

Etcheson, Craig. *After the Killing Fields: Lessons from the Cambodian Genocide.* Westport, CT: Praeger, 2005.

Heder, Stephen, and Judy Ledgerwood, eds. *Propaganda, Politics, and Violence in Cambodia: Democratic Transition under United Nations Peace-keeping.* Armonk, NY: M.E. Sharpe, 1996.

Kiernan, Ben. *The Pol Pot Regime: Race, Power and Genocide in Cambodia Under the Khmer Rouge, 1975–79.* New Haven: Yale University Press, 1996.

Ledgerwood, Judy, ed. *Cambodia Emerges from the Past: Eight Essays.* Dekalb: Center for Southeast Asian Studies, Northern Illinois University, 2002.

Ngor, Haing, with Roger Warner. *Survival in the Killing Fields.* New York: Carroll & Graf, 2003.

Peou, Sorpong, ed. *Cambodia, Change and Continuity in Contemporary Politics.* Aldershot, UK, and Burlington, VT: Ashgate, 2001.

_____. *Intervention and Change in Cambodia, Towards Democracy?* New York, Bangkok and Singapore: St. Martin's Press, Silkworm, and Institute of Southeast Asian Studies, 2000.

Welaratna, Usha. *Beyond the Killing Fields: Voices of Nine Cambodian Survivors in America.* Stanford: Stanford University Press, 1993.

– 4 –

LAOS

A Country at the Crossroads

Laos is at the crossroads of mainland Southeast Asia in both a literal and a figurative sense. Each year brings new additions to the country's growing network of highways, bridges, airports, and other transportation facilities, nearly all of it funded by foreign governments of the Asia-Pacific region. There clearly is some immediate value for Laos and its people in all this new construction. It creates more jobs for skilled and unskilled workers and more opportunities for all kinds of businesses from cement plants to hotels and restaurants. But will it help to unite the country and create better lives for the Lao people? Or will it mainly benefit China, Thailand, and Vietnam (the surrounding countries) and make it easier for them to exploit adjacent areas of Laos?

The Laotian government is figuratively at a crossroads too. Although the communist party is most unlikely to give up its control of the political system, it can decide how fast to move on political and economic reforms that could make a huge difference for the country and its people. In 2006 and 2007, Prime Minister Bouasone Bouphavanh declared that he had no plan to introduce multiparty democracy, but he did sponsor efforts to curb cronyism, crack down on illegal logging, and resolve the status of Hmong refugees in Thailand. A prominent Hmong woman has been added to the ruling Politburo, and government-paid journalists have been given a role in deciding the rules that govern their profession. They have also been encouraged to support the communist party's efforts to expose high-level corruption in the government. In 2009, Prime Minister Bouasone passed a decree allowing the formation of local non-governmental organizations in a further relaxation of restrictions on civil society. But the government also announced plans for a communications surveillance center to monitor telephone calls and e-mail messages.[1]

Reforms in trade and fiscal policy and efforts to broaden the range of private-sector industries lead the list of recent economic reforms. But Laos remains one of the poorest countries in Asia, and it tends to adopt the same policies as Vietnam, its communist neighbor, on many political and economic issues.[2]

People and Cultures

Laos has a population of only 6.5 million people. The country is as large as the United Kingdom, but 90 percent of the terrain is mountainous. The best farmland is limited to a narrow plain along the Mekong River. Vientiane, the largest city, had 633,000 residents in 2002. In spite of achieving high economic growth in recent years, the population also grew at a high rate, so per capita gross domestic product was only $572 in 2006. As Table 4.1 shows, almost two thirds of the population were living on the equivalent of two dollars a day or less, and more than a third of the population could not afford an adequate diet.[3]

Table 4.1
Laos: Demographic Overview

Population (2007 estimate): 6.5 million
Annual Growth Rate of Population (2007): 2.4%
Ethnic Groups (2007): Lowland Lao 66%, Upland Lao 23%, Highland Lao 10% (includes the Hmong and Yao), ethnic Vietnamese and Chinese together approximately 1%
Religious Affiliations (2007): Theravada Buddhist 65%, animist 30%, Christian 1.3%, Muslim 1%
Literacy (2007): 69%
Personal Computers (2001): 16,000
Primary School Students (2002–03): 85%
Secondary School Students (2002–03): 35%
Students in Universities (2002): 5,273
Students in Other Post-Secondary Education (2002): 7,459
Life Expectancy (2007): 56 years
Infant Mortality Rate (2007): 81.4 per 1,000 live births
Income per Capita (2006): U.S. $572 ($1,050 purchasing power parity)
Percent of Population Living on $2 a Day (2007): 63.4%
People Unable to Afford 2,100 Calories of Food a Day (2007): 39%

Sources: World Bank, "East Asia & Pacific Update," April 2007.

Ethnic Groups

There are sixty-eight distinct ethnic groups recognized by the Lao government. Roughly two-thirds of the people belong to the dominant ethnic group known as Lao Loum ("Lowland Lao"), who mainly occupy the towns and farmland along the Mekong River. About nine percent of the people belong to various mountain tribes (including the Hmong, Yao, Akha and Lahu), and live in the high mountains of northern Laos. They are known collectively as Lao Soung or Highland Lao. In the central and southern mountains, Mon-Khmer tribes (known as Lao Theung or Mid-slope Lao) are found.

CHINESE AND VIETNAMESE

There are also a few thousand Vietnamese and Chinese living in the towns and villages along the Mekong, but many left in the 1940s or after the communist victory in 1975. (See historical chronology in Table 4.2) Vietnam had 45,000 troops in Laos at the beginning of 1985 but reduced the number to between 10,000 and 20,000 by the end of the year and withdrew all of its troops a short while later.

China is the leading foreign investor in Laos, concentrating mainly on construction projects and developing rubber plantations in the northern provinces. As in Myanmar, the northern provinces of Laos have a rapidly growing Chinese presence. There are plans for making the border area between Yunnan province and northern Laos a major gateway for trade between China and Southeast Asia.[4]

Table 4.2
Events in Laotian History

1353	Kingdom of Lan Xang founded by Fa Ngum.
1700s	Siam gains suzerainty over all Lao kingdoms.
1893	France establishes suzerainty over all of present Laos.
1936	Lao section of Indochina Communist Party formed.
1942–45	Japanese (with Vichy French) occupy Laos.
1954	Laos regains its independence at Geneva Conference of all governments with an interest in Indochina.
1955	Pathet Lao (communist party) formed with Kaysone Phomvihane as its leader, and struggle for control of Laos begins.
1957	First coalition government includes Pathet Lao.
1962	Geneva conference recognizes second coalition government.
1964	Coalition collapses; U.S. begins "secret war" in Laos.
1972	Pathet Laos renamed Lao People's Revolutionary Party.
1973	Cease-fire and third coalition government formed.
1975	Kaysone Phomvihane becomes prime minister of Lao People's Democratic Republic. The monarchy is abolished.
1977	Treaty of friendship and cooperation signed with Vietnam.
1979	Collectivization of agriculture fails and program is ended. *1986*, Economic reform on Vietnamese model begins in Laos.
1992	Death of Kaysone Phomvihane, Laos' first communist leader.
1997	Laos joins ASEAN; financial crisis causes high inflation.
2006	General Choummaly Sayasone is named president and party head.

Kaysone Phomvihane, the long-serving first head of the communist party (LPRP), had a Vietnamese father and attended school and university in Hanoi. Many of the communist leaders have Vietnamese wives or other strong links to Vietnam, and there are very close official ties between the Lao and Vietnamese governments. But the Lao people, like the Cambodians, tend to resent Vietnamese influence in their country. The Chinese in Laos are not as well assimilated as the Chinese in Thailand, and there is a tendency for the Lao to regard China and its people with suspicion.

Hmong

The Hmong are the most alienated ethnic group in Laos, and they have been blamed for much of the instability there since the communist victory in 1975. About 20,000 Hmong tribesmen were recruited and trained by U.S. officers and fought under the command of General Vang Pao during the second Indochina war. The Hmong soldiers suffered horrendous casualties in battles that took place during and after the war. A large percentage of their troops were killed, including some by poison gas attacks. After the communist victory, over 132,000 members of hill tribes, including many Hmong, sought refuge in Thailand, and more than half that number (77,185) were resettled in the United States between 1975 and 1988.[5]

The Hmong who remained in Laos or settled in Thailand and other neighboring countries continued to mount armed attacks on various targets in Laos. Although the Lao government accused the United States of supporting these attacks, the United States firmly denied it. By 2005, the attacks appeared to have stopped for a combination of reasons, including the increased effectiveness of Vietnamese-trained Lao forces and offers of amnesty and free housing by the Lao government. Hmong communities in Laos reportedly enjoy improved social and economic conditions, and a Hmong woman named Pany Yathortou was nominated for the Politburo in March 2006. The daughter of a Hmong hero, she was the first woman and the first member of an ethnic minority to be elected to the Politburo.[6]

Status of Women

Like most women in Southeast Asia, Lao women play a strong and often dominant role in their families. There is a tradition of newly married couples living with the bride's family, and Lao women tend to have equal inheritance rights with men. Until recently, they had far fewer educational opportunities than Lao men, but during the 1990s the ratio of girls to boys in primary schools began to move from 40:60 toward 50:50. There are still far fewer girls than boys in secondary schools, but the relative strength of the Lao economy in recent years should help to equalize educational opportunities.[7]

As in most Southeast Asian countries, Lao women now work outside the home in quite substantial numbers, but they are underrepresented in the LPRP, the country's only political party. In the 2006 National Assembly election, 28 women were among the 115 successful candidates. In addition to one woman Politburo member, there are several women in the LPRP Central Committee. Women also serve as teachers, nurses, and mid-level administrators in the bureaucracy.[8]

The Middle Class

Besides a small number of professionals, Laos's middle class is mainly composed of government officials who are usually also members of the Lao People's Revolutionary Party. They are concentrated in Vientiane and other urban areas. After the communist victory in 1975, many senior government officials and officers of the defeated army were sent to "reeducation" camps. To avoid such treatment, thousands of middle class Lao fled the country after the communists took over in 1975.[9] Replacing their knowledge and skills has been a long, slow process because of the poor educational system in Laos. Those middle class Lao who remain in the country generally keep any criticisms they have of the communist regime to themselves for fear of retribution.

Historical Background

The Lao people have seldom been united in one large independent kingdom of their own. The only time this happened was when Phaya Fa Ngum founded the kingdom of Lan Xang in 1353, and his son extended its borders to include most of present-day Laos and Northeast Thailand. Internal wrangling over succession to the throne made Lan Xang vulnerable to intrigues by the rulers of Siam, Myanmar, and Vietnam. After reaching a "golden age" during the reign of King Souligna Vongsa, who died in 1694, Lan Xang split into three kingdoms centered on Luang Prabang, Vientiane, and Champassak.

During the eighteenth century, all three Lao kingdoms came under Siamese suzerainty. But by the end of the nineteenth century, the French were in control of Vietnam and Cambodia and looking for a commercial route up the Mekong River to southern China. They sent a resourceful man named Auguste Pavie to Luang Prabang, where he was caught in the middle of a battle between Siamese protectors of the city and Chinese invaders who proceeded to burn Luang Prabang to the ground. Pavie commandeered a canoe and rescued King Oun Kham from the burning city. After this exploit, he had no trouble persuading the king that France was a more useful protector than Siam.[10]

French Colonial Rule

Under a treaty signed in 1907 by France and Siam, the Mekong River became the boundary between Laos and Northeast Thailand and remains so today. Some of the Lao people were living on the eastern side of the river in what is now Laos, but more of the Lao people were in Siam on the western side of the Mekong. The fact that many of the Lao people still live on the Thai side of the border explains why Laos and Thailand have a difficult relationship.

As far as France was concerned, the only value Laos had was as a possible staging area for trade with China or for making further territorial inroads into Siam. The French governed Laos, a country as large as the United Kingdom, with fewer than 600 French administrators. But they brought in thousands of Vietnamese to staff the lower ranks of their administration, and the Vietnamese were resented in much the same way they were in Cambodia.[11]

To limit the cost of administering Laos, the French imposed heavy taxes on the Lao people and required them to perform unpaid labor on the roads. As a result, the Lao frequently rebelled against French rule. The French also skimped on health and educational services and did little to develop the Lao economy beyond building 5,000 kilometers of roads with unpaid labor. A few wealthy Lao families sent their sons to be educated in France, and some were recruited by the French Communist Party. When they returned to Laos, many joined the Indochinese Communist Party, which was founded by Ho Chi Minh in 1930.

When World War II came, the Vichy French regime allowed Japanese troops to cross Indochina to invade Myanmar, Malaysia, and Singapore, but French administrators remained in charge in Indochina until they were interned by the Japanese in the final months of the war. After World War II, France fought an eight-year war to regain control of the Indochina states but was defeated by the communist Viet Minh forces. Laos was only a minor theater of that war, but the decisive battle was fought near Laos at Dien Bien Phu. Laos regained its independence in 1954 as a result of agreements reached at Geneva by all the countries with interests in Indochina.

The Second Indochina War

Over the next twenty years, Laos would have three coalition governments composed of communist, right-wing, and neutralist leaders, but none of them lasted more than a year or two before either the communist or right-wing forces seized power. The communist Pathet Lao was formed in 1955 and led by Kaysone Phomvihane, who directed guerrilla activities from a cave near the Lao-Vietnamese border. In 1972, the Pathet Lao were renamed the Lao People's Revolutionary Party (LPRP). They were closely allied with

North Vietnam and supported by China and the Soviet Union. In 1975, they gained control of the Lao government, and Kaysone became prime minister.[12] He served in that role and had very little contact with western officials until 1991, when he became president just a year before his death.

U.S. Involvement in the War

From the early 1960s, the United States provided large-scale military and economic aid in an effort to shore up a series of neutralist Lao governments and prevent a communist take-over of the country. The United States waged a secret guerrilla war in the mountains of Laos with 18,000 U.S.-trained Hmong soldiers. The United States also carried out one of the most intensive bombing campaigns in history in an unsuccessful effort to cut off the "Ho Chi Minh Trail," a major Vietnamese supply route through eastern Laos. Large amounts of unexploded ordinance, including cluster bombs, still remain in Laos, and the United States is aiding the clean-up effort.

Shortly after seizing power in 1975, the Lao People's Revolutionary Party followed Vietnam's example and collectivized most of the farms in Laos. This move was as deeply unpopular with the Lao people as it was with the Vietnamese. In Laos, the experiment ended even more quickly than in Vietnam. In 1979, Kaysone announced that the frantic rush to build socialism would be slowed down, and most of the hated cooperatives would be abolished. Buddhism was restored to its central place in Lao society, and people had more freedom to worship as they pleased. There was even a small role allowed for a private sector of the economy. In 1986, the LPRP introduced free market reforms in Laos which were similar to one that were announced a few months earlier in Vietnam.

The Asian financial crisis in 1997 caused the Laotian economy to grow more slowly for several years because Thailand, the main trading partner of Laos, was severely harmed by the crisis. Insurgent attacks by Hmong dissidents in rural areas of Laos led to frequent clashes with the Lao army. But by 2006, the economic and the political situation had stabilized, and the Eighth Party Congress (in April 2006) emphasized a continuing commitment to cautious reform. A number of Lao and Hmong organizations, some based inside the country and some in Thailand and overseas, continued to oppose the LPRP government, but there was little likelihood they could overthrow it.[13]

Political System

As in Vietnam, the communist party (LPRP) maintains a tight hold on political power. According to Laos's 1991 constitution, the LPRP is the "leading nucleus" of the political system. Key political and economic decisions are made by the party's Politburo, and many LPRP officials hold corresponding positions in the government. Because of the shortage of educated personnel in Laos, this kind of overlap between the party and government is even more common in Laos than in Vietnam.

The Executive Branch

The positions of state president and secretary general of the LPRP are sometimes held by the same person. The state president is also head of the armed forces. At the

Eighth Party Congress in March 2006, Lt. General Choummaly Sayasone replaced General Khamtay Siphadone as secretary general of the LPRP. The following month, Choummaly also replaced Khamtay as president. Choummaly was the top choice of the military for both jobs.[14]

The prime minister is the head of government, and his role is to carry out the policy decisions of the Politburo. In March 2006, Bounyang Vorachit was replaced as prime minister by Bouason Bouphavanh, a Soviet-trained political economist and former deputy prime minister. Bounyang had previously served as Finance Minister, and he was brought in to stabilize the economy after the 1997 financial crisis.

After the Eighth Party Congress and national assembly elections, the eleven members of the Politburo in rank order were:

1. Choummaly Sayasone, Secretary-general of the ruling LPRP and President. A former army general, he had previously served as Vice President. He was regarded by analysts as conservative but willing to accept reforms.
2. Samane Viyaket, President of the National Assembly.
3. Thongsing Thammavong, Mayor of Vientiane.
4. Bounyang Vorachit, Vice President.
5. Sisavath Keobounphanh, President of the Lao Front for National Construction.
6. Asang Laoly, Deputy Prime Minister.
7. Bouasone Bouphavanh, Prime Minister.
8. Thongloun Sisoulith, Deputy Prime Minister.
9. Dousangchay Phichit, Minister of Defense.
10. Somsavat Lengsavad, Deputy Prime Minister and Minister of Foreign Affairs.
11. Pany Yathortou, Vice President of the National Assembly and a member of the Hmong ethnic group. As noted earlier, she was the first woman and ethnic minority member to be appointed to the Politburo.

CENTRAL COMMITTEE

The Central Committee of the LPRP is composed of fifty-five senior party members from across the country. It meets several times a year to discuss policy initiatives including those proposed in the Politburo. It nominates candidates for senior offices and provides the party leadership with feedback on policies. The Central Committee includes an increasing number of women and ethnic minority members.

National Assembly

This legislative body is not as politically assertive as the Vietnamese National Assembly. Its role is basically to rubberstamp legislation that has been approved by the LPRP, and it serves mainly as a training ground for LPRP leaders. Elections usually take place every five years. All candidates for the National Assembly are approved by the LPRP, and all are party members except for an occasional independent candidate. There are no other political parties in Laos besides the LPRP.

In the 2006 election, 175 candidates (all LPRP) were nominated for 115 seats. LPRP members won 113 seats, and two were won by candidates who were nominally independent. Seventy-one new members were elected, and forty-four who served in the previous legislature were reelected. In the previous election, LPRP candidates campaigned vigorously and sometimes criticized each other. They also tended to say little about the LPRP's goals. This may be why the LPRP leaders replaced so many of the former members of the assembly in the 2006 election.[15]

The Military

The Lao armed forces reportedly numbered 29,100 in 2004, with the army comprising 25,600 of the total. Senior army officers were mostly LPRP members, and they have held the majority of Politburo positions since 1975. The Lao military has extensive economic interests like the armies of Indonesia, Myanmar and several other Southeast Asian countries. There has been talk of the military getting rid of these interests (which pay a sizable portion of the army's expenses) but there has been little action in that regard.[16] The National Police are a branch of the military, but they do not play an important role in politics.

The Bureaucracy

Laos has approximately 65,000 civil servants. Most of the senior members belong to the LPRP, and they constitute a large portion of the Lao political elite. In 1996, responsibility for the bureaucracy was transferred from the Prime Minister's Office to the Central Committee of the LPRP, which illustrates the overlap between the party and government. The bureaucracy has never been well educated or very effective, and the great exodus of civil servants after the communists gained control of the government in 1975 (and the sentencing of many to reeducation camps) left Laos with badly weakened state institutions.

Local Administration

Laos is divided into provinces, municipalities, districts, and villages. Provincial governors and mayors of municipalities are appointed by the state president. Deputy provincial governors, deputy mayors and district chiefs are appointed by the prime minister. Administration of villages is conducted by village headmen.

The Judiciary and Rule of Law

Judges are appointed by the standing committee of the National Assembly on the advice of the Justice Ministry and are essentially political appointees.

When the LPRP took control of the government in 1975, they abolished the existing constitution and governed by fiat. In 1986, when the LPRP adopted the policy of trying to attract foreign investment, the party realized that a legal structure to protect private property was needed to attract foreign companies. So a surprisingly liberal investment law was enacted, but the rule of law has not been firmly established. Corruption in the judiciary and most other branches of government is almost impossible to control when the government pays its junior officials less than ten dollars a month.[17]

Civil Society

The LPRP does not tolerate opposition parties, a free press, or nongovernmental organizations (NGOs) that are critical of LPRP policies, so there is little in the way of civil society in Laos. Nevertheless, a number of exile groups based outside Laos have continued to attack the government's policies. These groups included the Lao Student Movement for Democracy, the Council of Lao Overseas Representatives, and the Lao Human Rights Council.[18]

Groups that are or have been in armed opposition to the government include: the Democratic Chao Fa Party of Laos; the Free Democratic Lao National Salvation Force; the United Front for Liberation of Laos; and the United Lao National Liberation Front. The latter group was reportedly based in Sayabouri province with an estimated 8,000 members who were mostly Hmong tribesmen.[19] Although the Lao government has accused the United States of supporting some of these groups, the U.S. has denied it.

The Media

As noted earlier, almost all Lao journalists are essentially government employees, but they have been encouraged by the government to participate in setting standards for their profession and urged to support the LPRP's policy of exposing corruption in the government.

About twenty newspapers, newsletters, and magazines are published at various intervals by different Lao government agencies in Vientiane, and several provinces have their own newsletters. The circulation of most of these is under 10,000, but the Federation of Lao Trade Unions publishes *Lao Dong* (Labor) which claims a circulation of 46,000, and the LPRP Central Committee publishes a daily newspaper, *Pasason,* which is an authoritative source on government policy. The English-language daily *Vientiane Times* specializes in publicizing opportunities for foreign investors.[20]

The electronic media are also largely government-controlled. Lao National Radio has a domestic and international service and broadcasts in Lao, French, English, Thai, Khmer, and Vietnamese. A government TV station broadcasts from Vientiane, and another one broadcasts from Savannakhet in the south. Also, a Thai firm, International Broadcasting Corporation, owns 70 percent of a TV station that broadcasts in Lao on a third channel. The government owns 30 percent. Thai stations that broadcast in Thai and Lao can also be received in areas near the Thai border.[21]

Economic Development

Starting from a very low base, Laos now has one of the fastest-growing economies in Southeast Asia. The economic development policies which LPRP leaders have followed resemble those of their Vietnamese mentors. In both countries, the communists sought to create a Soviet-style economy by collectivizing agriculture, abolishing private property, and forcing out the entrepreneurial class (i.e., Chinese in Vietnam, Chinese and Vietnamese in Laos). Because of the hardship this caused, piecemeal reforms soon followed in both countries, but Laos abandoned the hated communes in 1979 while Vietnam kept them for several more years.

In 1986, Vietnam changed course sharply and adopted its *doi moi* reforms to rebuild public support for the Vietnamese Communist Party and try to normalize relations with the West. Laos followed Vietnam's example, and by the early 1990s, the economies of both countries were growing rapidly.

The 1997 financial crisis caused severe damage to the Thai economy which led to a surge of inflation in Laos when basic necessities that are normally imported from Thailand became scarce.[22] Both countries recovered, and the Laos economy achieved 7.3 percent growth in 2005. This rapid growth continued through 2008, but 2009 saw a sharp reduction in growth to 3 percent because of a sharp drop in exports (mainly of electricity) to Thailand. Recovery to 5 percent growth was expected by 2010.

Table 4.3
Laos' Economy, 2007–10
(figures are percentages unless otherwise indicated)

	2007	2008	2009	2010
GDP Growth	7.5	7.5	3	5
Agricultural Production Growth	3.2	3.0	3.0	3.2
Inflation	4.5	8.6	3.4	5.8
Government Budget Balance	-2.8	-2.8	-3	-3.1
Exports (U.S. $B)	0.9	1.2	1.1	1.1
Imports (U.S. $B)	-1.1	1.4	-1.3	-1.4

Source: Economist Intelligence Unit, "Laos, Country Report," March 2009. Figures for 2009 and 2010 are EIU forecasts.

Manufacturing (mainly the garment industry) has benefited from temporary U.S. and EU restrictions on Chinese imports, but in its present state the Laotian workforce is unable to compete with workers in neighboring countries. One of the keys to continued high growth in Laos will be greatly increased investment in education and public health care to bring the Laotian population up to the standards of the rest of the region. The government's aim is to reduce the number of people living in poverty to 15 percent by 2011 and to make Laos poverty free by 2020. In 2006, the United Nations Development Programme ranked Laos near the bottom (133 out of 177 countries) on its Global Human Development Index.[23]

Foreign Investment

Laos has been attracting surprisingly large amounts of foreign investment; $2.5 billion was received in the first half of the 2005–6 fiscal year. Most investment has gone to the urban economy, particularly the area around Vientiane, and much more needs to be done to help the rural areas, where most of the population lives. For example, the building of major highways across the country has done little for rural villages because of the lack of feeder roads connecting them to highways. There has also been a lack of coordination of major aid projects funded by the EU, Japan, and the United Nations partly because they operate in different languages.[24] Some of the highways built across Laos have had very little use or maintenance and are already beginning to deteriorate.[25]

Unless there is improved planning of the country's overall development, Laos could end up with only marginal benefits from all the projects being implemented on its territory. For example, construction of roads, bridges, and major dam projects has provided employment for Laotians, and electricity produced by hydropower has been a major Lao export to Thailand. But all of this construction has meant moving tens of thousands of villagers off their traditional lands, and some critics argue that it has benefited the surrounding countries more than Laos because it tends to divide Laos into regions dominated by Thailand, China, and Vietnam.[26]

Tourism

The tourist industry has grown steadily as the amount of unrest in the country has been reduced. In 2005, the number of tourist arrivals passed the one million mark with over half (603,000) coming from Thailand. The Vietnamese were next with 165,000 arrivals, followed by Americans (47,427), Chinese (39,210), and French (35,371).[27]

Foreign Relations

Laos joined the Association of Southeast Asian Nations in 1997 in order to diversify its contacts within the region and to benefit from ASEAN's bargaining strength in dealing with the major powers of Asia and the West. ASEAN membership made Laos a better candidate for foreign investment, and most of Laos' trade is with other ASEAN states (two-thirds with Thailand alone).

Laos has hosted a successful ASEAN summit and it has been an active participant in the various committees and organizations aimed at developing the Mekong River basin, which links southern China with Laos, Myanmar, Thailand, Cambodia, and Vietnam. Of the six riparian countries, Laos arguably has the most at stake, because it is the most vulnerable to exploitation by China and Thailand and to the impact of their development strategies.[28]

The Laotian government's closest political ties are with Vietnam as a fellow communist state. But Thailand has much closer economic and cultural ties with Laos. Because there are new roads linking Laos with Vietnam and China, Thailand can no longer shut off Laos's trade with the outside world as completely as it did in the 1980s. But the railroad through Northeast Thailand to the port of Bangkok is still the cheapest and best route for Laotian exports.

Like Vietnam and Brunei, the Laotian government has tried conscientiously to fulfill the responsibilities of ASEAN membership. It has developed closer ties with Cambodia and Myanmar through exchanges of high-level visits, seminars on common problems, and agreements on joint development projects, including two more bridges connecting Laos to Thailand and Myanmar.[29] Although the Lao ruling party has no intention of allowing multi-party democracy, it does not embarrass ASEAN the way Myanmar does by its treatment of ethnic minorities.

Relations with the United States

The United States normalized its relations with Laos in the early 1990s at about the same pace at which it normalized relations with Vietnam. The United States and Laos have cooperated on counter-narcotics programs, on the search for the remains of U.S. military personnel, and on finding and removing unexploded ordnance in Laos. The Lao government has accused the United States of supporting insurgent groups in Laos, but the United States has denied giving them any support and in 2007 it arrested Vang Pao, the former leader of a U.S.-trained Hmong army.[30] Normal trade relations were reestablished in 2004, and a trade agreement was implemented in 2005. Bilateral trade, although still very limited, is growing, and U.S. aid and private investment are increasing.

Relations with China

Because Laos was closely allied with Vietnam in the 1970s and 1980s, China (which was fighting with Vietnam) had no diplomatic or party-to-party relations with Laos. Relations were restored in 1989, after China agreed to withdraw support from Laotian resistance groups operating from Chinese territory. In 1992, Laos and China signed an agreement on the delineation of their common border. In 1996, they opened a section of their common border to highway traffic, and in 2000, President Jiang Zemin became the first Chinese head of state to visit Laos.

Conclusions

The Southeast Asian region is benefiting from the new roads and bridges connecting Laos to its neighbors and the growing volume of trade that passes over them. So far, these connecting links may have helped the surrounding states more than the Laotian people. But with more effective planning by the Laotian government and donor states, Laos could gain important advantages from its new ties to the outside world and its greatly increased access to foreign investment.

Most analysts agree that Laos needs to invest heavily in improving healthcare and educational opportunities for its people and upgrading the standards of the bureaucracy. The ruling party clearly has no interest in sharing political power with other groups in Laos, but the apparent improvement in the government's relations with the Hmong minority is a positive development. The fact that Laotian journalists are encouraged to expose corruption is also a plus. But it is unfortunate that Laotian leaders have sided with Vietnam on a joint policy of tightly controlling religious groups.

Further Reading

Brown, MacAlister, and Joseph J. Zasloff. *Apprentice Revolutionaries: The Communist Movement in Laos, 1930–1985.* Stanford: Hoover Institution Press, 1986.

Evans, Grant. *Lao Peasants Under Socialism.* New Haven: Yale University Press, 1990.

_____, ed. *Laos, Culture and Society.* Chiang Mai, Thailand: Silkworm Books, 1999.

Goudineau, Yves. *Laos and Ethnic Minority Cultures: Promoting Heritage.* Paris: UNESCO, 2003.

Gunn, Geoffrey C. *Rebellion in Laos: Peasant and Politics in a Colonial Backwater.* Boulder, CO: Westview Press, 1990.

Hamilton-Merritt, Jane. *Tragic Mountains: The Hmong, the Americans and the Secret Wars of Laos, 1942–1992.* Bloomington: Indiana University Press, 1992.

Osborne, Milton. *The Mekong: Turbulent Past, Uncertain Future.* New York: Grove Press, 2000.

– 5 –

MYANMAR

ASEAN's Problem State

Since colonial rule ended in 1948, Myanmar has known only a brief interlude of democratic government. From 1962 to the present, a series of military dictators generally blocked Myanmar's economic growth and engaged in brutal repression of all who stood in their way.[1] The United States and some other Western powers responded with sanctions aimed at forcing the military junta to loosen their grip on the country, but the sanctions have had the unintended effect of isolating Myanmar from the forces of modernization, including trade, tourism, foreign travel, and educational exchange. Thus, the sanctions have penalized ordinary Burmese citizens economically while making it easier for the military to isolate the country from western influence.[2]

To gain access to Myanmar's rich resources, including large reserves of natural gas, China has provided economic and military aid that has helped to keep the military junta in power. ASEAN leaders opposed the U.S. and EU sanctions and instead tried to promote change through political and economic engagement with Myanmar. But in 2007 when the junta responded to mass demonstrations by Buddhist monks by firing on them and arresting thousands, ASEAN leaders seemed unable to agree on a strategy to promote political change.

In early 2008, the Burmese junta announced they would hold a referendum on a new constitution, which had clearly been designed to legitimize their hold on power. The referendum would be followed by parliamentary elections in 2010. The Singapore government called this a positive development, but the Indonesian foreign minister said the constitution would have to be amended to allow broader participation by opposition leaders.[3]

In May 2008, a cyclone ripped through the main city of Rangoon and the Irrawaddy delta, killing up to 100,000 people and destroying a large portion of Myanmar's best rice-growing area. At least two million people were left homeless and without food or medical supplies as torrential rain continued to flood the region. Burmese who survived the cyclone and dozens of foreign governments struggled to aid the victims. But the junta chose to limit aid workers' access to Myanmar and diverted initial aid shipments to the army. The military also went ahead with their referendum in parts of Myanmar that were not hit be the cyclone, and they announced that 92 percent of the voters supported the pro-military constitution. With the main rice-planting season less than two months off,

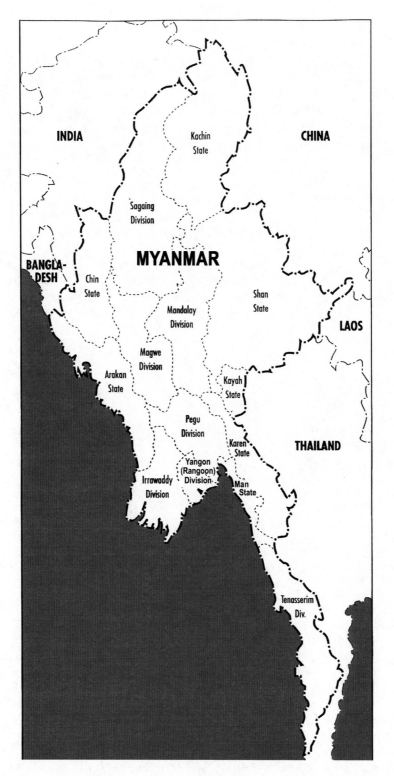

Figure 5.1.

the junta needed more than $250 million worth of foreign aid to restore the rice-growing areas that were destroyed.[4]

In 2009, Aung San Suu Kyi, leader of the main opposition party the National League for Democracy (NLD), was put on trial by the military junta because an American citizen entered the compound where she was under house arrest. It seemed very unlikely that she would be allowed by the junta to take part in the 2010 election. In Myanmar's last election, in 1990, she had led her party to victory in spite of being under house arrest, but neither she nor the NLD was allowed by the junta to take power.

People and Cultures

Ethnic Groups

Myanmar is about the size of Texas with a population in 2007 estimated at 57.6 million people. Ethnic Burmans make up more than two-thirds of the population (as shown in Table 5.1), while a large number of ethnic minorities comprise the remaining third. The most numerous minority groups are the Shans, Karens, Arakanese, Chinese, Mons, and Indians.

Table 5.1
Myanmar: Demographic Overview

Population (2007 estimate): 57.6 million
Annual Growth Rate of Population (2005 estimate): 0.8%
Ethnic Groups (2007): Burman 68%, Shan 9%, Karen 7%, Arakanese 4%, Chinese 3%, Indian 2%, Mon 2%, others 5%
Religious Affiliations (2007): Buddhist 89%, Christian 4%, Muslim 4%, animist 1%, others 2%
Human Development Ranking (2005): 129 out of 177 countries
Literacy (2003 estimate): females 86.4%, males 93.9%
Personal Computers (2003): 300,000
Internet Users (2005): 32,000
Est. Percentage of Children Who Complete the 4th grade (2002): 25%
Est. Number of Primary School Students (2000–02): 4.8 million
Est. Number of Secondary School Students (2000–02): 1.6 million
Est. Number of University Students (2000–02): 587,300
Life Expectancy (2000 estimate): females 64.2 years, males 57.6 years
Infant Mortality Rate (2005 estimate): 75 deaths per 1,000 live births
GDP per Capita (2005 estimate): $200

Sources: International Monetary Fund; United Nations Development Program, *Human Development Report*; World Health Organization; International Telecommunications Union.

The map in Figure 5.1 shows how Myanmar is divided into fourteen administrative units. Seven units called "divisions" are home to most of the ethnic Burmans, although some also live in the seven states that are named for the largest minority groups. These states were created in the British colonial period to give the minority groups some autonomy, but many Mons, Karens, and other minorities live outside the ethnic states.

BURMANS

For at least a millennium, Burmans have been the dominant ethnic group in Myanmar. They speak Burmese and are Theravada Buddhists. They immigrated from southern China, and historians once believed they were introduced to Indian culture by the Mons, who arrived in Myanmar before them, but they may have encountered Indian cultural influences much earlier.[5] Each Burmese government since Myanmar regained its independence in 1948 has been dominated by ethnic Burmans who have pursued policies aimed at creating a uniform national culture. But so far none of these governments has found a formula for relations between the ethnic groups that is acceptable to all concerned.

KARENS

Many Karens were converted to Christianity by American Baptist missionaries in the nineteenth century. During the colonial era, they were one of the most pro–British ethnic groups in Myanmar, and were recruited for the Burmese army while Burmans generally were not. During World War II, hundreds of Karens were executed as British sympathizers by the pro–Japanese Burmese Independence Army, setting off a chain of retaliatory actions.

In 1947, the Karens were offered a state of their own, but they also wanted special arrangements for Karens living outside the area of Karen state to be represented in parliament. After Myanmar regained its independence in 1948, Karens were among the first to rebel, and they have been fighting government forces ever since.[6] Most of the 160,000 Burmese living in refugee camps in Thailand and Bangladesh are Karens, while others live in makeshift camps on the Burmese side of the border. Burmese army offensives against the Karen National Union have often led to the destruction of Karen villages.

MONS

The Mons are Theravada Buddhists and related to the Khmer in Cambodia. They settled in Myanmar and neighboring countries before the Burmans migrated into Southeast Asia, and they have resisted assimilation by the Burmans for centuries. After Myanmar regained its independence in 1948, the New Mon State Party fought for political and cultural autonomy, and they were one of the last groups to agree to a cease-fire with the junta in the 1990s.[7]

SOUTH ASIANS

The British opened Myanmar to immigration from the Indian subcontinent in 1937, and thousands of people came, attracted by the possibility of obtaining land or jobs in the army and civil service. In 1947, as Myanmar prepared for independence, the various South Asian groups each responded differently. Gurkhas who had been recruited for the army were eager to become citizens of Myanmar and continue to serve in the army, while many of the Muslims in Arakan State fled to Bangladesh. Chettiars from Madras, who were money-lenders and resented by many Burmans because they foreclosed on their farms, returned to India after independence.[8]

CHINESE

The families of many of the Chinese in Myanmar immigrated from Yunnan province during the British colonial period. But another large influx began in the 1990s when the border between China and Myanmar was opened. It is estimated that over a million Chinese have settled in Myanmar since 1990, and they are now a dominant economic presence in Mandalay and much of northern Myanmar.[9] They play an important role in the internal economy and in cross-border trade with China, but they are much less powerful, economically and politically, than the Chinese in Thailand.[10]

Chinese Nationalist units retreated into Shan state after losing the Chinese civil war to Mao's forces. They took over control of the opium trade and became a serious problem for the Burmese government (and for the United States, which supported them). In the 1960s, China tried to export its Cultural Revolution to Myanmar, and this (plus resentment of their economic power) led to violent anti–Chinese riots in Rangoon.[11]

The Middle Class

An urban middle class composed of government officials, business people, and other professionals probably constitutes between 5 and 10 percent of the total population, but it is much less affluent than the middle class in Thailand or Malaysia. Several million middle class and working class Burmese have felt compelled to leave the country for political or economic reasons since the military seized power in 1962.[12]

Middle class students have traditionally been leaders of the pro-democracy movement, but the universities have been closed much of the time since the early 1960s to prevent student political demonstrations, and the junta's informer network has made any kind of political activity dangerous. The generals who rule Myanmar claim the middle class has accepted the inevitability of military rule, and they greatly exaggerate Myanmar's economic performance. But middle class Burmese know their country has failed to keep pace with the rest of the region, and their anger at the junta's misrule sometimes explodes in massive demonstrations, like those in 1988 and 2007.[13]

Status of Women

Burmese women have had access to education much longer than most women in Asia. Today, they are beginning to outnumber men in some university programs, and they are active in business and most of the professions, but they play no role in the military government. It has been well documented that the Burmese army has used rape as a weapon of war against minority women.[14]

Burmese women have traditionally been excluded from politics. Exceptions include the leader of the pro-democracy movement, Aung San Suu Kyi, and her mother, who served as ambassador to India, because they were related to Aung San who led Myanmar's campaign for independence. Aung San Suu Kyi clearly has the qualities of a major political leader, including intelligence, charisma, courage, and determination. The junta attacks her foreign connections and claims she no longer has broad public support, but the fact that she is kept under house arrest proves they do not believe their own propaganda.[15]

Religion

Theravada Buddhism is the religion of most of the Burmese people, and it plays a central role in their culture, as it does in Thailand, Cambodia, and Laos. Before his death in 1947, Aung San promised the minorities (including non–Buddhist Karens) that everyone would enjoy religious and cultural freedom and that religion and politics would be kept separate. The junta has gone to great lengths to present themselves as patrons of Buddhism, spending large sums of public money on restoring Buddhist temples. But by arresting and mistreating thousands of Buddhist monks and nuns in 2007, the junta enraged the Burmese people.

Historical Background

The first great dynasty at Pagan (1044–1287) was Myanmar's golden age in which Theravada Buddhism was introduced and a great many pagodas and monasteries were built to adorn the capital city (see Table 5.2). The Toungoo and Konbaung dynasties that followed were often at war with neighboring kingdoms and with non–Burman minorities in Myanmar such as the Mons and Karens. The country's present military rulers draw the lesson from Myanmar's history that only a strong army can hold the country together and protect it from foreign invaders. This is their main rationale for refusing to share political power.[16]

Table 5.2
Events in Burmese History

984–1287	Myanmar's "golden age" in which Theravada Buddhism is introduced at capital city of Pagan.
1824–85	British conquer Myanmar and annex it to India.
1920	University strike launches nationalist movement.
1937	Myanmar is separated from India, and constitution provides elected parliament and substantial self-government.
1942–45	Myanmar invaded and occupied by Japanese army.
1947	Britain and Burmese prepare Myanmar for independence. Aung San, the intended prime minister, is assassinated by rival.
1948–62	U Nu serves as independent Myanmar's first prime minister. He is deposed by military coup in 1962.
1962–88	General Ne Win's anti-foreign military regime tries to make Myanmar self-sufficient. Result is economic chaos.
1988	Huge demonstrations against military regime provoke violent crackdown. Aung San Suu Kyi becomes opposition leader.
September 1988	Military junta (SLORC) seizes power; kills 3000 demonstrators but promises elections and new economic policy.
May 1990	Election won by Suu Kyi's National League for Democracy, but SLORC regime refuses to convene parliament.
Mid–1990s	Opening economy to foreign investment brings some GNP growth, but SLORC unable to manage economy effectively.
1988–2008	Nobel Peace Prize winner Aung San Suu Kyi under house arrest for most of period. SLORC (renamed SPDC) says it plans to create constitutional but military-dominated government.

One way to summarize Myanmar's recent history is to look at how the British colonial administration and successive Burmese governments have dealt with the problems of ethnic diversity and economic development. The problems are closely linked, because economic growth is impossible in areas plagued by ethnic conflict, while the distribution of economic rewards and opportunities is often a major source of conflict between ethnic groups.

British Colonial Rule

Between 1824 and 1885, the British Raj in India, provoked by border conflicts with various Burmese forces, conquered all of Myanmar in order to gain access to its resources and to an overland trade route to China. British rule brought sweeping changes to Myanmar, including the creation of an export-based economy and a Western style bureaucratic government. By 1939, Myanmar was the world's leading rice exporter, and the country was evolving toward self-rule within the British Commonwealth, although not as rapidly as Burmese nationalists wanted.[17]

Rangoon University was founded in 1920, and students there became leaders of the movement for Burmese independence. In the years just before World War II, the British gave an elected parliament and mostly Burmese cabinet broad political powers. But major social unrest was created by the breakdown of traditional political and religious authority as large numbers of people moved to the cities and to new rice-growing areas. The crime rate soared, and ethnic conflicts were common.[18]

To protect the rights of the minorities, the British created a separate administrative service to deal with the states inhabited by minorities, and a certain number of seats were reserved for them in the national parliament. By opening Myanmar to immigration from South Asia, a new class of foreign merchants, money-lenders, and land owners was created. Indians gained possession of land that had belonged to Burman families for centuries, and they competed with Burmans for jobs in the civil service and army. Burmans were largely excluded from service in the army because they were seen as anti–British.[19]

Aung San

A young student leader named Aung San took part in Japan's 1942 invasion of Myanmar and was appointed defense minister in the puppet government set up by the Japanese. But he became disillusioned with the Japanese because of their brutality, and in 1945 he led Burmese troops in support of the Allied liberation of Myanmar. He presided over the newly formed Anti-Fascist People's Freedom League (AFPFL), which included many anti–Japanese and anticolonial groups, and he demanded immediate independence for Myanmar after World War II.[20]

The British Labour government agreed to give Myanmar its independence as soon as a constitution could be written and approved by the Burmese people, but they wanted to avoid the kind of violent ethnic and religious conflict that had rocked the Indian subcontinent. So in 1947, Aung San met with leaders of the ethnic minority groups at Panglong in the Shan state and tried to persuade them to join the Union of Myanmar in return for almost complete autonomy in running their own affairs. The Shans, Kachins, and Chins agreed, but the Karens and other minority groups remained uncommitted. In July 1947, Aung San was murdered along with six members of his cabinet by a political rival, who was arrested and later executed for his crime.[21]

U Nu and Equal Rights

U Nu, a leading nationalist and close friend of Aung San, was named prime minister and president of the AFPFL, and Burmese independence went ahead on schedule in January 1948. Initially, the Burmese government controlled very little of Myanmar except the capital city of Rangoon. The small and poorly equipped army was far outnumbered by insurgents, including Burmese communists, ethnic minorities, and Chinese nationalists, who took refuge in Myanmar after losing the Chinese civil war.

U Nu thought it was a mistake to create semiautonomous states for the minority groups, but he accepted it as part of the constitution, and he believed that all indigenous races (as well as Indians and Chinese who supported the constitution) should have equal rights.[22] As a deeply religious person, U Nu also believed that Buddhism could be a powerful force for social cohesion and might reduce the amount of crime and violence in modern Myanmar, but he supported the right of non–Buddhists to religious freedom.[23]

U Nu also tried to promote economic development in ways that encouraged social cohesion, but little economic growth took place during his administration because of the turmoil caused by insurgent groups. Neither the Burmese bureaucracy nor the army were trained to carry out economic development projects, and the army was preoccupied with fighting insurgents. Faced with the possibility of civil war and an economy in chaos, U Nu stepped aside in 1958 and allowed General Ne Win, the army commander, to form a caretaker government.

Ne Win's Burmese Socialism

Over the next two years, the army received public support for high impact projects like cleaning up the badly littered streets of Rangoon and reducing crime. But in the 1960 election, the public voted overwhelmingly for U Nu and a return to democratic government. Nevertheless, in 1962 Ne Win staged a military coup, had U Nu arrested, and imposed a military dictatorship. The constitution, parliament, and political parties were abolished and replaced with a fascist-style mass party called the Burmese Socialist Programme Party (BSPP).

Deeply suspicious of foreign powers, Ne Win tried to make Myanmar economically self-sufficient, even though the livelihood of many Burmese farmers depended on exports. The resulting poverty and economic chaos resembled what Sukarno achieved with a similar policy in Indonesia. Realizing the need to institute some of the reforms recommended by the World Bank, Ne Win accepted aid from foreign governments (but not private investment), and occasionally the aid funds were put to good use, as when high-yield strains of rice were introduced. But by the late 1980s, when many Southeast Asian countries were enjoying high rates of export-driven growth, the UN ranked Myanmar along with Chad, Ethiopia, and Bangladesh as one of the world's least developed countries.[24]

In 1987, possibly acting on the advice of his astrologer, Ne Win issued a decree canceling the value of large denomination bank notes, which wiped out the savings of almost everyone in Myanmar. This kind of chaotic economic management forced many of Myanmar's most able people to go abroad in order to earn a decent living.[25]

1988 Demonstrations

In 1988, a student fight in a Rangoon tea shop led to a confrontation with police in which a student was shot and killed. The incident marked the start of six months of antigovernment demonstrations by people from all walks of life who were angered by the government's brutality and the worsening economic conditions. On August 8, soldiers shot an estimated one thousand demonstrators. Shortly after this massacre, Aung San's daughter, Aung San Suu Kyi, addressed a large crowd near the Shwedagon Pagoda. It was her first political speech, but she electrified the crowd and was soon chosen to lead the newly-formed National League for Democracy (NLD).[26]

The SLORC-SPDC Junta

On September 18, 1988, while NLD leaders were trying to decide whether to form an interim government, a group of army officers preempted them by establishing a junta which they called the State Law and Order Restoration Council (SLORC). Although they were younger than Ne Win and "overthrew" his government, it was generally believed Ne Win guided their actions from behind the scenes. They sent their troops to clear the streets of Rangoon where demonstrations were continuing, and the troops killed as many as 3,000 people. An estimated 10,000 students fled to the border areas to join the ethnic insurgents.[27] Many members of the NLD were arrested and sent to prison. Aung San Suu Kyi was placed under house arrest, where she would spend most of the next twenty years.

In an effort to legitimize their regime without relinquishing control, SLORC announced that multi-party parliamentary elections (the first since 1960) would be held in 1990. The junta tried to engineer a victory for the Myanmar Socialist Programme Party, which they renamed the National Unity Party (NUP), but the opposition NLD won more than 80 percent of the parliamentary seats even though its leader was under house arrest. The generals were stunned, and they refused to convene parliament. Instead, they invited hundreds of delegates to meet and write a new constitution under their close supervision.[28]

To revive the economy after years of stagnation, the SLORC adopted new strategy, which Ne Win recommended in a July 1988 speech. It roughly followed the example of Suharto's New Order regime in Indonesia. Private enterprise was allowed, but a large state sector was retained, and Myanmar was opened to foreign investment and international tourism. This strategy produced modest economic growth in the 5 percent range during the mid–1990s, but the junta lacked economic expertise, and they failed to recruit a group of technocrats (as Suharto did) who could manage Myanmar's development on a sustained basis. To support a greatly enlarged army, the junta often resorted to printing more money, and they tried to curb the resulting inflation by halting rice exports, with disastrous consequences for Burmese farmers.[29]

Cease-Fire Agreements

By intimidation and negotiation, the junta achieved cease-fire agreements with seventeen of the insurgent groups the army had been fighting since the 1950s. Increased security encouraged some foreign investment, but the Karen insurgency continued, and the army's brutal response included rape, genocide, and destroying whole villages.[30] This led the United States and European Union to apply economic sanctions that hobbled Myanmar's economic recovery without compelling the SLORC to relax its grip on power. Thus, the SLORC's failure to deal effectively with Myanmar's problem of ethnic conflict handicapped its efforts to restore economic growth.

Political System

Since seizing power in 1988, the SLORC junta (later renamed the State Peace and Development Council) has tried to create a constitution that would provide the appearance of civilian government while maintaining the army's hold on power. In 2008, the junta announced that a constitution had been drafted and would be submitted to a referendum, followed by parliamentary elections in 2010. But Aung San Suu Kyi would not be allowed to run for office because she had been married to a foreigner.[31]

A list of 104 "constitutional principles" drawn up by the junta for the National Convention to approve shows the type of government the junta planned to implement. The military would have the power to appoint the head of state and a quarter of the members of parliament. In all likelihood, General Than Shwe or some other general would be named head of state, perhaps after retiring from the army. Key positions such as Minister of Defense, Minister of Home Affairs, and Minister of Border Development would be reserved for military officers, so the army would continue to control the government.[32]

The SLORC/SPDC Junta

The military junta that seized power in 1988 is composed of officers who entered the army after independence in 1948. Ne Win probably continued to wield influence behind the scenes until his death in 2002. Analysts believe the eleven-man junta is divided on important policy issues.[33] They have tried to follow Suharto's strategy in Indonesia by combining military dictatorship with policies aimed at producing steady economic growth. But the economy has stagnated under their leadership, because they lack economic expertise and seem unwilling to trust non-military experts.[34]

UNSTABLE LEADERSHIP

In 1997, many army officers were purged after being charged with corruption. Prime Minister Khin Nyunt was purged in 2004 (two years after the death of Ne Win, his patron). Along with Khin Nyunt 8,000 military officers and bureaucrats considered to be his supporters were purged, and the military intelligence directorate which he headed was abolished. Khin Nyunt was probably the most capable person in the SLORC/SPDC junta. International press reports often described him (erroneously) as "pro–Western" because his policies seemed more rational than those of his colleagues. He devised the junta's "road map" to constitutional government, negotiated cease-fire agreements with insurgent groups, and engaged in a dialogue with Aung San Suu Kyi.[35] He was probably also one of the few members of the junta who understood the importance to Myanmar of being a member of ASEAN and having good relations with neighboring countries.

The purging of Khin Nyunt was a result of longstanding rivalry between officers of

Myanmar's regular army and the military intelligence corps. Khin Nyunt was a general and chief of intelligence, but he was junior to many army generals and he had no combat experience. His intelligence officers often clashed with regional army commanders over political issues, and occasionally the clashes were so heated that shots were exchanged.[36]

The National Convention

When it was first convened in 1993 to write a new constitution, the National Convention consisted of 702 delegates all of whom were chosen by the junta. Only 99 of the delegates were people who had won parliamentary seats in the 1990 election, and only 81 of these delegates were members of the National League for Democracy, which had won 392 seats in the 1990 election. When they learned that the junta intended to exercise tight control over the convention and dictate the results of their work, the NLD and some of the other delegates chose to boycott the convention. Delegates who continued to participate reportedly believed that "something was better than nothing," even if the junta wouldn't allow much in the way of political reform.[37]

When the convention met in December 2005, it included 1,071 delegates: 50 representatives of political parties; 99 winners of seats in the 1990 election; 215 members of ethnic minority groups; 93 peasant farmers; 48 workers; 41 intellectuals; 92 civil servants; and 57 other invited delegates.[38]

Political Parties and Elections

Table 5.3
Results of the 1990 Burmese Parliamentary Election

Party	Seats	% of Vote
National League for Democracy	392	59.9
Shan Nationalities League for Democracy	23	1.7
Arakan League for Democracy	11	1.2
National Unity Party	10	21.2
National Democratic Party for Human Rights	4	0.9
Chin National League for Democracy	3	0.4
Kachin State Nat. Congress for Democracy	3	0.1
Party for National Democracy	3	0.5
Union Pa-O National Organization	3	0.3
Patriotic Old Comrades' League	1	12.8
Shan State Kokang Democratic Party	1	—
Mro (or) Khami National Solidarity Org.	1	—
Independents	6	—
Total	485	100%

Source: Europa World Year Book 2004, London, pp. 2,013–14. Note: Parties shown in italics were legally registered as of 2005. Three other parties (which did not contest the 1990 election) were also registered: Wa National Development Party, Union Karen (Kayin) League, and Kokang Democracy and Unity Party.

Table 5.3 shows the number of seats won by the various parties in the 1990 election and their percentage of the national vote. In a bizarre effort to divide the opposition, the junta encouraged the creation of over 200 political parties, and 93 parties actually took part in the election. Any group could register as a political party, and those that did were allowed to open offices and were given telephone lines and extra rations of gasoline at the subsidized government price. The junta also gerrymandered electoral districts and forced large numbers of people to move from one district to another in an effort to secure victory for their National Unity Party.[39] If the junta holds an election in 2010, it will probably have complete control over the ground rules, and opposition parties will have to decide whether it is in their interest to take part.

The New Administrative Capital

In November 2005, the junta suddenly announced plans to move the government to Nay Pyi Taw, a sparsely populated district near the township of Pyinmana about halfway between Rangoon and Mandalay. Most government workers were forced to move to Nay Pyi Taw over the next six months despite the lack of adequate housing, transportation, or communication facilities. Diplomatic missions remained for the time being in Rangoon. The official explanation given for the move was that it would facilitate economic development because of Nay Pyi Taw's central location. But there was speculation that the junta acted on the advice of an astrologer or that they might be afraid of an invasion by a foreign power. Burmese civil servants were said to be appalled by the difficulties created by the junta's arbitrary decision to move the capital.[40]

Legislature

Except for the single-party legislature that was convened in 1974, Myanmar has not had one since 1962. Some of the winners of the 1990 parliamentary election were invited to take part in the National Convention, but the NLD and a number of other parties boycotted the convention, because their leaders were in prison or under house arrest. The junta has said they plan is to have a bicameral parliament with a 440-member lower house elected from equal size electoral districts plus a 224 member upper house with twelve seats allocated to each of the 7 divisions and 7 states. In each chamber, the military would appoint a quarter of the members.[41]

The Judiciary

Since seizing power in 1988, the junta has failed to establish the rule of law. They have used any convenient legal rationale to support their arbitrary actions. Thousands of people whom the junta regarded as opponents have been arrested and imprisoned under inhumane conditions after sham trials in which they were not allowed lawyers to defend themselves. There is a Supreme Court, with all judges appointed by the junta, and several levels of courts from the state or division level down to the township. But Myanmar's judiciary has no independence, and many of the judges have little or no legal training. As David Steinberg notes, "Law under the military is conceived of not as a protection of rights but as a means of control."[42]

Civil Society

During the 1988 demonstrations against Ne Win's military government, hundreds of nongovernmental organizations (NGO's) sprang up to promote political reform or to provide make-shift social services. A large number of new publications appeared in Myanmar, spreading news of the uprising around the country. But the events of 1988 made far less of an impression on the rest of the world than the 2007 demonstrations, because very few images of the 1988 demonstrations were transmitted out of Myanmar, and the crumbling Soviet empire held the world's attention at that time. By contrast, in 2007, the Internet and digital photography ensured that pictures of monks marching in Rangoon were on TV screens and newspapers all over the world at a time when the UN General Assembly was meeting.[43]

NGOs

Of the hundreds of nongovernmental organizations that sprang up in Myanmar during the 1988 uprising, some managed to carry on in spite of intensive efforts by the junta to suppress them. Burmese pro-democracy groups were also active in Thailand, Europe and the United States, and their web sites have helped to keep alive the Burmese people's hope for change. Approximately forty international nongovernmental organizations provide a channel for humanitarian aid from abroad, much as they have done in Cambodia.[44]

In 2005 and 2006, the United States extended its economic and financial sanctions and (because of Burmese government travel restrictions) discontinued funding for the UN's Global Fund which helps to combat HIV/AIDS and malaria. The United States also threatened to withhold funds from the UN program that funds poppy replacement unless the UN agreed to report on human rights violations in the parts of Myanmar where it operates. Some Burmese groups opposed to the military regime, including the NLD, have supported sanctions. But the United States has also been criticized for politicizing humanitarian aid.[45]

The Media

The electronic and print media in Myanmar are controlled by the junta, which uses them to glorify the army's reputation and warn of the alleged dangers posed by foreign powers. But the junta's effort to limit the Burmese people's knowledge of the world is a losing battle. Many Burmese have managed to travel abroad and see how other people live. Several million Burmese now live abroad, and they keep in touch with family and friends in Myanmar. As of 2004, there were 3.2 million radios in Myanmar, and TV dishes were widely used.[46] The web sites of overseas Burmese NGO's, such as the National Coalition Government of the Union of Burma (www.ncgub.net), helped to keep opponents of the junta informed and in touch with one another.

Economic Development

After seizing power in 1988, SLORC abandoned Ne Win's anti-foreign economic strategy known as "Burmese Socialism" and (as Ne Win himself advised) replaced it with a policy of opening the country to foreign investment. But the junta's human rights violations caused many aid donors to cancel their programs, and foreign investors were reluctant to enter such an unstable country. Of those companies that came despite the risk, a considerable number (including Apple, Levi Strauss, and Pepsi-Cola) eventually left to avoid offending their share-holders and customers.

Despite the SLORC/SPDC's efforts to attract tourists and stimulate border trade with its neighbors, economic growth was only in the 1.5 percent range during the early 1990s, but it increased to 5 percent in the middle of the decade as several companies invested in the oil and natural gas sector.[47]

The 1997 financial crisis caused neighboring countries to reduce their investment in Myanmar, and it weakened demand for Burmese exports. The junta's practice of printing money to meet its current spending requirements caused serious inflation, and the currency plummeted in value. As the junta began to reverse its policy of economic liberalization, most imports were banned, foreign exchange dealers were arrested, and gasoline was rationed. Having defaulted on the repayment of loans to the World Bank, the junta took the position in 1998 that it would only repay old loans if the World Bank supported the junta's policies, which the bank was unwilling to do.[48]

The U.S. policy of imposing economic and financial sanctions on Myanmar was partly based on a report by the International Labor Organization which cited the junta's use of forced labor to develop Myanmar's tourist sites.[49] Some European governments also imposed sanctions, but Asian governments did not, because they believed sanctions would be contrary to their own economic interests and would not force the junta to change its ways. Table 5.4 shows a sharp drop in Myanmar's economic growth in 2008 which was due to reduced production and export of natural gas, crude oil, plywood, and cotton yarn. But a slow recovery was expected in 2010 as the worldwide recession eased.

Table 5.4
Myanmar's Economy, 2007–10
(figures are percentages unless otherwise indicated)

	2007	2008	2009	2010
GDP Growth	3.4	0.9	0.3	1.2
Agriculture Production Growth	1.4	-3.0	-1.2	0.5
Inflation	35	26.9	13.51	10.6
Government Budget Balance	-3	-3.6	-4.3	-4.7
Exports (U.S. $B)	$6.2	6.3	4.9	5.2
Imports (U.S. $B)	$3.1	3.8	4.0	

Source: Economist Intelligence Unit, "Myanmar (Burma), Country Report," March 2009. Figures for 2009 and 2010 are EIU forecasts.

In the event of disasters like the 2008 cyclone in Myanmar, in which the national government proves unable (or unwilling) to aid the victims, Western governments tend to support the principle that the UN should step in and do the job whether the national government agrees or not. Asian governments generally oppose UN intervention without the host government's approval.[50]

Despite Myanmar's rich natural resources, foreign investment was only in the range of $50 million to $160 million annually during the years 2002–06, largely because of foreign government sanctions and the junta's failure to establish the rule of law. Investment during 2008 was largely in the oil and gas sector.[51] But Myanmar's future economic prospects would depend on implementing a wide range of reforms, such as curbing the inflationary practice of borrowing money from the central bank to fund the annual budget.[52]

Foreign Relations

Myanmar and ASEAN

The Thai government wanted to include Myanmar in ASEAN partly for commercial reasons, while the leaders of the island countries of Southeast Asia were probably more concerned with countering China's growing influence in the country. Most of the Burmese generals seem to have had little interest in ASEAN, but Prime Minister Khin Nyunt probably saw that membership in the organization would help to legitimize the junta's rule. Myanmar also joined the ASEAN Free Trade Area (AFTA) and the ASEAN Regional Forum (ARF). In 2000, the junta hosted a meeting of the ASEAN economic ministers, which was attended by ministers from China, Japan and south Korea. In 2005, the Burmese foreign minister announced that Myanmar would forego its turn to chair ASEAN during the coming year.

This came as a surprise, although Singapore and Malaysian leaders had already stated publicly that Myanmar should give up the chair unless it improved its international image.[53] As already noted, the ASEAN members (like most Asian governments) favored a policy of "engagement" with Myanmar for a mixture of economic and political reasons. This involved a cautious modification of ASEAN's basic principle of noninterference in member states' affairs. Meeting in Kuala Lumpur in December 2005, ASEAN leaders assigned the Malaysian foreign minister the task of visiting Rangoon to urge the release of Aung San Suu Kyi from detention as well as other political reforms. In what seemed a related move, the ASEAN leaders also agreed to draft a formal ASEAN Charter.[54]

2008 Cyclone Relief

Great natural disasters can sometimes produce important changes in relations between neighboring states. As the death toll from the 2008 cyclone mounted, ASEAN leaders called on the Burmese junta to relax restrictions on foreign aid workers. ASEAN Secretary-General Surin Pitsuwan said "I think it is a defining moment for ASEAN. We have to demonstrate that we are relevant, that we can help each other, that we can solve the problems that occurred in our landscape." He added that, if relief efforts were not speeded up, an epidemic could spread from Myanmar to neighboring countries. World Health Organization officials said that plague could easily break out among the storm survivors, many of whom were stranded in areas that were infested by rats.[55]

Myanmar and China

Myanmar was one of the first Southeast Asian countries to recognize the communist government of China, and the junta has become more dependent on Chinese trade, aid, investment and political support than any other Southeast Asian country. In return for Chinese aid and diplomatic support, Myanmar provides China with raw materials which China needs for its development. During the 1990s, China reportedly supplied Myanmar with more than a billion dollars worth of military equipment, including fighter aircraft, tanks, artillery, signals intelligence equipment, and electronic warfare equipment. The Chinese are also believed to have listening posts in Myanmar to intercept Indian military communications.[56] Although China provides military aid designed to keep the junta in power, Chinese leaders are no doubt aware that Myanmar's misuse of this aid can produce instability on China's southwestern border.

Myanmar and India

After Britain linked Myanmar to its Indian empire in the nineteenth century, the steady flow of immigrants from India began to transform Myanmar. Britain separated the two countries in 1937 and began preparing them both for independence. As described earlier, the Burmese resented the presence of South Asians in their country, and many of them left after Myanmar regained its independence.

In the 1990s, India became concerned about China's role in Southeast Asia and began to rebuild its ties with the region. India now hopes to import large quantities of natural gas from Myanmar, but it stopped supplying arms to the junta after the generals crushed the demonstrations by Buddhist monks in 2007. The junta probably considers it desirable to have India competing with China and other Asian countries for influence in their country.[57]

Myanmar and Thailand

Thaksin Shinawatra, Thai Prime Minister from 2001 to 2006, had lucrative economic ties with Myanmar and reversed his predecessor's policy of pressing the junta to reform. But the presence of more than a hundred thousand Karen refugees in Thailand and even larger numbers of Burmese illegal workers make for tense relations between the two neighboring states.[58] Although poppy cultivation has been reduced in Myanmar, drug shipments continue, and Myanmar is a major producer of amphetamines, which add greatly to Thailand's drug problem.[59]

Myanmar and the United States

Responding to strong pressures from Congress, the United States has used a comprehensive array of economic sanctions to try to prod the Burmese junta to implement political reforms.[60] While the junta has not changed its policies as a result of U.S. sanctions, it has accused the Unites States of planning an attack on its country. Beginning in 2005, there have been some bombings in Rangoon and Mandalay which a spokesman for the junta suggested were inspired by the U.S. government. But according to visitors to Rangoon, residents there suspected the junta might have planted the bombs to reinforce their claim that Myanmar was being threatened by a foreign country.[61]

During 2005 and 2006, the United States tried to persuade the UN Security Council to adopt a resolution calling on the Burmese junta to release political prisoners and hold a dialogue with democracy groups and ethnic minorities, but China and Russia both opposed the resolution. In 2007, the United States changed its approach after appointing a new ambassador to the United Nations. The United States reintroduced the resolution knowing it would be vetoed, but a senior State Department official issued assurances that the United States was not seeking regime change in Myanmar. At the same time, the United States sought China's support in pressing the Burmese junta to adopt a more moderate policy. After vetoing the U.S. resolution, the Chinese ambassador to the UN publicly urged the junta to "consider constructive recommendations" from ASEAN and also "listen to the call of its own people."[62]

Conclusions

The Burmese junta will not voluntarily relax its grip on Myanmar's political system, and its management of the economy is unlikely to improve. The U.S. sanctions have produced none of the political or economic changes they were intended to produce. Unfortunately, they have helped the junta isolate Myanmar from foreign influence by denying the Burmese people the benefits of foreign trade, aid, investment and contact with foreign cultures.

ASEAN leaders do not believe that sanctions will force the junta to change its policies, but they know that ASEAN's reputation will suffer if they fail to find a way to persuade the junta to change course. Some leaders of ASEAN states have warned the junta that Myanmar might be expelled from ASEAN, but it is not clear that this threat would weigh very heavily on the Burmese generals, whose main concern is preserving their grip on power. Besides, Myanmar's participation in ASEAN development programs and in the hundreds of ASEAN meetings that take place each year tends to reduce Myanmar's isolation. China and the ASEAN states may have helped persuade the junta to hold a referendum on the constitution followed by parliamentary elections. But this process will only serve to give the Burmese regime a veneer of legality unless the generals allow their opponents to take part in a free election.[63]

Further Reading

Callahan, Mary P. *Making Enemies: War and State Building in Burma*. Ithaca: Cornell University Press, 2003.

Lintner, Bertil. *Burma in Revolt: Opium and Insurgency Since 1948*. Boulder, CO: Westview Press, 1994.

Rotberg, Robert I., ed. *Burma: Prospects for a Democratic Future*. Washington, D.C.: Brookings Institution, 1998.

Selth, Andrew. *Burma's Armed Forces: Power Without Glory*. Norwalk, CT: EastBridge, 2002.

Steinberg, David I. *Burma: The State of Myanmar*. Washington, D.C.: Georgetown University Press, 2001.

Taylor, Robert H. *The State in Burma*. London: Hurst, 1987.

_____, ed. *Political Economy Under Military Rule*. London: Hurst; New York: St. Martin's Press, 2000.

– 6 –

MALAYSIA

Politics of a Plural Society

Malaysian politics has always been about balancing competing interests, usually those of the Malay half of society versus those of the Chinese who make up a quarter of the population. In the 1950s, the Federation of Malaya gained its independence on the basis of a bargain between the largest ethnic communities. In return for Malay control of the government and preferred access to schools and jobs in the bureaucracy, the Chinese and Indians would continue to enjoy economic and cultural freedom. Since then, the Malay-dominated government has increased affirmative action programs for Malays while sometimes defending and sometimes undercutting the rights of minorities.[1]

The year 2007 was marked by several large protest demonstrations by ethnic minority parties, but Prime Minister Abdullah Badawi called a snap election in March 2008, hoping to gain public support for his reform agenda.[2] Instead, the ruling National Front coalition suffered its worst electoral setback since independence. Although it won the election, its share of seats in parliament dropped from 90 percent to below 63 percent (the amount needed to amend the constitution). In state elections, the National Front also lost control of five of Malaysia's thirteen state governments.

However, the opposition would have difficulty maintaining their unity. Their coalition included the Islamic Party of Malaysia which had called for the imposition of Islamic law and the Democratic Action Party, whose Chinese supporters strongly opposed such a move.

Because of the opposition's unprecedented gains, Prime Minister Abdullah resigned in April 2009 and handed over power to his deputy, Najib Razak. Mr. Najib began to dismantle the affirmative action rules (known as the New Economic Policy) which benefited Malays, the largest ethnic group. These rules were put in place by Najib's father in 1971, and they were still strongly supported by most of the Malay population and by leaders of UMNO (United Malays National Organization), the leading party in the ruling coalition. But Mr. Najib and many other Malaysians believed that the Malay community no longer needed this affirmative action. Moreover, it impeded the country's economic growth by denying equal economic and educational opportunities to all Malaysian citizens. Mr. Najib was also determined to break the opposition coalition, which was led by Anwar Ibrahim. Thus, Najib had Anwar put on trial for sodomy, a crime for which he had been tried and acquitted a few years earlier.[3]

People and Cultures

Ethnic Groups

Malaysia is a classic example of a plural society in which politics is dominated by competition between the main ethnic groups. As Table 6.1 shows, people classified as Malays make up just over half of the population of 26.9 million people. The Chinese comprise about a quarter of the total and Indians about 7 percent. The ratio varies in different parts of the federation, with indigenous tribes and Chinese Malaysians outnumbering Malays in Sabah and Sarawak. (See map of Southeast Asia in Figure 6.1) The percentages also change over time because of the different birth rates of the various ethnic groups.

Table 6.1
Malaysia: Demographic Overview

Population (2009): 26.9 million
Annual Growth Rate of Population (2008): 2%
Ethnic Groups (2008): Malay 53.3%, Chinese 26%, indigenous tribes 11.8%, Indian 7.7%, non–Malaysian citizens 1.2%
Religions (2006): Islam 60.4%, Buddhism 19.2%, Hinduism 6.3%, Christianity 9.1%, Confucianism 2.6%
Literacy (2007): 93.5%
Personal Computers (2001): 3,000,000
Internet Users (2001): 6,500,000
Percentage of Students in Primary Schools (2007): 90.1%
Percentage of Students in Secondary Schools (2007): 82%
Life Expectancy (2007): females 76.4 years, males 71.9 years
Infant Mortality Rate (2007): 5.1 per 1,000 live births
Income per Capita (2007): $5,610

Sources: United Nations, *Demographic Yearbook*; *Europa World Year Book*; Embassy of Malaysia, Washington, D.C.; United Nations Development Program, *Human Development Report*; U.S. Department of State, "Background Notes: Malaysia."

Until the 1960s, there was little contact between the Malays, who lived mainly in rural areas, and the more urbanized Chinese and Indians. That has changed as large numbers of Malays have moved to the cities, where there is a great deal of social and economic interaction between the various ethnic groups, but for religious reasons there is still very little intermarriage between Malays and non–Muslims.[4]

Indigenous tribal people who comprise about 11 percent of the Malaysian population live mainly in Sarawak and Sabah (East Malaysia) although a much smaller number live on the Malay peninsula, mainly in the mountainous interior. Migrant workers from Indonesia, the Philippines, and South Asia comprised almost 6 percent of the population who are not Malaysian citizens, and the rest are from Europe or the Middle East.

MALAYS

The Malaysian constitution defines what it means to be a Malay (in Malaysia) in cultural rather than ethnic terms. A Malay is "a person who professes the Muslim reli-

Figure 6.1. Malaysia and Brunei Darussalam.

gion, habitually speaks the Malay language, [and] conforms to Malay custom." Virtually all Malaysian Malays are Muslim and speak Malay.[5] But "conforming to Malay custom" may no longer necessarily describe the lifestyles of urban Malays.

CHINESE

The Chinese are the largest minority group in Malaysia, and they play a major economic role, but they are much less socially integrated than the Chinese minority in Thailand. Their political role is also very limited, except when they happen to hold the balance of power between the two main Malay parties, as happened in the 1999 national election.

During the nineteenth and early twentieth centuries, thousands of Chinese men were recruited to work in Malaya's tin mines. They lived in company quarters and had no contact with Malays. Many of them returned to China after earning some money. Those who stayed in Malaya married Chinese women when the male-female ratio among Chinese immigrants gradually evened up.[6]

STRAITS CHINESE

An interesting subgroup of Chinese immigrants married with Malays and became partially assimilated to Malay culture, although they did not convert to Islam. This group, known as Straits Chinese, learned English and many of them were employed by the colonial administration. But after Malaysia's independence, the Straits Chinese community began to fade away, because many of the young people chose to marry ethnic Chinese.[7]

INDIANS

The British also brought Tamil Indians from southern India to build railroads and work on rubber plantations. As the Chinese and Indian communities grew, a whole range of services (restaurants, schools, and newspapers) were created by enterprising members of these communities to cater to their countrymen's needs. Eventually, many of the towns and cities on the Malayan peninsula contained a majority of Chinese and Indians. The newest group of urban poor in Malaysia are Indians who lost their jobs when rubber plantations closed.[8]

INDIGENOUS GROUPS

Indigenous tribal groups live mainly in Sabah and Sarawak where they constitute a majority of the population. About a hundred thousand *Orang Asli* ("original peoples") also live in isolated areas in the interior of the Malay peninsula. Because they are classified as "indigenous," all of these groups are entitled to affirmative action programs like the Malays. In recent decades, they have received increased educational opportunities, but they have the highest poverty rates in Malaysia. In 1997, 81 percent of the *Orang Asli* were living below the national poverty line, while the poverty rate for Malaysia as a whole was 7.5 percent.[9]

New Economic Policy

In 1971, the government adopted the New Economic Policy (NEP) a major expansion of affirmative action for Malays. The policy aimed at breaking down the occupational separation of Malays and Chinese by giving Malays a much greater presence in the modern sectors of the economy and a much larger role as shareholders in publicly traded companies. These goals have largely been achieved. Malays now comprise about a quarter of the work force in the manufacturing and service sectors, and they form less than a quarter of the agricultural work force. Malays own about 20 percent of the shares in corporations.[10]

Malay household incomes have risen sharply and are closer to parity with households of the Chinese community. The Chinese have also benefited from economic growth, but the disparity of incomes between the two communities has decreased. One unintended result of affirmative action programs is that the disparity of incomes within the Malay community has increased very sharply. A Malay professional and business class has emerged, and most of the students enrolled in state-supported universities are Malays because of affirmative action.[11]

Table 6.2
Poverty in Malaysia, by Region and Ethnic Group
(figures given are percentages)

	1970	1980	1999
Rural Residents	58.7	21.8	10
Urban Residents	21.3	7.5	1.9
National Poverty Rate	52.4	16.5	5.5
Malays and Other Indigenous Groups	65.9	20.8	10.2
Chinese Malaysians	27.5	5.7	2.6
Indian Malaysians	40.2	8.0	1.9

Source: Malaysian national economic plans.

Poverty has been sharply reduced in Malaysia, with Malays as the main beneficiaries, as Table 6.2 shows. But it is hardly surprising that affirmative action programs for Malays are resented by non–Malay citizens. Chinese families have been forced to send their children abroad for higher education or enroll them in private institutions in Malaysia which are often substandard.

Former Prime Minister Mahathir and his successor, Prime Minister Abdullah Badawi, both believe that affirmative action saps the initiative of recipients and undermines the concept of advancement by merit, thus making Malaysia less able to compete in the global economy. But politically it is extremely difficult for a Malay politician to reduce any of the privileges enjoyed by his Malay constituents.[12]

The Middle Class

Mahathir's policies played a major role in creating an urban middle class in Malaysia composed of Malays, Chinese, and Indians. The three groups interacted much more frequently than in the past, but Malays and Chinese seldom married because Malay law required that anyone marrying a Muslim must convert to Islam. Although middle class Malays tend to be grateful to the government for the affirmative action programs that have helped them advance socially and economically, they are not directly dependant on UMNO's political patronage like the wealthiest Malay businessmen.[13]

Status of Women

Women in Malaysia (both Muslims and non–Muslims) enjoy a greater degree of freedom and equality with men than women in most other Muslim countries. A Malay woman is likely to wear a headscarf, but she can drive a car, and she has far more career options than her Saudi counterpart.[14] Although they are greatly underrepresented in government (as in all Southeast Asian countries), a small but growing number of Malaysian women have served as ambassadors, members of Parliament, and senior bureaucrats.

For example, Rafidah Aziz was the longest serving trade minister in Asia (until she was removed from the cabinet in 2008), and Dr. Wan Azizah, the wife of Mahathir's former deputy, became the first Malay woman to head a political party. Examples like these are rare, but middle and upper class Malaysian women of all ethnic groups are active in business, the professions, and nongovernmental organizations.

Religion

Malays and Islam

Malays tend to be more orthodox in their religious beliefs than the *abangan* Muslims of Indonesia but far less orthodox than many Muslims in Middle Eastern countries such as Saudi Arabia. Prime Minister Mahathir responded to his country's Islamic revival in the 1980s by appointing Anwar Ibrahim to serve as Education Minister and allowing him to require religious education in schools and universities.[15] But Mahathir opposed making Malaysia an Islamic state, and he showed political courage when he acknowledged that Islamic terrorists were a threat to the region. He favored a modernizing version of Islam and warned that his political opponents in the Islamic Party of Malaysia (Pas) would impose Islamic law and restrict religious freedom.[16]

Mahathir's successor, Abdullah Badawi, was an Islamic scholar whose doctrine of *Islam Hadhari* ("civilizational Islam") calls for tolerance of religious differences, less emphasis on Islamic law, mastery of scientific knowledge, and individual piety (as opposed to obeying community standards). In the 2004 election, Abdullah's moderate version of Islam struck a responsive cord with Muslims and non–Muslims alike and helped his coalition achieve a record-breaking victory. But Abdullah's slow implementation of reforms led to the coalition's worst showing in fifty years in the 2008 election.

Historical Background

From the seventh century to the end of the thirteenth century, Malaya was at the center of the Srivijaya empire, which had strong commercial ties to China. But the golden age of Malayan history was the century (1400–1511) when the Sultan of Melaka controlled the Strait of Melaka (formerly spelled Malacca) between Sumatra and the Malay peninsula, the most direct route between the Pacific and Indian Oceans. This is still one of the world's busiest sea lanes, with oil having replaced spices as the most valuable commodity in east-west trade. In the 1400s, Melaka was a cosmopolitan city with many Malay, Chinese, Indian, and Arab residents, and it dominated the other sultanates on the Malay peninsula.

Table 6.3
Events in Malaysian History

7th–13th centuries	Hindu-Buddhist Srivijaya empire.
1400s	Golden age of Malayan history and Sultanate of Melaka.
1786–1819	British acquire Melaka, Penang, and Singapore.
1874–1915	All of Malaysia brought under British rule.
1942–45	Japanese army occupies SE Asia in World War II.
1946	UMNO formed to oppose British plan for Malayan Union.
1952–54	UMNO is allied with Malayan Chinese Association.
1957	Federation of Malaya gains independence with UMNO leader Tunku Abdul Rahman as prime minister.
1963	Federation of Malaysia created by adding Sarawak, Sabah, and Singapore. Philippines and Indonesia oppose.
1965	Singapore expelled from Malaysia after Lee Kuan Yew campaigns for the support of the Chinese in Malaya.
1969	Emergency rule imposed after race riots break out.
1971	New Economic Policy and affirmative action for Malays.
1974	National Front (Barisan Nasional) is created.
1981	Mahathir becomes Malaysia's fourth prime minister.
1987	Mahathir barely survives as head of a badly divided UMNO. Arrest of 119 oppositionists creates severe tension.
1988	Mahathir sacks chief judge and two high court judges.
1998	Mahathir jails his deputy and rival, Anwar Ibrahim.
2003	Abdullah Badawi succeeds Mahathir; launches reforms.
2008	National Front suffers its biggest electoral setback, losing five states and a third of its seats in parliament.

In 1511, the Portuguese captured Melaka after a long battle which marked the beginning of European colonial penetration of Southeast Asia. The Dutch ousted the Portuguese in 1644, and during the Napoleonic wars they asked the British to protect Melaka from falling into French hands.

Straits Settlements

In addition to Melaka, the British acquired two strategic islands: Penang at the northern entrance to the Strait of Melaka in 1786, and Singapore at the southern end of the Strait in 1819. Both islands were largely unpopulated when the British acquired them from local rulers, but they were soon settled by mainly Chinese immigrants, who prospered under the orderly administration and free trade regime established by the British.[17] In 1826, Penang, Melaka, and Singapore became known as the Colony of the Straits Settlements.

Between 1874 and 1915, the British established protectorates over the sultanates on the Malay peninsula. Under the treaties providing for "indirect rule," the sultans formally retained sovereignty over their states, but British Residents assigned to the states had the power to "advise" the sultans, and their advice was seldom rejected.

Sarawak and Sabah

On the island of Borneo, the Sultan of Brunei ceded Sarawak to a British adventurer named James Brooke in 1843. Brooke and his descendants were known as the "white rajas," because they ruled the territory until World War II, although it was a British protectorate from 1888. In 1881, a British commercial firm took over the territory of North Borneo (later renamed Sabah), and it became a British protectorate the following year. Both Sabah and Sarawak became British colonies after World War II and joined the Federation of Malaysia in 1963.[18]

Impact of British Colonialism

British rule in Malaya and Borneo laid the foundations for western-style bureaucratic administration. In Malaya especially, new roads, harbors, railroads, and banking systems helped transform a subsistence economy into one based on export of food and natural resources. But Sabah and Sarawak were much less developed than Malaya during British rule, and this relative neglect has continued since independence. As noted earlier, British rule brought a large influx of Chinese and Indian workers, and they made major contributions to Malaya's development.

But British rule failed to produce a harmonious multiethnic society. Instead, the Malay, Chinese, and Indian communities were physically and occupationally separate from each other during the colonial period. The British believed that the Malays were the main indigenous race in Malaya and needed to be protected from the more energetic Chinese. So land was reserved for Malays, and they were given preference for educational opportunities and jobs in the colonial administration.[19]

The Rise of Nationalism

The Japanese occupation of Malaya during World War II encouraged the development of nationalist sentiment among Malays and support for the (largely Chinese)

Malayan Communist Party among the Chinese in Malaya. In 1946, the United Malays National Organization (UMNO) was organized to resist British plans to create a Malayan Union, which would have granted equal rights to all the main ethnic groups. In 1948, the British created the Federation of Malaya with nine Malay states plus Penang and Melaka, an arrangement that was more acceptable to UMNO. The British promised to give the Federation independence if and when there was evidence of national unity. But from 1948 to the mid-fifties, British and Commonwealth forces were busy suppressing the Malayan Communist Party insurgency.

Meanwhile, UMNO formed an alliance with the Malayan Chinese Association which won the 1952 municipal elections. When the Alliance added the Malayan Indian Congress in 1955 and won the election for local rule, the British decided Malaya was ready for independence. The Alliance was based on a bargain in which the Malays ran the government and retained their special privileges but the Chinese and Indians were promised that their economic and cultural freedom would not be tampered with. The independent Federation of Malaya was launched in 1957 with Tunku Abdul Rahman as prime minister. Rahman was so intent on preserving the Alliance he was accused by some Malays of not fighting hard enough for their interests.[20]

Formation of Malaysia

In 1963, the Federation of Malaya was expanded to include Singapore, Sabah, and Sarawak, which the British believed were incapable of surviving on their own. The federation, renamed Malaysia, faced challenges on all sides. The Philippine government disputed Malaysia's claim to Sabah, and Indonesian President Sukarno launched a military campaign against Malaysia, which he viewed as a British plot to challenge his country's preeminence in the region. "Confrontation," as the campaign was called, lasted until General Suharto replaced Sukarno as Indonesian president in 1966 (see chapter 8).

But the most serious challenge of all came from Singapore's leader, Lee Kuan Yew, who campaigned for equal rights of citizenship for the Chinese minority in Malaysia. Prime Minister Rahman feared this would destabilize the political balance in Malaysia, so he expelled Singapore from the federation in 1965. In spite of their economic interdependence, relations between the two countries have never fully recovered since the split.

And Malaysia's troubles were not yet over. In 1967, the National Language Act made Malay the sole national language but permitted the continued use of English "for official purposes as may be deemed fit." Chinese Malaysians welcomed the compromise, which was arranged by Prime Minister Rahman, but many Malays saw it as a sellout. Race riots broke out in the predominately Chinese state of Penang, and the language issue was hotly debated in the 1969 elections in which opponents of the Alliance scored major gains. Although they did not win enough seats to form a government, they celebrated their moral victory in a manner that led to race riots in the capital, and the army had to be called in to restore order.[21]

The constitution was suspended, and for the next two years, Deputy Prime Minister Tun Abdul Razak ran Malaysia by decree. In 1971, the New Economic Policy was instituted. As discussed earlier, it was designed to raise the incomes of Malay households, which were much lower than those of Chinese households, and end the link between race and occupation by giving Malays a greater presence in the modern economy. Also during the 1970s, political freedoms were restricted by constitutional amendments, and most political parties joined the *Barisan Nasional* (National Front), which was led by UMNO. Malaysia's second and third prime ministers, Tun Abdul Razak and Hussein Om, who ran the country in the seventies, were English-educated Malay aristocrats like Tunku Abdul Rahman.

Mahathir Mohamad

Malaysia's fourth prime minister served for twenty-three years (1981 to 2003) and greatly expanded the powers of the office by constitutional amendments and by other means.[22] Unlike his predecessors, Mahathir was not of aristocratic lineage or temperament. Early in his premiership, he fought with Malaysia's nine sultans who take turns serving as king (Yang di-Pertuan Agong). He also clashed with leading judicial figures and imprisoned 119 academics and others who opposed his policies.

During the 1997–98 financial crisis, Mahathir imprisoned his deputy (and rival) Anwar Ibrahim on trumped up charges of corruption and sexual misconduct. This transparent effort to destroy Anwar's reputation weakened Mahathir's support among Malays, and he would have lost the 1999 election without the support of ethnic parties allied with UMNO.[23]

In 2003, Mahathir resigned and handed over power to his deputy, Abdullah Badawi, who launched a reform campaign and angered Mahathir by canceling some of his wasteful showpiece projects. The public gave Abdullah a resounding victory in the 2004 election, but UMNO party leaders were much less enthusiastic about reforms that would destroy their patronage networks. As noted earlier, Abdullah called a snap election in March 2008 in which UMNO's support hit a forty-year low point. Instead of strengthening his political position, it revealed how angry Malaysians were at the slow pace of reform.

Political System

A coalition of parties led by UMNO has controlled the Malaysian government since independence. But after its setback in the 2008 election, the coalition's future was in doubt. Would UMNO leaders respond by increasing authoritarian controls or by instituting reforms? The noted analyst Harold Crouch describes Malaysia's semi-democratic political system as "incremental authoritarianism," but he adds that "democratic political structures were maintained and [they] encouraged, even forced, the government to respond to societal pressures."[24]

UMNO leaders have retained some aspects of parliamentary democracy that were prescribed in the 1957 constitution. But they have often rationalized an authoritarian disregard for civil liberties as essential for keeping order in a multi-ethnic society. For example, the government broke up a series of human rights rallies in 2007 and 2008, using water canons on at least one occasion.[25]

Elections

Under the 1957 constitution, national elections must be held at least every five years, although the prime minister can and sometimes does call an election sooner. Most state elections are held at the same time as national elections, but Sabah and Sarawak can choose when to hold their elections. Opposition parties are allowed to contest the national and state elections and have gained power in some of the thirteen states in spite of numerous handicaps such as limits on their access to media.[26]

Political Parties

In Malaysia, most of the parties are supported by only one ethnic group (e.g., Malays, Chinese, or Indians). Thus, the ruling coalition (the *Barisan Nasional*), is led by UMNO (Malaysia's largest Malay party) and includes the Malaysian Chinese Association (MCA) and the Malaysian Indian Congress (MIC).

In the 2008 election, an opposition coalition (*Barisan Alternatif*) was led by Anwar Ibrahim of the People's Justice Party (PKR), which is Malaysia's only multi-ethnic party. This coalition included the Chinese-based Democratic Action Party (DAP) and the conservative Islamic Party of Malaysia (PAS). DAP and PAS are uneasy bed-fellows, because PAS has wanted to make Malaysia an Islamic state under strict Islamic law. DAP supporters fear this will lead to anti–Chinese discrimination. Table 6.4 compares the success of the National Front and opposition parties in the 2004 and 2008 elections.

Table 6.4
Malaysian National Elections, 2004 and 2008

	Seats Won in 2004	*Seats Won in 2008*
National Front	199	140
Opposition Parties		
People's Justice Party	1	31
Democratic Action Party	12	28
Islamic Party of Malaysia	6	23
Independent Candidates	1	0
Total Seats in Parliament	219	222

Source: Data compiled by the *Financial Times*, March 10, 2008.

THE UNITED MALAYS NATIONAL ORGANIZATION

UMNO was founded in 1946 to resist British plans to create a Malay Union in which minority groups would have the same rights as Malays. In the 1950s, UMNO formed an Alliance with the Malayan Chinese Association and Malayan Indian Congress. The Alliance, which was expanded to include other parties and renamed the National Front, has won every national election since 1957.

UMNO's political control has been buttressed by the power to amend the constitution and dispense an unlimited amount of public funds as patronage. The National Front also controls the media and draws the map of electoral districts. During elections, UMNO relies on the police for political intelligence and on the bureaucracy for support in preparing policy initiatives.

MCA AND GERIKAN

These two Chinese parties are both in the National Front coalition, but they compete for the votes of the Chinese community. The Malaysian Chinese Association (MCA) is led by Chinese businessmen, and their ability to connect with the Chinese community varies from one election to the next. Gerikan (which means "Movement") held power for many years in the Chinese-majority state of Penang. In the 1999 election, the relatively strong performance of these two parties played a key role in keeping the National Front in power.

People's Justice Party (PKR)

This party was formed by Dr. Wan Azizah when her husband, Anwar Ibrahim, was imprisoned by Mahathir in 1998. In the 1999 election, the party supported Anwar's call for political and economic reform (an echo of the Indonesian reform movement), and Dr. Wan Azizah won a seat in the national parliament. Anwar did not run for the presidency of the party in 2007, because he had been banned from politics. But he played an active role in the 2008 election even though the ban was still in effect. As a devout Muslim, he had good relations with the Islamic Party of Malaysia (PAS). But he also had the confidence of Chinese leaders of the Democratic Action Party, so he served as a bridge between these two parties.[27]

Democratic Action Party

The DAP is an opposition party that competes with the MCA and Gerikan for Chinese votes. It split off from the Singapore-based People's Action Party (PAP) after Singapore left the federation of Malaysia in 1965. DAP formed a tactical alliance with the conservative Islamic Party of Malaysia (PAS) in the 1999 election, but the alliance fell apart because the Chinese community was opposed to PAS's goal of instituting Islamic law in Malaysia. In the 2004 election, DAP outpolled PAS and took over the leadership of the opposition in parliament.

The Islamic Party of Malaysia (PAS)

Ever since PAS broke away from UMNO in 1951, it has been UMNO's main competitor for Malay votes. Its strength is concentrated in the most conservative Malay states, and in the 2008 election, PAS and its allies won control of the governments of five states: Penang, Selangor, Perak, Kedah, and Kelanton, plus Kuala Lumpur, the national capital.

Although PAS tends to alienate non–Malay parties by favoring Islamic law, it campaigned on the need for political reform in 1999 and won its greatest number of seats at the federal and state levels. After losing badly in the 2004 election, PAS leaders appointed younger, more media-savvy members to leadership positions, and they have tried to broaden the party's appeal to non–Muslims by calling for the establishment of an "Islamic society" rather than an Islamic state.[28]

The Monarchy

Every five years, Malaysia's nine hereditary sultans meet and elect one of their own number as king (*Yang de-Pertuan Agong*). The king (or Agong) serves as ceremonial chief of state and has little political influence, unlike King Bhumipol of Thailand, whose role as a stabilizing force in Thai politics is described in chapter 1.

In 1983, Prime Minister Mahathir sponsored legislation that would take away the Agong's power to declare a state of emergency. The same bill removed the necessity for the Agong to sign acts of Parliament. When the Agong refused to sign this particular bill, Mahathir orchestrated a media campaign against the sultans, and they eventually agreed to follow government advice when they declared emergencies, but they gained the power to delay legislation by sending it back to Parliament. In 1993, Mahathir resumed his campaign against royalty, and the sultans lost their immunity from prosecution and their power to bestow pardons except on the government's advice.[29]

The Judiciary

Malaysia's first three Prime Ministers all had legal training, and their relations with senior judges were close. Although the High Court theoretically had the power to rule on the constitutionality of parliamentary acts, it did not try to exercise this power, even though certain acts of parliament restricted the constitutional rights of citizens. For example, the Sedition Act was often used to suppress criticism of government policies, and the Printing Presses and Publications Act required all publications to be licensed annually.

During his long reign, Mahathir steadily increased his authority by adding new laws and amending the constitution in ways that reduced citizens' rights or the ability of other institutions to block his agenda. His lack of legal training and his abrasive manner probably contributed to a souring of relations with the judiciary. In 1988, the High Court declared UMNO an illegal organization, but this enabled Mahathir to reorganize the party.

It also gave him an excuse to introduce constitutional amendments to weaken the judicial branch, which led to a confrontation with the chief judge of the High Court, Tun Mohamed Salleh Abas. Mahathir succeeded in having Tun Salleh suspended and then dismissed. Five other senior judges who became involved in the conflict were suspended, and two were dismissed. The whole matter attracted international attention and raised serious doubts about the independence of Malaysia's judiciary.[30]

Armed Forces

The Malaysian armed forces have never intervened in politics, but most of the senior officers have been Malays (usually close relatives of the prime minister), and they would undoubtedly support the government in the event of another emergency like the 1969 race riots.[31] The army numbers about 89,000 and the navy and air force about 12,500 each. Joint Malaysian and Indonesian naval patrols take place in the Strait of Melaka, where piracy is a serious threat to shipping. Malaysia is also concerned about protecting the territorial and mineral rights which it claims in the South China Sea.

Police

The Home Affairs Ministry is in charge of the police force, which includes a paramilitary Field Force numbering 20,000 and a Federal Reserve Unit of 2,500 which is trained to deal with civil disturbances. There is a higher percentage of non–Malay officers in the police than in the military, but almost all enlisted police personnel are Malay. The Special Branch is in charge of countering subversion and providing the government with political intelligence. As in Thailand and Indonesia, police corruption is a major concern of the Malaysian public.[32] A 2005 report on the subject commissioned by Prime Minister Abdullah listed more than one hundred reforms that were urgently required. Since Abdullah had served as Minister of Home Affairs, he was criticized for being slow to implement the reforms.

Bureaucracy

As a result of affirmative action programs, Malays hold most of the senior positions in the bureaucracy and a majority of junior posts as well. Four out of five places in the elite Administrative and Diplomatic Service are reserved for Malays. The bureaucracy serves the interests of the ruling party, and it has never been politically neutral. The bureaucracy was the main recruiting ground for UMNO leaders until the 1980s, when there began to be more educated Malays in other professions.[33]

Civil Society

The urban middle class in Malaysia (as in Thailand) wants to make religious values more relevant to their daily lives and to their society, so they have been the backbone of civil society. Malaysian NGO's tend to be linked to specific ethnic groups (like Malaysian political parties), so they focus on the main concerns of their group, such as language policy and the role of religion in society.[34]

As noted earlier, the intense dispute between Chinese and Malays over the use of Malay as the national language led to race riots in the 1960s. The government responded by tightening restrictions on civil society and the media and by making it a criminal offense to debate or discuss government policies on ethnic relations in public. But the expansion of higher education opportunities in the 1970s led to the formation of new NGO's that campaigned on issues such as women's rights and protection of the environment.

In the 1990s, organizations like Hakam, the National Human Rights Society and JUST, the International Movement for a Just World, were formed. And when the financial crisis hit Malaysia in 1997, critics of Mahathir's policies ignored government censors for a few months and filled the newspapers and air waves with stinging attacks on his government.[35]

The Media

The Malaysian government exercises tight controls over the country's electronic and print media, which are either run by the government or owned by UMNO supporters. Under the Broadcasting Act, which was approved during Mahathir's first major crackdown on civil society, the Minister of Information was given powers to control and monitor all radio and television broadcasting. As noted earlier, Mahathir complained bitterly, after he left office, when the government-controlled media ignored his complaints about Abdullah's policies.[36] The government has steadily increased its control over print news media, which are now run by the government or its supporters. Political party newspapers can only be sold to party members, a restriction that was aimed at *Harakah*, the newspaper of PAS.[37]

The Internet

With more than three million personal computers in use in Malaysia and many Internet cafes, cyberspace provides a powerful alternative to the government-controlled media. Online newspapers such as *Malaysiakini.com* and *MGG Pillai* provide a steady stream of editorials and news stories about sensitive issues such as government corruption, neglected social issues, and environmental problems. The Internet has also enabled NGO's and opposition groups to keep in touch with each other.

Economic Development

Malaysia in the 1950s and sixties had an economy that was based on import substitution and exporting primary products. By the early nineties, high economic growth had been achieved by manufacturing increasingly sophisticated goods such as computers and air-conditioners for export. This change happened during Mahathir's premiership, but the government also became heavily involved in managing the economy during that period.

The ruling party, UMNO, supported the growth of government-linked corporations, which were run by a new class of wealthy Malay managers who often lacked the necessary business skills to survive without large government subsidies. UMNO leaders developed powerful patronage networks, which they defended jealously. They also used the revenue from the state oil and gas company to reward their political supporters, and they resisted any reduction in affirmative action programs for Malays. This prevented the economy from reaching its full potential.[38]

1997–98 Financial Crisis

Because of weaknesses in the Malay economy which included a very high level of deficit spending, currency speculators tried to profit by forcing a devaluation of the Malay ringgit. In September 1998, the government introduced capital controls to limit the repercussions of the regional crisis and ensure stability in domestic prices and exchange rates. The ringgit was fixed at 3.80 to the U.S. dollar and was made non-convertible overseas.[39]

This enabled the government to reduce interest rates and raise domestic demand without destabilizing the currency. The Malaysian economy was the first to recover from the regional economic crisis, and capital controls for non-residents were removed in 2001. In 1998, Malaysia had 6 percent negative economic growth, but the economy grew by 6 percent in 1999 and 8.5 percent in 2000.[40] Malaysians suffered much less from the financial crisis than their neighbors in Thailand and Indonesia. Although Malaysian workers had to accept pay cuts, unemployment only reached 4.9 percent at its highest point in 1998.

By contrast, foreign workers in Malaysia (mostly Indonesians and Filipinos) were laid off in much larger numbers, and the Malaysian government began to arrest and deport undocumented foreign workers. This put a strain on Malaysia's relations with Indonesia and the Philippines and led to a shortage of workers in some sectors of the economy. Yet rules governing the employment of foreign workers were tightened in 2008.[41]

When Mahathir left office in 2003 the economy was growing steadily at a rate of close to 5 percent, thanks largely to high prices for Malaysian exports, including oil. Soon after he took over, Prime Minister Abdullah cancelled some of Mahathir's expensive show-piece projects, and the economy performed well during Abdullah's first four years in office.

Retail and wholesale trade and the tourist industry now account for 60 percent of Malaysian economic growth. Tourists are arriving at a rate of over 10 million a year, spending about $10 billion a year in Malaysia, and making the service sector the leading source of new jobs.

As Table 6.5 shows, Malaysia's economy was expected to contract by at least 3 percent in 2009, the steepest decline since the 1997–98 financial crisis. The 2009 decline was caused by weak global demand for Malaysia's exports. The Malaysian government enacted a U.S.$17 billion stimulus package, and world demand for Malaysian exports was expected to begin to recover in late 2009. For 2010, economic growth was expected to increase slowly to a level of 1.1 percent.

Table 6.5
Malaysia's Economy, 2007–10
(figures are percentages unless otherwise indicated)

	2007	2008	2009	2010
GDP Growth	6.3	4.6	-3.0	1.1
Agriculture Production Growth	2.2	3.8	-1.0	0.5
Industrial Production Growth	2.1	0.5	-8.9	2.8
Unemployment	3.2	3.4	5.0	5.3
Inflation	2.0	5.4	-0.7	1.7
Government Budget Balance	-3.2	-4.8	-8.7	-10.1
Exports (U.S. $B)	176.4	198.9	140.5	144.1
Imports (U.S. $B)	-139.1	-154.7	-106.8	-111.0

Source: Economist Intelligence Unit, "Country Report, Malaysia," April 2009. Figures for 2009 and 2010 are EIU forecasts.

Government investment was being channeled to the long-neglected agricultural sector and to the development of small and medium enterprises. Approved foreign investments reached a level of about $4 billion in 2006, down 14 percent from the previous year, but the budget deficit was declining. One possible result of the 2008 election might be a reform demanded by opposition parties: allowing companies other than those that support the National Front to bid on government contracts. The United States pressed for this reform in its trade negotiations with Malaysia.[42]

Foreign Relations

Malaysian leaders have supported measures to strengthen ASEAN including the practice of inviting the leaders of China, Japan and South Korea to attend the annual ASEAN summit meetings. Prime Minister Abdullah and Foreign Minister Syed hosted the ASEAN summit in Kuala Lumpur in December 2005 to which India, Australia, and New Zealand were also invited. Thus, ASEAN + 3 became ASEAN + 6.[43] These meetings have begun to focus on the long-term goal of creating an Asian union, which might eventually include a common market and common currency.[44] At the 2005 summit in Kuala Lumpur, ASEAN leaders also agreed to move ahead with the drafting of an ASEAN Charter, and Tun Musa Hitam was named chairman of an "eminent persons group" with the task of recommending basic principles for the charter, which was signed by the leaders of ASEAN in November 2007.

Malaysia is also an active member of the Non-aligned Movement and the Organization of Islamic Conference (OIC). Mahathir was chairman of these two organizations during his final year in office, and he vigorously denounced the United States for waging war in Iraq. His final speech to the OIC included anti–Semitic remarks that received international media attention, but his speech mainly focused on support for Islamic causes.[45]

Abdullah has proved to be a more skilled diplomat than Mahathir with an instinct for quiet diplomacy and focusing on the national interest. He developed good working relations with the new leaders of Singapore and Indonesia who were elected in 2004, and he has helped to resolve longstanding issues with these countries.

Mahathir's most constructive foreign policy initiative was helping to mediate the conflict between the Philippine government and the Muslim separatists in the southern Philippines. Mahathir also acknowledged the existence of a terrorist problem in Malaysia and in Southeast Asia generally, but he has been a vocal critic of President Bush's "war on terrorism." Acknowledging the seriousness of the threat posed by Jamaa Islamiah, the Al Qaeda affiliate in Southeast Asia, took courage, because Mahathir risked being falsely accused by his political opponents of taking sides with the West in a global struggle against Islam.[46]

Islam and Foreign Policy

Malaysian leaders, including Mahathir and Abdullah, have resisted pressure at home and abroad to declare that Malaysia is an Islamic state. But they support Islamic causes in the Organization of Islamic Conference (OIC). Prime Minister Abdullah has said, "Many Muslims aspire to set up an Islamic government. I don't think Islam is the only way to solve all problems. A government that is just, a government that is trustworthy, that becomes people-centered, that is Islamic.... A government can have Islamic values without the label Islamic."[47]

Malaysian-Burmese Relations

As noted in chapter 5, Malaysia has played a leading role in ASEAN's efforts to promote political reform in Myanmar. At ASEAN's December 2005 summit in Kuala Lumpur, the leaders of member states asked Malaysian Foreign Minister Syed to visit Rangoon on a fact-finding mission. Myanmar's military leaders eventually agreed to the visit, but Syed cut his mission short when the Burmese leaders refused to let him meet with Aung San Suu Kyi, who was under house arrest.[48]

Malaysian-Thai Relations

Relations between Malaysia and Thailand have generally been close and friendly. But the secessionist movement by Malay-speaking Thais that erupted in 2004 was a serious problem for Prime Minister Abdullah, and it was complicated by the repressive methods used by Prime Minister Thaksin's government. Abdullah insisted on raising the subject with Thaksin at ASEAN summit meetings. When Thai military leaders overthrew Thaksin's government in 2006, they promised Abdullah they would try to reach a political agreement with the separatists.[49] But the Thai military regime made no progress on this front during 2007.

Conclusions

As the people of Malaysia and their government struggle to overcome a history of ethnic separation, affirmative action programs for Malays have been a major source of tension between the country's ethnic groups, and they prevent advancement based on merit in universities and in the economy generally. But UMNO's conservative leaders oppose any change in policies that benefit Malays. Prime Minister Abdullah took on the huge task of reforming the country's political and economic system. But his instinct was to proceed much more cautiously than Mahathir did in domestic and foreign affairs.[50]

The 2008 election showed that many Malysians faulted Abdullah for not pressing harder for reform after winning a major electoral victory in 2004. Anwar Ibrahim's success in the 2008 election marked him as a potential future leader who might have the strength to carry out badly needed reforms.

Religion is clearly one of the wild cards in Malaysia's future, capable of provoking tension between Muslims and non–Muslims and between traditional and modern believers. But the moderate form of Islam espoused by Prime Minister Abdullah struck a responsive cord with Malays and non–Malays alike, and this is one of the strongest reasons for optimism about Malaysia's future.

Further Reading

Clapper, John. *Straits Chinese Society.* Singapore: Singapore University Press, 1980.

Funston, John. *Malay Politics in Malaysia: A Study of UMNO and Party Islam.* Kuala Lumpur: Heineman Educational Books, 1980.

Khoo, Boo Teik. *Paradoxes of Mahathirism: An Intellectual Biography of Mahathir Mohamad.* Kuala Lumpur: Oxford University Press, 1995.

Milne, R.S., and Diane K. Mauzy. *Malaysian Politics Under Mahathir.* London and New York: Routledge, 1999.

Mohamad, Mahathir. *The Malay Dilemma.* Singapore: Federal Publications, 1970.

Suryadinata, Leo, ed. *Ethnic Chinese as Southeast Asians.* Singapore and New York: Institute of Southeast Asian Studies and St. Martin's Press, 1997.

— 7 —

SINGAPORE

City with a Siege Mentality

Singapore is a small island city-state with a mainly Chinese population surrounded by a vast Muslim archipelago as large as the United States. The entire country is smaller than metropolitan Jakarta, and most of its food and drinking water must be imported. When Lee Kuan Yew formed his first government in 1959, race relations were tense, communists ran the labor movement, and half the population was still living in makeshift shanties. Now, Singapore is one of the richest nations in Asia with the world's busiest port, and 7,000 multinational firms conduct business in its gleaming office towers.

Yet the People's Action Party which has run Singapore for nearly fifty years has a siege mentality. In his autobiography, Lee Kuan Yew said he wanted to remind his people of how vulnerable Singapore was in the early days of independence and why it was still vulnerable to forces it could not control.[1]

Singapore's only resources are its 4.5 million people and its location astride one of world's busiest sea-lanes. Thanks to the remarkable adaptability of the government and work force, Singapore's economy is one of the richest in Asia, but it faces increased regional competition. To attract and retain the highly qualified people it needs to maintain its competitive edge, the country's leaders know they must make the social and political system more open. But they are afraid of releasing racial, religious, or class tensions that could destroy their remarkable creation.[2] This chapter explores how they are seeking to reconcile these conflicting needs for freedom and security.

People and Cultures

Ethnic Groups

Singapore has a predominately Chinese population and sizable Malay and Indian minority groups, as Table 7.1 shows. The Chinese and Indian categories consist of many subgroups based on dialect, religion, or place of origin. The population is aging, and each year some of the most highly educated people leave because of the restrictive social and political systems. This also makes it hard to attract well-qualified foreign workers.[3]

Table 7.1
Singapore: Demographic Overview

Population (2007 estimate): 4.68 million (including permanent residents and foreign workers)

Annual Growth Rate of Population (2007): 4.4% (all population groups), 1.8% (permanent residents)

Ethnic Groups (2007): Chinese 75%, Malays 14%, Indians 9%

Religious Affiliations (2007): Buddhist, Taoist, Muslim, Christian, Hindu

Literacy (2007): 95.4%

Income per Capita (2005): $27,490 ($29,780 purchasing power parity)

Personal Computers per 1,000 People (2001): 458

Percentage of Children in Primary School (2007): 94%

Number of Students in Universities (2003): 55,426

Number of Students in Polytechnics (2003): 62,206

Life Expectancy (2007): females 81.8 years, males 78 years

Infant Mortality Rate (2007): 2.1 per 1,000 live births

Income Distribution (2007): top 20% receive 50% and bottom 20% receive 2.8% of national income

Percentage of Population Living in Public Housing (2007): 86%

Sources: Economist Intelligence Unit; Embassy of Singapore, Washington, D.C.; United Nations, *Demographic Yearbook*; U.S. Department of State, "Background Notes: Singapore."

RACIAL INTEGRATION

While Singapore's main ethnic groups tended to live in separate neighborhoods before independence, the government's public housing policy was designed to bring them closer together. Yet interethnic marriages make up less than 4 percent of all marriages in a given year. The main reason is that it is difficult for a non–Muslim to marry a Muslim without converting to Islam, which most Chinese Singaporeans are reluctant to do.[4]

CHINESE IN SINGAPORE

Almost all of the Chinese now living in Singapore were born there, and they are gradually developing a Singaporean identity through social contact with other races in school, public housing, the army, and their workplace. But they tend to consider themselves "Chinese Singaporeans" rather than simply Singaporeans. Many still speak the dialect of the region in China where their families originated. The main dialect groups are the Teochews, Cantonese, Hainanese, and Hakkas. Ties to their dialect group in Singapore are important to them and are often strengthened if they return to their parents' home town in China as tourists or to work or invest there.[5]

The Chinese living in most other Southeast Asian countries play a major role in the commercial and manufacturing sectors but only a marginal role in politics and government. By contrast, Chinese Singaporeans dominate the Singapore government and armed forces. They also play an important role as managers in the Singapore offices of multinational firms. But those who operate their own businesses often do so on a smaller scale than Chinese in Thailand or the Philippines. This is because the Singapore government prefers to attract multinational firms to the city-state rather than risk creating a local class of powerful Chinese entrepreneurs who might compete with the PAP.

MALAYS

The Singaporeans whom the government classifies as Malays are mostly Muslims whose families originally came from what is now Malaysia or Indonesia. Many of them serve in the police force, in lower-ranking bureaucratic positions, and in manual trades. Malays also make up a large percentage of the unemployed and poorest classes.[6]

SOUTH ASIAN SINGAPOREANS

The Singaporeans who are classified as Indians include many Tamils and other ethnic groups from India, but the category also includes people from Pakistan, Bangladesh, Sri Lanka, and Nepal. They tend to feel their access to top positions in the government and civil service is limited by their race. Yet two Indians have served as foreign minister, and two others have been elected to the largely ceremonial position of president of Singapore.

FOREIGN CONNECTIONS

One of the things that keeps Singapore's many ethnic minorities and subgroups together (and may impede the development of a Singaporean identity) is their ability to maintain close ties with their own or their family's homeland. This has always been the case with people classified as Malays and Indians and also for smaller Asian groups such as the Thai, Filipinos, and Japanese. However, Singaporeans could not visit China from 1950 (when the communists gained power) until 1990, when Singapore and China established diplomatic relations. Since then, tourist and business travel between China and Singapore has increased steadily, with over half a million visitors from China arriving in Singapore in 2006.

Languages

The four official languages in Singapore are Malay (the national language), Mandarin Chinese, Tamil, and English, which is the language used in government. English is also the language that is most widely used by the public on most occasions. Education is bilingual at all levels in Singapore, with instruction given in English and in the student's "mother-tongue" (i.e., Malay, Tamil, or Mandarin, whichever is nearest to the actual language spoken in his or her home).

An increasing number of Chinese Singaporeans also choose Malay, because Mandarin Chinese is not their mother-tongue. Declining enrolments in schools that teach Mandarin has caused the government to fear that Chinese culture in Singapore is being neglected, with the implication that "Western values" are gaining in popularity over "Asian values." To counter this trend, the government has outlawed the use of Chinese dialects in government and instituted intensive campaigns to induce Chinese Singaporeans to speak Mandarin.[7]

Status of Women

Singapore has been widely praised for allowing both sexes more or less equal opportunities for education. One result has been that girls and young women outperform their male counterparts in many areas of study, and women university graduates are finding a shortage of well-educated men to go around. Singaporean women now play the leading role in teaching at the school and university levels, in many areas of medicine, and in some key areas of the bureaucracy. The leader of the opposition Workers' Party, Sylvia Lim, is a former police officer turned university lecturer. She drew enormous crowds of young Singaporeans to her party's rallies during the 2006 election campaign.[8]

Religion

The government generally allowed religious freedom until the late 1980s because it was felt that religion tended to reinforce moral behavior, family values, and respect for authority. During the 1980s, religious education was mandated in all schools, and children were assigned to classes where the religion officially linked to their racial group was taught. But the classes were stopped in the late 1980s when the government realized that certain religious groups, including those who espoused "liberation theology," were criticizing government policies.

The government responded by jailing some of the activists, expelling the Christian Conference of Asia, placing the Student Christian Movement under close watch, and passing the Maintenance of Religious Harmony Act in 1990. This act restricted the practice of religion except in approved forms, and banned any political expression of religion. At about the same time, the government produced a national ideology called Shared Values which was loosely based on Confucianism.[9]

Historical Background

For 2,000 years or more, ships trading between China and India anchored in Singapore's fine natural harbor while they waited for the monsoon winds to change direction and carry their vessels on the remainder of their voyage. Over the centuries, the island attracted people of many races and nationalities, including Chinese, Malays, Thais, Indians and Arabs. In the fourteenth century A.D., it was a flourishing port called Temasek. The *Malay Annals* recall that it was "a great city to which foreigners came in great numbers." But around 1390, Javanese invaders destroyed Singapore, and for the next four centuries it was little more than a haven for pirates.[10]

Raffles

In 1819, Sir Thomas Stamford Raffles persuaded the Sultan of Johore to cede the island to the East India Company. The entire population was said to consist of 120 Malays and 30 Chinese, but within a few years, the city Raffles planned was again drawing immigrants from Malaya and Sumatra and from as far away as China, India, and Arabia.

Straits Chinese

During the nineteenth century, most Chinese immigrants to Singapore were men, and many of them planned to return to China after earning and saving some money. But

Table 7.2
Events in Singaporean History

1300s	Singapore was a flourishing port called Temasek.
1819	Stamford Raffles acquires Singapore as a British port.
1826	Singapore becomes part of the Straits Settlements.
1867	Straits Settlements become a British crown colony.
1942–45	During Japanese occupation, many Chinese murdered.
1955	Constitution allows partially elected legislature.
1959	Lee Kuan Yew forms semi-independent government.
1963	After gaining independence, Singapore joins Malaysia.
1965	Singapore expelled from Malaysia.
1966–81	PAP monopolizes all seats in the parliament.
1981	Workers Party candidate wins a seat in parliament.
1984	PAP begins allocating some seats to opposition to quell unrest over its increasingly authoritarian rule.
1988	PAP wins 80 out of 81 seats in election.
1990	Lee Kuan Yew passes premiership to Goh Chok Tong.
1991	PAP wins 77 seats and opposition wins 4.
1997	Asian financial crisis has mild impact on Singapore.
2001	PAP wins 84 out of 86 seats in parliamentary election.
2004	Goh Chok Tong passes premiership to Lee Hsieng Loon.
2006	PAP wins 84 out of 86 seats in parliamentary election.
2008	Singapore opposes sanctions against Burmese junta.

some married Malay women and became partly assimilated to Malay culture, although they did not convert to Islam. Their descendants, including Lee Kuan Yew, were known as Straits Chinese, and many of them learned English in order to serve in the colonial administration. But today the Straits Chinese culture is fading away, because many members of the younger generation prefer to marry outside the Straits Chinese community.[11]

British forces failed to stop the Japanese invasion of Singapore in World War II. More than 25,000 Chinese were massacred by the invaders, and thousands of other residents were killed or imprisoned. When the British regained control in 1945, Singapore's infrastructure was in ruins, nearly half the people were living in make-shift housing. Unemployment was a serious problem, and pro-communist sympathy was on the rise because of communist victories in China.

Lee Kuan Yew

Lee entered politics in postwar Singapore after earning degrees at Oxford and Cambridge. He and his English-educated friends formed the People's Action Party (PAP) in 1954, but since they lacked a mass base they allied themselves with Chinese communist labor unions. After PAP won a landslide victory in the 1959 election, Lee headed Singapore's first home rule government.

In 1961, Lee and his colleagues provoked a break-up with the communists by calling for the merger of Singapore with the anti–communist Federation of Malaya. The communists walked out and formed the opposition *Barisan Socialis* (Socialist Front), but Lee's faction still controlled the government, so they were able to use the police to crush the communist labor movement.

Troubled Ties with Malaysia

In 1963, Lee led Singapore into a merger with Malaya to form the Federation of Malaysia. But he soon angered Prime Minister Tunku Abdul Rahman by campaigning for equal rights of citizenship for the Chinese Malaysians. Fearing this might destroy Malaysia, Rahman expelled Singapore from the federation in 1965. This was perhaps the greatest disappointment of Lee's career, and he never quite managed to repair relations with Singapore's closest and most important neighbor.[12]

Rebuilding

After this near-fatal blow, the Singapore government showed remarkable determination in the face of adversity. The Housing and Development Board (HDB) was created to replace the shanty-towns and slums where many people lived. Soon, entire new towns were being created. By the 1990s, 86 percent of the population were living in public housing built by the HDB, and most Singaporeans owned the apartments they occupied. But apartments designed so working class families could afford them were very small, and many people disliked living in high-rise buildings which lacked the character of their former neighborhoods. Also, PAP leaders kept track of how the different housing units voted. People who failed to support PAP were warned that their developments were in danger of becoming slums.[13]

Goh Chok Tong

When Lee's deputy, Goh Chok Tong, became Prime Minister in 1990, he was expected to serve only briefly until Lee's eldest son, Lee Hsien Loong, was ready to govern. But the younger Lee had some health problems, and he probably benefited from a longer apprenticeship. During his fourteen years as prime minister, Goh proved to be a tough but extremely able leader. He piloted Singapore through the Asian financial crisis that destabilized much of Southeast Asia, and he took some small but positive steps toward opening his country's political system. Goh also proved to be an effective diplomat, and he worked hard at improving relations with Malaysia. In 2009 he called on Myanmar's military junta to allow Aung San Suu Kyi, the imprisoned pro-democracy leader, to take part in the general election which was due in 2010.[14]

Lee Hsien Loong

In 2003, Goh announced that he would hand over power to Lee Hsien Loong, who promised in a speech at Singapore's Harvard Club to promote political "openess" after he took office.[15] Yet apart from defying his father's wishes by introducing casinos to attract foreign tourists, the younger Lee has made few changes of note in the political or social systems of Singapore.

Political System

There are many similarities between the Singapore and Malaysian political systems. Each of these countries has been ruled by an authoritarian party since independence, and national elections are held at least once every five years in both countries. The ruling party in both places enjoys a huge advantage over its opponents, because it controls the media, the timing of the election, and the courts (so it can ruin an opponent by suing him or throwing him in prison). In both countries, the ruling party has unlimited government funds to spend on keeping itself in power while the opposition has few resources to draw on. But the dominant party is under constant pressure to justify its rule by managing the economy effectively. Thus, the parties that run both Singapore and Malaysia must be responsive to voters' concerns to a certain degree.[16]

Despite these similarities, PAP controls the political, economic, and social agenda in Singapore much more completely than UMNO does in Malaysia. This is partly because Singapore is so much smaller than its neighbor, and most Singaporeans live in government-maintained buildings that can be turned into slums if the people vote against PAP candidates.[17] Malaysia is a much bigger country, and the relative strength of UMNO and the opposition parties varies from state to state, making election results much less predictable. In the 2008 election, UMNO and the National Front coalition suffered a far greater setback than most people expected. The opposition parties could even gain control of the government if they could persuade just thirty members of parliament to defect to their side of the aisle.[18] In Singapore's, ruling party is much more securely in control.

People's Action Party

Since all cabinet ministers and senior bureaucrats are members of PAP, they work together closely on major policy issues. Senior officers in the armed forces and police and leaders of government-linked corporations are also members of PAP. Little is known about the internal policy debates of PAP members, which take place in private, and factional disputes are almost never aired in public. Such tight party discipline is not difficult to maintain, because the party is small and cohesive, with a membership that is largely male, Chinese, and highly educated.[19]

Although it is not a mass-based party, PAP controls much larger organizations like the National Trades Union Congress (NTUC), the armed forces, police, and civilian bureaucracy, and it relies on these and other organizations for support during elections. A small number of party cadre are assigned responsibility for electing the party's twelve-member Central Executive Committee. The leader of the party (who also heads the government) works with the Executive Committee to select candidates for Parliament and key bureaucratic appointments.[20] Members of PAP hold most of the seats in Parliament, and they routinely approve whatever the government proposes. But Parliament serves as a training ground for future government ministers, and PAP members of Parliament are expected to keep in touch with their constituencies and serve as a link between them and the party.

CORRUPTION

Unlike its neighbors, Singapore is consistently rated one of the least corrupt countries in the world by Transparency International, a nongovernmental organization based in Berlin. The government's success in controlling corruption is largely due to the fact that pay scales and incentive awards for public officials are very generous, because the government must compete for scarce talent with multinational firms, many of which have regional offices in Singapore.[21] Salaries for top-level officials in Singapore are so lavish they contribute to the huge disparity of incomes between rich and poor Singaporeans.[22]

The Presidency

Lee Kuan Yew realized in the 1980s that there was nothing to prevent PAP leaders from spending Singapore's large foreign currency reserves exactly as they pleased. So he amended the constitution to give Singapore's ceremonial president control over the currency reserves, and he made the presidency an elective office. Some people thought that Lee might want to be president himself after stepping down as prime minister, but even the enhanced presidency did not appeal to him, and he was far less interested in accumulating wealth than autocrats like Ferdinand Marcos in the Philippines or Suharto in Indonesia.[23]

Opposition Parties and Elections

In 1961, the Socialist Front (*Barisan Socialis,* BS) broke away from PAP, and in the 1963 election, the BS won fourteen seats to thirty-seven for PAP. After PAP used the police to destroy the Barisan's influence and jail its leaders, the party began a boycott of Parliament in 1966, and PAP won every seat in Parliament in the next four elections, as shown in Table 7.3.

Table 7.3
Singapore Parliamentary Elections, 1959–2006

Election	Seats Contested in Parliament	Seats Won by PAP	PAP's Percentage of the Vote	Opposition Seats Won
May 1959	51	43	54.08	8
Sept 1963	51	37	46.93	14
April 1968	7 (51)*	58	86.72	0
Sept 1972	57 (8)	65	70.43	0
Dec 1976	53 (16)	69	74.00	0
Dec 1980	38 (37)	75	77.66	0
Dec 1984	49 (30)	77	64.83	2
Sept 1988	70 (11)	80	63.17	1
Aug 1991	40 (41)	77	60.97	4
Jan 1997	36 (47)	81	64.98	2
Nov 2001	29 (55)	84	75.3	2
May 2006	29 (55)	84	67.0	2

*The number of seats not contested by the opposition are in parentheses. *Source:* Singapore government election data.

In 1984, PAP's percentage of the vote dropped by almost 13 percent, and the opposition won two out of seventy-nine seats in Parliament. In most countries, PAP's 64 percent of the vote and seventy-seven seat win would be considered a landslide, but PAP's control of the media and election rules gave it an overwhelming advantage. PAP leaders realized that voters were angry about the lack of an opposition in parliament. To ensure that some non–Chinese candidates were elected to parliament, they adopted a new electoral system using multimember constituencies in which one member had to be non–Chinese. They also guaranteed that at least the three top vote-getters in the opposition parties would be given seats in parliament.[24]

A further small drop in PAP's percentage of the vote in the 1988 election may have been caused by diminished confidence in PAP's economic management and the increasingly autocratic tone of Lee's administration. In any case, PAP leaders concluded that more adjustments in the electoral system were needed. So they introduced a system in which up to six eminent people from various professions would be appointed as members of Parliament (without the right to vote on money matters or constitutional issues).

A group of the most active opposition parties formed a coalition called the Singapore Democratic Alliance (SDA) in 2001 in the hope of improving their chances in that year's election, but their strategy failed. PAP increased its victory margin in 2001, because the SDA could not offer a realistic alternative to PAP's economic development policies.

With almost no access to the media, the opposition parties tend to drop out of sight between elections, and they have difficulty attracting qualified people to run for office. Singaporeans are reluctant to play an active role in politics, and even PAP has difficulty recruiting able people to run for office. Those who take the risk of running against PAP candidates usually lose, and they are often accused of libel and sued for enormous sums in the courts, which always side with the ruling party.[25]

The Judiciary

Singapore's courts have a reputation for independence in trying civil cases, but penalties for criminal offenses tend to be much harsher than in western countries, and the courts invariably support the government in cases that become politicized.[26] The Chief Justice, senior judge, and six judges of the High Court are appointed by the president on the government's recommendation. Trial by jury was abolished in the 1960s, and the right of appeal to the Privy Council in London was abolished in 1994 after the leader of the Workers Party won an appeal to the Judicial Committee of the Privy Council on the issue of his disbarment.

When the Law Society criticized certain legislative proposals in the late 1980s, they were forced to get rid of their president, Francis Seow, and abstain from further criticism of government policies. When Francis Seow ran for Parliament in 1988, he was arrested, accused of tax evasion, and subjected to vicious personal attacks by government leaders. To escape harassment, he finally moved to the United States. Meanwhile, the first secretary of the American embassy was expelled from Singapore for meeting with Seow and other potential opponents of the government.[27]

Civil Society

The Singapore government makes it nearly impossible to express opposition through the kind of civil society that has developed in Thailand, the Philippines, and Indonesia.

Nongovernmental organizations (NGOs) exist, but they must be approved by the Registrar of Organizations, and they are quickly brought in line or abolished if they overstep the bounds set by the government. A favorite technique used by the government to suppress criticism is to co–opt the leaders of NGOs and turn them into tame supporters, but critics can also be imprisoned without trial under the Internal Subversion Act.[28]

Examples of NGO's include the women's group AWARE which opposes sexism in advertising, the Nature Society which is concerned with ecological issues, and the Singapore Heritage Society, which is interested in conservation of historic buildings. The membership of these organizations is elite, and they have close ties with the government.

The Media

Like Malaysia, the Singapore government has gained nearly complete control over the media. In 1966, Singapore issued regulations for the "control of publications and safeguarding of information," and charged the editor of a Chinese-language newspaper with sedition. A reporter for the *Far Eastern Economic Review* became the first of many to be ordered out of Singapore for the crime of reporting information obtained from Amnesty International. In 1983, the government took over the management of all domestic publications.[29]

Singapore has four daily newspapers that are published in English and three in Chinese, plus one each in Tamil and Malay. The English-language papers (with a combined circulation of over half a million) include the *Straits Times,* which provides useful coverage of political and social issues in spite of being government-controlled. The Media Development Authority supervises radio and TV broadcasting. Although Singapore is a leading manufacturer and exporter of satellite dishes, Singaporeans are not allowed to own one.[30]

The Singapore government tries to control the flow of information in the city-state, but this obviously conflicts with its goal of becoming a leading world business center in the information age. It also seems rather futile, because almost every household in Singapore is connected to the Internet. Singaporeans are free to travel abroad and many of them do, while some eight million visitors arrive at Changi Airport each year. Internet cafes are plentiful, and more than 55,000 Singaporeans attend the country's universities, while thousands more study abroad. So the government's effort to control the flow of information appears neither rational nor practical.

Economic Development

Fluctuating world demand for Singapore's exports continues to affect the economic growth rate, as Table 7.4 shows. Until the early 1960s, Singapore followed a policy of import-substitution, but when that approach proved unsuccessful, the government switched to an emphasis on export-oriented manufacturing using mainly foreign capital. In 1961, the Economic Development Board was created and work began on Jurong Industrial park where foreign corporations could build factories to produce for export and pay little or no taxes. Labor laws and tax codes were adjusted to attract multinational corporations from Japan, Europe, and the United States.

As Table 7.4 shows, Singapore's economic growth rate dropped to 1.1 percent in

2008, and the economic growth rate was expect to contract by 8.8 percent in 2009. Almost all the weakness was caused by reduced worldwide demand for Singapore's exports. The country was one of the most export-dependant countries in the world. Worldwide demand was expected to begin to recover in late 2009 or early 2010. By Singapore standards, unemployment was high in the city-state, but it was moderate to low by Western standards. Firms based in Singapore were anxious to retain their well-qualified workers, which were their most important asset, so they tended to resort to reducing pay or the length of the work week rather than laying off workers. As a result, there was no exodus of qualified Singaporeian or expatriate workers from the country, because job opportunities tended to be better there than in the West.

Table 7.4
Singapore's Economy, 2007–10
(figures are percentages unless otherwise indicated)

	2007	2008	2009	2010
GDP Growth	7.8	1.1	-8.8	-0.9
Industrial Production Growth	7.8	-4.2	-9.3	1.5
Unemployment	2.1	2.2	3.8	4.4
Inflation	2.1	6.5	-0.2	1.9
Government Budget Balance	3.3	0.8	-4.1	-4
Exports (U.S. $B)	303.1	342.7	222.4	231.1
Imports (U.S. $B)	254	309.6	189.8	200.4

Source: Economist Intelligence Unit, "Singapore, Country Report," April 2009. Figures for 2009 and 2010 are EIU forecasts.

Foreign Investment

By 2008, over 7,000 multinational corporations were operating in Singapore, providing most of the capital invested in manufacturing and producing more than two thirds of the island's manufacturing output and direct export sales.

Singapore's total (government and private) direct investment abroad was $111 billion by the end of 2005. China was the leading destination, receiving 13.8 percent of the total. Malaysia was next, with 9 percent, followed by Indonesia (8 percent), Hong Kong (7 percent) and the United States (5 percent).[31]

To maintain Singapore's competitiveness, the government has also invested heavily in education and health services while generally keeping extremely tight controls on the labor force and resisting demands for social benefit programs.[32] Workers were required to contribute a large percentage of their wages to the government pension plan, and these funds were steadily invested in Singapore's infrastructure and government-linked corporations (GLC). These now number about 500, and they are much more competitive than the GLCs in Malaysia or the state companies in Vietnam.

Economic Prospects

The major challenges Singapore faces include an ageing population, the need to upgrade its manufacturing sector, and increased competition with other Asian countries as a trade and transportation center and as a center for financial services. In 2007, Singapore launched a new stock market in an effort to encourage high-growth Asian companies to make their initial public offerings (IPOs) in Singapore.

Private consumption is likely to be an increasingly important factor in Singapore's economic growth because of lower unemployment, higher wages, and stable real estate values, which adds to the wealth effect for home owners.[33] Regional economic integration is an important goal of the Singapore government, and this requires strengthening relations with Malaysia, Indonesia and Thailand as well as China, Japan, South Korea, and Taiwan.

Foreign Relations

As a major trade and transportation hub, Singapore has done more to link the economies of Southeast Asia than most other countries in the region. Its diplomats and scholars have been among the most effective proponents of regional integration. The Singapore government is also an important investor in developing countries, and their sociopolitical system is admired by conservative leaders in China and the West. But the main weakness in Singapore's diplomacy has been its relations with its neighbors, particularly when Mahathir, Suharto and Lee Kuan Yew were running their respective countries.

Singapore has not faced a conventional military threat from its neighbors or anyone else since the early 1960s, but it spends between 5 and 7 percent of its GNP on its defense forces, which are among the best equipped in the region. They have played a useful role by taking part in numerous UN peacekeeping missions. They also create some good will by training with the forces of every ASEAN country plus Australia, New Zealand, Taiwan, India, and the United States.

Singapore's security policy recognizes a variety of non–military threats, including organized crime, piracy in surrounding waterways, Islamic terrorism, natural disasters like the 2004 tsunami, and epidemics that can frighten away tourists. The other ASEAN states face similar threats, and Singapore has been one of the leaders of efforts to develop security programs on a regional basis.

Relations with Malaysia

After Singapore was expelled from Malaysia in 1965, relations between the two countries were strained for decades, usually over economic issues that were allowed to harden into political problems. Relations were handled at the most senior level, but this often seemed to make matters worse. The long-serving leaders of Singapore and Malaysia, Lee Kuan Yew and Mahathir Mohamed, were regarded by many as world class statesmen but they seldom bothered to be diplomatic when speaking of each other's countries.[34] Relations began to improve under their successors, Goh Chock Tong and Abdullah Badawi, who took over as Malaysia's Prime Minister in 2003 after serving as Foreign Minister.

When Lee Hsien Loong succeeded Goh in 2004, he made his first overseas visit to Malaysia and he sensibly asked Goh to continue playing a key role in relations with that country. Singapore offered to release Malaysians' pension fund contributions in exchange for access to Malaysian airspace. The Singapore government's investment agency was allowed to acquire a 5 percent stake in Telekom Malaysia and in Proton, Malaysia's national car maker. The Singapore investment agency also joined with a Malaysian bank to form a real estate investment fund, but a considerable number of bilateral issues remained unresolved, perhaps because both sides have tried to link too many issues together.

Relations with Indonesia

In years past, Singapore's relations with its other Muslim neighbor, Indonesia, were also strained for reasons that were partly personal. For example, Lee Kuan Yew had a particularly poor opinion of President B.J. Habibie. Singapore leaders also believed undocumented Indonesian workers contributed to the crime problem in Singapore, but the rise of Islamic terrorism in Indonesia was their greatest concern, and they wanted an extradition treaty so they could bring terrorists to trial in Singapore. For their part, Indonesian leaders also wanted a treaty so they could extradite Indonesians who fled to Singapore after being accused of corruption and embezzlement, but Singapore was not eager to give their neighbors access to Singapore bank records.

After new leaders took office in both countries in 2004, they agreed to expedite work on an extradition treaty, and agreement was finally reached in 2007. They also signed a defense agreement in 2007, but opposition parties in Indonesia's legislature tried to postpone ratification of the necessary implementation agreements in order to embarrass the administration of President Yudhoyono.[35]

Singapore responded quickly with aid when the Indonesian province of Aceh was destroyed by a tsunami, and agreement was reached in 2004 on a security issue of great symbolic as well as practical importance. Singapore, Malaysia and Indonesia began to coordinate patrols in the Straits of Malacca, where pirates and terrorists threaten more than a quarter of the world's seaborne trade. Other ASEAN members joined these three countries in making formal commitments to a common regional approach to the problem of terrorism. But there was undoubtedly still a great deal of work to be done to build mutual trust among the security and intelligence services of these and other ASEAN states.[36]

Relations with China

In 1990, after many years of regarding China as a potentially hostile and subversive nation, Singapore finally established diplomatic relations with Beijing. A surprisingly close relationship was soon formed between the world's most populous nation and the small city-state. Millions of people now travel each year between Singapore, China, Hong Kong, and Taiwan. After stepping down as prime minister of Singapore in 1990, Lee Kuan Yew became a trusted advisor to the Chinese leadership, who seemed to regard Singapore as an interesting experiment in combining capitalism with one-party rule. Lee's concept of "Asian values" also has much in common with the neo-Confucianism that has all but replaced Maoism in China.

Nevertheless, Singapore's relations with China, Taiwan, and Hong Kong contain some interesting contradictions. Singapore recognizes the government in Beijing as the sole government of China while continuing to have an unofficial but active economic, political, and military relationship with Taiwan. Singapore's leaders know it would destabilize the entire region if Taiwan were to declare its independence or if China seized Taiwan. China's broad claims to the islands and resources of the South China Sea do not conflict with Singapore's interests directly, but (like the tensions in the Taiwan Strait) they could lead to a dangerous conflict in the region. Singapore also competes with China for foreign investment and for western export markets, and at the same time, the Singapore government and private citizens have invested heavily in China's development.[37]

Relations with the United States

Singapore's first free trade agreement (FTA) was signed with the United States, and large amounts of trade and investment capital flow in both directions. Some 1,500 American multinational companies have regional operations based in Singapore. Defense agreements with the United States provide for visits by U.S. Navy ships and the use of Paya Lebar Airbase by U.S. fighter aircraft. A 2005 Strategic Framework Agreement with the U.S. provides for annual strategic talks, additional joint military exercises, and cooperation in military research and development. These agreements and the Five-Power Defense Arrangement with Britain, Australia, New Zealand, and Malaysia help the United States and Australia maintain the balance of power in the western Pacific.[38]

Conclusions

Singapore's leaders believe their island city-state is vulnerable to a range of external threats, but their greatest fear is that social instability will return and weaken Singapore's ability to survive in a hostile world environment. Because of their remarkable economic achievements, PAP leaders may think that they alone are capable of running Singapore, and they probably believe the electorate will keep them in power as long as they maintain a high rate of economic growth. They see any loosening of political and social controls as risky, but they realize there is pressure for liberalization, particularly from the younger generation. Thus, they may believe that a very cautious opening of the system may gain some added support from the electorate, and it may help attract foreign tourists.

But these advantages are seen as minor compared with the need to maintain social stability. If they see a need for it, PAP leaders are just as willing to tighten political and social controls as to loosen them.

In a rare televised confrontation during the 2006 election campaign, a group of young journalists told Lee Kuan Yew that the PAP had become "arrogant" and "power crazy." Mr. Lee dismissed them as "English-educated radicals" and said they did not represent more than 20 or 30 percent of Singapore's younger generation.[39] His response shows that political controls are unlikely to be loosened very much over the short term. But PAP leaders are determined to keep Singapore competitive by building a knowledge-based economy. So they may see a long-term need to allow their people more freedom.

Further Reading

Ho, Khai Leong. *The Politics of Policy-Making in Singapore*. Singapore: Oxford University Press, 2000.

Lee, Kuan Yew. *The Singapore Story: Memoirs of Lee Kuan Yew.* Singapore: Times Editions, 1998.
Leifer, Michael. *Singapore's Foreign Policy, Coping with Vulnerability.* London and New York: Routledge, 2000.
Low, Linda. *The Political Economy of a City-State: Government-Made Singapore.* Singapore: Oxford University Press, 1998.
Milne, R.S., and Diane K. Mauzy. *Singapore: The Legacy of Lee Kuan Yew.* Boulder, CO: Westview Press, 1990.

– 8 –

INDONESIA

A Shallow-Rooted Democracy

For Indonesia, more than any other country in Asia, the 1997 financial crisis was a watershed event. It ended three decades of autocratic rule by General Suharto during which living standards rose (for some people spectacularly) but no political dissent was allowed, and racial and religious tensions simmered beneath the surface calm. The swift collapse of the "miracle economy" in 1997 revealed the weakness of Suharto's New Order institutions, and jolted the political elite into accepting some badly needed reforms. But *reformasi* took place against a backdrop of racial and religious conflict, especially in Maluku and Sulawesi, plus serious human rights violations by the military in East Timor and Aceh. Some analysts even wondered if the world's fourth largest country might be on the verge of breaking apart.

Yet within a few years the situation stabilized. In two successive national elections, 1999 and 2004, Indonesian voters opted for a democratic change of government. In December 2004, a tsunami devastated the province of Aceh with enormous loss of life. But reconstruction began with billions of dollars of international aid and investment. President Yudhoyono and Vice President Kalla used the opportunity to negotiate peace with the Aceh secession movement and to improve relations with many foreign governments including the United States.

For the next three years, economic growth was in the 5 to 6 percent range, and exports increased substantially in 2008 despite the global recession.[1] Democracy seemed to have scored a major victory, but like many developing countries, Indonesia emerged from the shadows of autocracy with political institutions that were still dangerously weak. Corruption, cronyism, and nepotism remained deeply embedded in the system. The armed forces adopted a lower profile in politics, but they were seldom held responsible for their human rights abuses. Relations between religious and ethnic groups improved, but intolerance by militant Islamists remained a problem. Much needed to be done to strengthen the rule of law as a basic precondition for sustained economic development.

In the 2009 election, Yudhoyono won a second five-year term as president, defeating his two main rivals, Jusuf Kalla and former president Megawati Sukarnoputra. Thus, Yudhoyono gained a new mandate to tackle the country's major problems of poverty and corruption. By late 2009, analysts expected the Indonesian economy to achieve modest growth in the 2 to 4 percent range during 2009 and 2010, and the poverty rate actually dropped from 15.4 percent in March 2008 to 14.2 percent in March 2009.[2]

People and Cultures

Indonesia has 245 million people (half the population of Southeast Asia) spread over 13,000 islands and speaking more than 200 local languages. But this ethnic and geographic complexity is not such an obstacle to national unity as the numbers suggest. Most of the islands are uninhabited, and three quarters of the Indonesian people belong to four main ethno-linguistic groups, as shown in Table 8.1. Many of the smaller linguistic groups are concentrated in Papua, and most Indonesians speak a form of Malay called *Bahasa Indonesia* as their first or second language.

Table 8.1
Indonesia: Demographic Overview

Population (2006 estimate): 245 million
Rural Population (2006 estimate): 69%
Urban Population (2006 estimate): 31%
Annual Growth Rate of Population (2009 estimate): 1.136%
Ethnic Groups (2006 estimate): Javanese 45%, Sudanese 14%, Madurese 7.5%, Coastal Malays 7.5%, Chinese 3%, others 2.3%
Religious Affiliations (2006 estimate): Muslim 88%, Protestant Christian 5%, Catholic Christian 3%, Hindu 2%, Buddhist 1%
Percentage of Students in Primary School (2004 estimate): 92% (but far fewer attend school full-time)
Percentage of Students in Secondary School (2004 estimate): 44% (but far fewer attend school full-time)
University Students (1999–2000): 3.13 million in 1,634 institutions with 194,828 teachers
Literacy (2007 estimate): 90.4%
Personal Computers (2002 estimate): 2.5 million
Internet Users (2002 estimate): 8 million
Life Expectancy (2009 estimate): 70.76 years
Infant Mortality Rate (2009 estimate): 29.97 per 1,000 live births
Per capita GDP (2005): $1,280 ($3,720 purchasing power parity)

Sources: Embassy of Indonesia, Washington, D.C.; United Nations Development Program, *Human Development Report*; Economist Intelligence Unit; World Bank, Washington, D.C.; U.S. Department of State, "Background Notes: Indonesia."

Religion

Although Indonesia has the largest Muslim population in the world, there has never been broad support, even among Muslims, for making Indonesia an Islamic state.[3] Indonesia's first President, Sukarno, insisted on a secular state based on the five principles of *Pancasila:* monotheism, humanitarianism, national unity, democracy by consensus, and social justice. President Suharto's New Order regime supported this (deliberately non–Islamic) ideology and required all citizens to receive instruction in one of five state-authorized religions.[4]

ISLAM

Indonesian Muslims have a reputation for being more tolerant of other religions than Middle Eastern Muslims. As Islam spread slowly from west to east across the archipelago, it only gradually made a deep impression on the lives and belief systems of Indonesians. Hinduism and Buddhism had gained acceptance before the arrival of Islam, which did not so much displace the earlier religions as add another strand of religious belief.

Many Indonesians are *abangan* Muslims, whose faith includes elements of Hinduism or native animism and is sometimes called the "Javanese religion," because its stronghold is in Central and East Java. But a growing number of Indonesians, who may now constitute a majority, are *santri* Muslims, meaning they have studied their religion more deeply and are more observant of Islamic rules and restrictions. The Muhammadiyah organization was founded in 1912 by urban, modernist Muslims who wanted to purge Islam of Hindu and Javanese influences. Rural, conservative Muslims formed the Nahdlatul Ulama (NU) organization in 1926, and both organizations now have about 30 million members.[5]

Traditionally, Muslims and Christians have lived peacefully in close proximity in many parts of Indonesia, but there have been serious flare-ups of religious conflict in Maluku and Sulawesi in recent years. One reason for this is that the New Order regime kept both Christians and Muslims on edge about their status by supporting first one group and then the other. Suharto was an *abangan* Muslim who distrusted *santri* Muslims. Initially, he gave preference to Christians in his administration, but later he sought the support of middle class *santri* Muslims to compensate for his waning popularity with the military.[6]

CHRISTIANITY

Portuguese missionaries brought Christianity to the eastern islands of Indonesia nearly 500 years ago, but the Dutch, who displaced them as colonists, were less intent on proselytizing. Although fewer than ten percent of the Indonesian people are Christian, their influence has been greater than their numbers would suggest. They often receive a superior education in Christian schools, and they were given preference by the Dutch (and later by the New Order regime) for positions in the army and civil administration.[7]

Ethnic Groups

In Indonesia, a person's ethnic identity is based on their place of origin and mother tongue rather than on physical traits (or religion, as in Malaysia). Thus, a Javanese is a person who was born in Java and whose mother tongue is Javanese. A person who is born in Bali to Javanese parents is also Javanese, and a person born of Madurese parents whose mother tongue is Madurese may spend his life in Java and not be considered Javanese. However, because of intermarriage between ethnic groups and migration within the country, a growing number of Indonesian citizens now identify themselves simply as "Indonesian."

THE JAVANESE

The island of Java is the size of New York state, but its population of over 100 million people makes it one of the world's most densely settled areas. The term "Javanese"

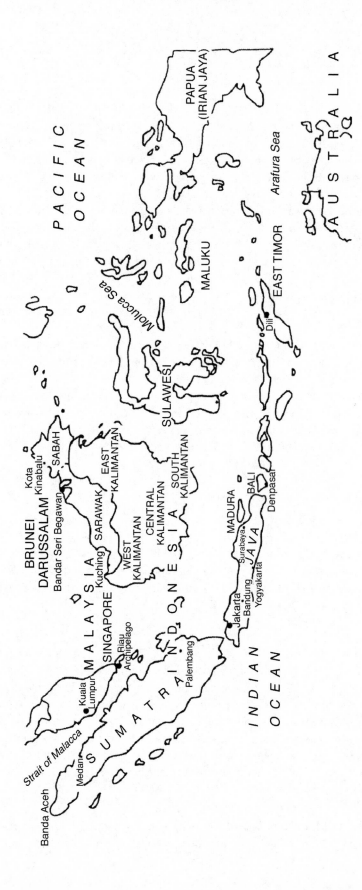

denotes a specific ethno-linguistic group which is by far the largest and most powerful in Indonesia, although they share the island of Java with other ethnic groups. Javanese are numerically dominant in East and Central Java, but they make up only a third of the eight million people in Jakarta and a tenth of the 44 million people in West Java.[8]

The traditional Javanese aristocracy, known as the *priyayi,* have a rigid code of personal behavior, which involves never showing anger or other strong emotions. The Javanese language has many different levels of formality to be used in speaking to people of different social classes. The Dutch colonial rulers co-opted the *priyayi* to assist them in exploiting the country's peasant class. The Dutch also favored the *abangan* Muslims because they were suspicious of the political motives of strict (*santri*) Muslims. Although Suharto was from a lower middle class background, his wife was of the aristocracy, and he ruled Indonesia like a Javanese sultan, adopting the *priyayi* forms of etiquette.[9]

THE SUNDANESE

The next largest ethno-linguistic group in Indonesia is the Sundanese, who are concentrated in West Java and number about 34 million. They tend to be more devout Muslims than the Javanese, but they are also considered to be more relaxed and contemplative. The capital of their region is Bandung, which is famous for its universities and intellectual life. Bandung's student leaders are regarded as among the most radical in Indonesia, and they helped foment the 1998 riots and demonstrations that ended Suharto's rule.

THE MADURESE

Numbering about 18 million, the Madurese are known as a seafaring and warlike people. Their home is the rugged island of Madura off the northeast coast of Java. This is the center of the spice trade, but the island is much less developed than Java, and many Madurese have emigrated to Java and other parts of Indonesia for economic reasons.

COASTAL MALAYS

Indonesia's 18 million Coastal Malays live in the Riau Islands near Singapore and in the city of Palembang on Sumatra. They are the Indonesians who are most closely related to the dominant Malay ethnic group in Malaysia. Palembang occupies the site of the ancient capital of the Srivijaya empire, which was founded thirteen centuries ago.

THE ACEHNESE

The people of Aceh in northern Sumatra are considered to be Indonesia's most devout Muslims. In the nineteenth century, they fought a thirty year war of resistance against the Dutch which cost over a hundred thousand lives. The Acehnese initially supported the Indonesian revolution and accepted inclusion in the Indonesian state. But an armed rebellion broke out in the 1950s when they felt their interests were being ignored by Jakarta, and the central government had to grant them virtual autonomy and make Aceh a Special District.[10]

In the 1970s, the Free Aceh Movement (Gerakan Aceh Merdeka, GAM) began a struggle for independence which lasted until a tsunami destroyed the province in December 2004. With international assistance, the newly elected Yudhoyono administration

Opposite: **Figure 8.1. Indonesia and surrounding countries.**

reached an agreement with GAM on autonomy for the province while mounting a multi-billion dollar reconstruction program.[11]

THE CHINESE

In 2004, the ethnic Chinese in Indonesia numbered about seven million or 3 percent of the population. They are the largest non–Malay ethnic group in Indonesia and have long played a major role in the economy (as Chinese do in most Southeast Asian countries), but they are one of the least assimilated overseas Chinese communities in the region. As in Malaysia, Chinese whose families have lived in Indonesia for generations are not considered indigenous (*pribumi*), and their political rights and participation remain limited.[12]

During the colonial period, thousands of Chinese immigrated to Indonesia as merchants or laborers and over time they came to be resented as a privileged class of merchants, money-lenders and tax farmers. When Mao Zedong's forces won control of China, many Chinese in Indonesia joined the local Communist Party or communist-influenced organizations.[13]

Race riots against the Chinese occurred frequently before and during the twentieth century. In the chaos that followed the 1965 Gestapu coup (described later in this chapter), thousands of Chinese were murdered, and many who could afford to leave did so, depriving Indonesia of their entrepreneurial skills.[14] Cultural assimilation was the policy of Suharto's New Order regime. (This was much like Thai policy until the 1960s.) The Chinese who remained in Indonesia were strongly encouraged to adopt Indonesian names, and the process for attaining Indonesian citizenship was simplified. Chinese schools and newspapers were closed, and Chinese characters could no longer be displayed on shop signs. Although Suharto made use of the commercial expertise of Chinese businessmen, he was careful to prevent them from gaining political influence, as many Chinese did in Thailand and the Philippines.

Historical Background

Twentieth century Indonesian nationalists like Sukarno were inspired by the great Southeast Asian empires of the past, but it was the Dutch colonial regime that unified the archipelago and created the beginnings of a modern central government, although they had no intention of granting the country independence.

Drawn by the lucrative trade in Asian spices, the Portuguese were the first European colonialists to gain a foothold in the region during the 1500s. But the Dutch drove them out of their base at Melaka in 1641 and gradually took over ports and then land areas in order to grow spices and other tropical crops. Under the "Culture System," Javanese peasants were required to grow commercial crops for the government, legally on a fifth of their land but often on two fifths or more.[15] Javanese aristocrats were enlisted to help run the system and became lower-ranking members of the colonial administration. Thousands of Chinese laborers were imported, and Chinese merchants were given a major role in running the economy, with the result that Indonesians often resented them even more than the Dutch.

Yet despite its negative aspects, Dutch rule laid the groundwork for the present Indonesian state by unifying the islands under one administration and linking the country together with roads, modern communications, and a shipping fleet. In the early twentieth century, a colonial legislature was created, and medical and educational facilities were gradually improved. But the Dutch had no intention of relinquishing the colony, and they did their best to repress any group that sought independence.

Table 8.2
Events in Indonesian History

600s–1300s	Srivijaya empire centered on Sumatra.
1293–1520	Hindu Majapahit empire based in Java.
1500s	Arrival of Islamic missionaries from the Middle East and Christian missionaries from Portugal.
1596	Dutch begin 350 year colonial expansion in Indonesia.
1942–45	Japanese occupation brings great hardship.
1945	Sukarno proclaims independence; anti–Dutch war begins.
1949	Indonesian forces win war of independence.
1955	Indonesia's first (and last) free election until 1999.
1959	Sukarno assumes dictatorial powers (Guided Democracy).
1963	Sukarno seizes Irian Jaya; "confronts" Malaysia.
1965–66	Gestapu coup; General Suharto replaces Sukarno as president and reverses his pro–China, anti–Western policies.
1966–98	Suharto and the Indonesian army run Indonesia. In return for steady economic growth, they rule autocratically.
1998	Economic crisis topples Suharto; Habibie begins reform.
1999	East Timor votes for independence; UN intervention halts rampage by anti-independence militias and Indonesian army.
1999	Ailing Muslim leader Wahid chosen president by MPR.
2001	Wahid is impeached; replaced by Megawati Sukarnoputri.
2004	Yudhoyono defeats Megawati in first direct election for president. Tsunami engulfs Aceh with great loss of life.
2004–06	Aceh is granted autonomy; separatist war ends.

Rise of Nationalism

The Islamic Association (*Sarekat Islam*) was formed in 1912 and evolved into a radical nationalist organization led by western-educated Indonesians. A communist faction split off and, although severely repressed by the Dutch, it survived to play a major role as the Communist Party of Indonesia (PKI) after World War II.[16] The secular Indonesian Nationalist Party (PNI) was formed in 1927 with a charismatic young engineering graduate named Sukarno as its leader. In 1929, when Sukarno and his colleagues called for independence, the Dutch arrested them and dissolved the PNI.

During World War II, the Japanese unintentionally laid the groundwork for Indonesian independence by co-opting many nationalist leaders and putting them in charge of mass organizations to support the Japanese occupation. Nationalist and Muslim organizations were kept separate and competed with each other, as they have continued to do ever since. When the Japanese finally realized they were losing the war, they removed all restrictions on independence movements and organized an Indonesian army to resist a possible Allied invasion.[17]

Revolution

On August 17, 1945, two days after the Japanese surrender, Sukarno proclaimed Indonesia an independent republic with himself as president and Mohammad Hatta as vice president. (Hatta, a Sumatran who had studied in Holland, was more pro–Western than Sukarno.) The two men drafted a constitution calling for a presidential form of government, created a Central National Committee of 135 people, and appointed a cabinet responsible to Sukarno. By year's end, there was sporadic fighting between Indonesian armed units and the Dutch and British forces who came to restore Dutch rule.

The next four years were marked by fighting and negotiating. The Dutch held some major cities on Java and Sumatra, but the republic's forces controlled the roads and countryside. The Dutch met less resistance in the outer islands, and began to set up states in what they hoped would become a federal system. Sukarno and Hatta surrendered to Dutch forces in 1948, but the Indonesian army continued to fight, thus establishing their claim to be the true defenders of Indonesia's independence. By 1949, the Dutch had lost the struggle, and they ceded the entire Netherlands Indies to the republic, except for the western half of New Guinea.[18] The Indonesians inherited a huge archipelago along with the $4.3 billion debt of the Netherlands Indies.

The Liberal Period

In 1950, a new constitution providing for a parliamentary form of government was adopted, and in 1955 the country's first democratic election was held. (It was also the last one until 1999.) With four major parties and dozens of minor ones competing for power, unstable coalition governments became the norm in the 1950s, and they failed to provide effective leadership or badly needed economic development. Throughout the decade, Indonesia's survival was threatened by a variety of destructive forces, including a large and active communist party, clashes between rival military commanders, and the Darul Islam insurgent movement which sought to create an Islamic state.

Guided Democracy

In 1959, Sukarno restored the 1945 constitution (thereby increasing his powers as president) and instituted what he called Guided Democracy. This resembled fascism, except that Sukarno relied increasingly on the Communist Party of Indonesia (PKI), which had attracted three million members. By cutting all foreign economic ties, he plunged the country deeper and deeper into recession.

In 1963, he launched an armed struggle ("confrontation") against the newly formed state of Malaysia, which he saw as a rival for political influence in the region. When Malaysia was elected to a seat on the UN Security Council, Sukarno withdrew Indonesia from the United Nations. He also sent troops to occupy West New Guinea, provoking a new conflict with the Netherlands. Finally, by leaning toward the communists, he provided the Indonesian military with an excuse to seize control of the country.

Gestapu Coup

On October 1, 1965, six leading generals were killed by army officers with links to the PKI, probably to forestall a military coup against President Sukarno. General Suharto, commander of the Army Strategic Reserve Command (Kostrad), took over as head of the armed forces, and there was a massive, nationwide slaughter of anyone who was accused of supporting the PKI. The killings were condoned by the armed forces, and most of the victims were indigenous Indonesians, but many Chinese were also killed, and the death toll rose to between 160,000 and half a million.

Although Suharto had only a grade school education and lacked Sukarno's charisma, he knew how to seize and hold power. He gradually moved Sukarno aside and had himself named acting president in 1967 by the People's Consultative Assembly (*Majelis Permusyarawatan Rakyat,* MPR).[19]

Suharto's "New Order"

During the New Order period (1966–1998), Indonesia's political system was dominated by President Suharto who made all the important decisions with the aid of a small circle of military and technocrat advisors. He used the rewards and sanctions at his diposal to keep the military and civilian elites divided and dependent on him. He also enriched his family and his cronies by giving them control of valuable state assets.

The parliament (*Dewan Perwakilan Rakyat,* DPR) provided the New Order regime with some democratic window-dressing, but it had no independence. Its role was to rubber stamp legislation initiated by the executive branch and to reelect Suharto as president every five years. Political parties were forced to merge into two groupings, the Indonesian Democratic Party (PDI) for secular parties and the Development Unity Party (PPP) for Islamist parties. The government's electoral machine, *Golkar,* functioned almost like an East European communist party during the cold war era.[20]

The judiciary was noted for its corruption and incompetence, but it faithfully protected the interests of the executive branch and the military. Political parties, elections, the media, and non-governmental organizations were tightly controlled by the executive branch, which was dominated by Suharto. He realized he had to provide steady economic growth in order to be accepted as the country's legitimate ruler. Since growth depended on foreign aid and investment, he did not indulge in anti–Western posturing like Sukarno. Instead, he sought close military ties with the U.S., and Washington generally saw him as a staunch anti-communist ally.

Role of the Military

New Order policies were carried out by the state bureaucracy, which included a large number of active duty and retired military officers who often had more authority than their civilian counterparts. The military claimed that their success in winning Indonesia's independence earned them the right to intervene in the country's socio-political affairs. The armed forces controlled an economic empire that provided an estimated two thirds of their budget, freeing them from civilian control. Their territorial command structure extended down to the village level, and one of its main functions was to manage military economic enterprises.[21]

Despite its many shortcomings, the New Order regime gave the Indonesian people a more stable social and political environment than they had known in the past. Although they enjoyed none of the democratic rights they were promised in the 1945 constitution, economic growth averaged about 6.5 percent a year during the New Order period.[22] People living in urban areas benefited far more than people in rural areas, but life under the

New Order offered a striking contrast to the previous decades of war, political instability, and economic stagnation.

POPULAR DISCONTENT

However, during the late 1980s and early 1990s, there was increasingly open criticism of the greed and corruption of Suharto's family and the incompetence of his inner
circle. The New Order measures aimed at suppressing communal conflict actually
increased tension between religious groups by creating uncertainty about whose side the
government was on. This led to outbursts of violence in Maluku and Sulawesi.

In response to pressures from the middle class, Suharto allowed some political activity, but any potential opponent was either co-opted or suppressed. The daughter of ex-
president Sukarno, Megawati Sukarnoputri, was allowed to become chairman of the
Indonesian Democratic Party, but when she attracted a following, a gang of army-sup-
ported thugs raided her headquarters and forced her to resign.[23]

But few people realized just how weak the system was or anticipated its sudden and
complete collapse.[24] Suharto himself was out of touch with the masses and blind to all
warning signals. Just two months before he was forced to resign, he was busy arranging
for parliament to elect him to a seventh term as president. When his family's greed and
corruption angered the elite, he tried to protect himself by building close ties with the
Muslim hierarchy. But this disturbed Christians, Chinese, and many Muslims who
opposed making Indonesia an Islamic state.

The End of Suharto's New Order

When the 1997 financial crisis spread to Indonesia, the sudden collapse of the Indonesian currency and stock market revealed the weakness of New Order institutions and created extreme hardship for millions of people.[25] Having failed to anticipate the crash,
Suharto and his cronies seemed powerless to cope with it. They were totally unprepared
for the massive demonstrations that forced Suharto to resign in May 1998.[26]

INSTABILITY AND REFORM

For the next four years, Indonesia was wracked by social turmoil and severe out-
breaks of violence, which probably made the elite more receptive to badly needed reforms
(*reformasi*). B.J. Habibie, Suharto's successor, freed the media, political parties, and nongovernmental organizations from New Order restrictions and called for elections in 1999.
Nevertheless, the pro-democracy movement saw him as protecting Suharto from prosecution, and the military resented his efforts to reduce their role in government.

Habibie's most radical move was to allow the people of East Timor to opt for independence in a 1999 referendum. When they voted overwhelmingly to reject Jakarta's offer
of autonomy and remain in Indonesia, government troops and Timorese militias under
their control went on a rampage, killing scores of people and destroying much of East
Timor's infrastructure.

ELECTIONS

Indonesia's first democratic election in 44 years was held in 1999. It was a parliamentary election, and the newly elected members of parliament were responsible for

choosing the president and vice president of Indonesia. Since the Indonesian Democratic Party-Struggle (PDI-P) won the parliamentary election, its leader would normally be chosen as president. Megawati Sukarnoputri, Sukarno's daughter, was the head of PDI-P, but the Islamic political parties refused to support her for president.[27]

Abdurrahman Wahid, the long-time head of Nahdlatul Ulama, was elected president, and Megawati was elected vice president to calm her supporters who were demonstrating in the streets outside parliament. Wahid delegated many of his responsibilities to Megawati because he was legally blind and in poor health. In July 2001, he was declared incapable of performing his duties by the parliament, and Megawati was sworn in as Indonesia's fifth president. She served until 2004 and was given credit for stabilizing the economy after the 1997 financial crisis. In September 2004, she lost her bid for reelection to retired General Susilo Bambang Yudhoyono, who had served in her cabinet as Coordinating Minister for Political Affairs and Security.

Political System

The new political system that emerged after Suharto's fall was a nearly complete reversal of the New Order regime. In the post–Suharto era, presidential powers are defined and limited, and the parliament is a nearly coequal branch of government. The political role of the armed forces has been reduced, but they continue to play an important behind-the-scenes role.

The revival of political parties, a free press, and free elections made Indonesia one of the most democratic countries in Southeast Asia. There was some strengthening of the judiciary and the rule of law, but much remained to be done in that area. Decentralization of powers down to lower levels of government was another potentially major change. But it remained to be seen how well the provincial administrations would handle their new responsibilities.

The Executive

Under the reformed political system, the President of Indonesia remains both head of government and head of state, but he or she is now elected by direct popular vote and is limited to two 5-year terms in office. The President is responsible to parliament but still initiates most legislation. Since Indonesia has a multiparty system with seven or eight parties having substantial representation in parliament, the president must put together a coalition of parties in order to achieve his legislative goals. President Yudhoyono's support in parliament was initially very weak, but it was greatly strengthened in 2005 when Vice President Kalla was elected chairman of Golkar, the largest party in parliament.[28]

The Armed Forces

The Indonesian Armed Forces (known as TNI for *Tentara Nasional Indonesia*) totaled about 346,000 active-duty personnel in 2006. This made it one of the smallest military forces in the world on a per capita basis. Its operations have been almost entirely confined to the Indonesian archipelago. The TNI has been used to suppress secessionist movements in East Timor, Aceh, and Papua, and its record of human rights violations has been strongly criticized at home and abroad. The TNI's reputation among Indonesians also suffered because of its failure to control violence against the Chinese in Jakarta and religious clashes in the eastern islands after Suharto's fall. Many Indonesians believe the TNI helped to instigate much of the violence.

Since 1999, military officers have been required to resign or retire before they can serve in the civilian government. The armed forces have also downplayed the "dual function" concept that they have a socio-political role to play in addition to their military duties. The national police are no longer under the control of the armed forces, having been placed directly under the Office of the President, but the separation of commands has led to serious rivalry between the two organizations.

The army's territorial command structure was abolished in 1999, when the police assumed responsibility for internal security. President Yudhoyono has said he wants to reform the military, but in 2005 he ordered the TNI to take a more active role in counterterrorism. The army responded by reactivating the territorial command structure by which they parallel the civilian bureaucracy down to the village level. There were also signs of backsliding on a major reform that required the military to place its extensive economic assets under government control and rely on official appropriations to fund its activities. In 2005, the government decided to let the military retain most of its assets, and officers were even allowed to sell some of the military assets for personal profit.[29]

Legislative Branch (MPR)

The MPR is now composed of two chambers. The lower one is the People's Representative Assembly (DPR) which has 550 seats. The other chamber is the newly created Regional Representative Council (DPD) which has 128 seats, four for each of Indonesia's 32 provinces. It is supposed to serve as a check on the DPR, but the entire legislative branch has a serious problem of corruption, and it has moved slowly to enact reforms.

Elections

Indonesia's first democratic election since 1955 was held in June 1999 to choose the members of the MPR who would then elect a president. The election was peaceful, and the voter turn-out was a remarkable 91 percent. Megawati Sukarnoputri's Democratic Party of Indonesia-Struggle (PDI-P) won 34 percent of the vote and 154 seats. Golkar (formerly the party of Suharto) supported President Habibie and came in second with 20 percent of the vote and 120 seats. Abdurrahman Wahid's National Awakening Party (PKB) was third with 59 seats. Amien Rais's National Mandate Party (PAN) won 7 percent of the vote and 35 seats.[30]

MEGAWATI VS. WAHID

Since the president was still being elected by the national parliament in 1999, Megawati's supporters expected the MPR to choose her as president, but her selection was blocked by Islamic parties. They questioned her competence for the job, and they may have had misgivings about electing a woman president, especially one who believed in the separation of religion and politics. Habibie withdrew from the race at the last moment after the MPR rejected his presidential record, so the election was between Megawati and Wahid. As former head of Nahdlatul Ulama, the traditionalist Islamic organization, Wahid was endorsed by many small Islamic parties as well as Golkar, and he won with 373 votes to Megawati's 313. But this led to violent protests by Megawati's supporters, so the MPR chose her as vice president in order to calm the situation.[31]

President Wahid also became Indonesia's first civilian defense minister and the first non-army commander of the armed forces. But his health was frail and his administrative style was erratic. He spent much of his time on official visits abroad. During his first year in office, he delegated many of his responsibilities to Megawati. In 2001, the MPR impeached him because he was unable to perform his duties, and Megawati was sworn in as the new president.

ISLAMIST PARTIES

The four largest Islamist parties together gained 20.5 percent of the vote in 2004, about 3 percentage points higher than in 1999, while the 7 largest nationalist (or Pancasila) parties together won 68.8 percent of the vote in 2004. This showed that Indonesian voters strongly favored maintaining Indonesia's status as a secular state and had no desire to adopt Islamic law. The best organized party in Indonesia was the Islamic PKS (Prosperous Justice Party), which won 7.3 percent the vote in the 2004 election, but it did not campaign for implementation of Islamic law. Instead, it campaigned for "clean and caring government," a far more popular theme.[32]

PRESIDENTIAL ELECTION

Two thousand four was also the year of Indonesia's first direct presidential election. No longer would the president be chosen by parliament. The first round of the election would take place in July 5, and five candidates were competing for the office. Susilo Bambang Yudhoyono was an ex-general who had served in the cabinets of Wahid and Megawati. He was well known to the political elite, but he had little name recognition among the general public. In the April parliamentary election, his new Democratic Party won 7.5 percent of the vote and 57 seats, a good start for a new party but hardly a landslide.

However, Yudhoyono was an effective speaker with a charismatic personality. He campaigned tirelessly, and the media made him a national celebrity. In the first round of the election he led the field of five candidates with 33.5 percent of the vote. Megawati was next with 26.6 percent, so a run-off election between the two of them was scheduled for September.

During the ten-week campaign, voters were able to compare the two candidates on television and at public rallies. Yudhoyono was forceful, articulate, and obviously intelligent. Megawati was shy and reserved in public, and she failed to make a strong case for her reelection as president. Yudhoyono won decisively with 60.6 percent of the vote. His victory was broadly based across the electorate. He even won the support of a third of the voters who normally would have voted for Megawati's party.

Nevertheless, Yudhoyono began his term as president with a weak base of support in parliament. He put together a coalition of parties that together received 42 percent of the vote in the April parliamentary election and held less than half the seats in parliament (232 out of a total of 550 seats). The opposition parties had 264 seats, and former

President Wahid's PKB held the balance of power with 52 seats. But during 2005, Vice President Kalla was elected chairman of Golkar, which moved from opposition to support for the administration, and the opposition coalition fell apart.

Decentralization

After Suharto's resignation, considerable power has devolved from the central government down to provincial, regency (district), and village legislative assemblies. In 2005, the newly elected provincial governors initiated a wave of prosecutions of local government officials on charges of corruption.[33] It remains to be seen how effectively these and other civilian provincial officials will use their new powers and how they will interact with their military counterparts.

The Judiciary

Opponents of the New Order regime insisted that Suharto and senior military leaders be punished for corruption and human rights abuses. This became a test of whether or not Suharto's successors were committed to democratic reform and whether the judicial system could provide impartial justice. As president, Habibie was unable to overcome suspicions that he was protecting Suharto from justice. President Wahid filed charges against Suharto, but they were dropped after a team of doctors decided Suharto was mentally and physically unfit to stand trial. Suharto's youngest son was given a fifteen-year prison sentence for murder, but he was released after five years. Suharto himself was sued for $1.54 billion in a civil case but he died of natural causes in 2008 before the case was settled.

None of the four presidents who succeeded Suharto has been willing to bring senior military officers to trial for human rights abuses. In 2000, some junior officers received sentences of up to ten years for a massacre in Aceh, but the Indonesian media tended to play down human rights abuses there and in East Timor, probably reflecting the public's strong opposition to surrendering any Indonesian territory.

REFORMING THE JUDICIARY

President Yudhoyono won praise from human rights groups for appointing Supreme Court Justice Abdul Rahman Saleh as attorney-general. Saleh had been the lone dissenter in a panel of judges that reversed the conviction of a Golkar chairman for embezzlement. During the Suharto years, the Ministry of Justice ensured that the judiciary supported the New Order. But since then the Supreme Court has been given greater responsibility for running civilian court system. Military courts are supposed to deal with cases involving military discipline, but they protect high-ranking officers, as already noted. Islamic courts (with jurisdiction over Muslims only) try cases involving family matters such as marriage, divorce, and inheritance.

Civil Society

The Suharto regime tried to prevent the rise of independent organizations that could challenge its authority. Policy-oriented groups and professional associations were forced to disband or submit to government control. In 1985, New Order legislation required Muslim organizations and all mass organizations to make *Pancasila* their "sole foundation." Nahdlatul Ulama and Muhammadiyah, each with around 30 million members, complied formally with the law. But they continued to serve as training grounds for opposition leaders like Wahid and Amien Rais. In 1999, Wahid was elected President and Rais became chairman of the MPR.

The government also created a variety of industrial and mass-based organizations and think-tanks such as the Center for Strategic and International Studies to support its policies.

Many NGOs were engaged in social work of various kinds which did not conflict with government programs, but as the New Order's grip began to weaken, some NGOs dared to offer alternative policies.

When opposition to New Order policies and corrupt practices began to grow in the military, Suharto turned to Islamic organizations for support. As in Malaysia, these have always been the most powerful non-governmental organizations in Indonesia. In 1990, the Suharto regime created ICMI (*Ikatan Cendekiawan Muslim se Indonesia*), an organization of Muslim scholars led by Dr. Habibie. ICMI and its think-tank CIDES (the Centre for Information and Development Studies), were among the few institutions that supported Habibie as Suharto's successor.

After Suharto resigned, the first reform initiated by President Habibie was to remove the New Order's restrictions on NGO's, opposition parties, and the media. This led to a sudden upsurge of political activity in a country that had been "depoliticized" for decades. Under pressure from forces he himself had released, Habibie agreed to hold elections to choose new representatives to legislative bodies at the national, provincial, and local levels. Parties that had long been moribund scrambled to prepare for the first meaningful elections since the 1950s, and the media amplified a national debate about how the reform process should proceed.

The Media

President Habibie's reforms led to an explosive growth of news sources. His administration issued 1200 publication licenses, 912 radio licenses, and five television broadcast licenses. Habibie also met frequently with the press, to the point where they began to joke about his chattiness. By contrast, President Wahid became petulant and threatened to sue the media for misrepresenting him when his administration began to fall apart in 2001. President Megawati was known for being ill at ease during her infrequent interviews with the press. But Yudhoyono's good relations with the media lasted well into his first term in office.

Economic Development

When Suharto seized power in 1965, the Indonesian economy had been battered by decades of war, unrest and mismanagement. Indonesia was one of the poorest countries in Asia, with annual per capita income below $100. The New Order regime reversed Sukarno's economic policy of striving for self-sufficiency and his political tilt toward

China and the PKI. Suharto needed Japanese and Western investment to develop export industries and achieve rapid economic growth. He believed that most of the Indonesian people would accept his autocratic rule as long as their standard of living was rising.

And rise it did. Per capita income increased from less than $100 in 1966 to $3,388 in 1995. During the New Order years, Indonesia made large gains in literacy and life expectancy, and the number of people in absolute poverty declined steadily.

But there were weaknesses in the New Order economic system that were present to varying degrees in other Southeast Asian countries as well. The state sector included many banks and companies that were poorly managed by Suharto's cronies who depended heavily on state patronage to survive. The military controlled a vast economic empire and frequently ignored or overruled the policies of Western-trained technocrats in the government. The Suharto family controlled major economic enterprises, and their greed and corruption set an example for the rest of the country, which was consistently rated one of the most corrupt in the world.[34]

Consequences of the Financial Crisis

The Asian financial crisis spread to Indonesia in mid–1997, coinciding with the country's worst drought in 50 years and falling world prices for its export commodities.[35] The Indonesian currency and stock market lost much of their value, and the overall economy *declined* by 15 percent in 1998 as foreign investors pulled their money out of the country. Forty million people were unemployed or working less than 15 hours a week, and millions of people were reduced to abject poverty.

Suharto tried to ignore the angry demonstrators who filled the streets of Jakarta and other major cities, but the armed forces refused to rally to his defense, and his own cabinet urged him to resign. On May 21, 1998, he handed over power to Vice President Habibie in what many saw as a desperate attempt to protect his family and the fortune they had amassed.

Economic Reforms

Neither Habibie nor Wahid were effective economic managers, but during Megawati's three years in office she achieved important progress in stabilizing the economy. By reducing inflation and the budget deficit, she was able to free the country from the strictures of the IMF's rescue program by the end of 2003. The rupiah's value rose 25 percent against the U.S. dollar and the Jakarta stock market rebounded strongly during her administration as foreign investment began to flow again and business confidence gradually recovered.

But serious problems remained to be addressed during Yudhoyono's first term as president (2004 to 2009). As Table 8.3 shows, unemployment and inflation remained much too high throughout this period. But those who had jobs in the increasingly sophisticated export industries demanded higher wages, reducing the competitive advantage Indonesia had once enjoyed. Fear of avian flu and terrorism kept the tourist industry from expanding.

To reduce the budget deficit, President Yudhoyono took the politically bold step in 2005 of reducing the fuel subsidy. Contrary to what many people feared, this did not trigger domestic unrest, partly because the poorest citizens received some compensation. But inflation soared during 2005 and 2006 before coming down in 2007. Although Indonesia has long been an oil and gas exporter, it is a net importer of oil. Basically, it is at the mercy of forces that cause the world price of oil to rise. When the price topped $100 a barrel in 2008, the Indonesian government felt compelled to let the local price rise sharply, knowing this would once again produce a sharp rise in inflation, but hoping it would come down as it did in 2007.[36]

Table 8.3
Indonesia's Economy, 2007–10
(figures are percentages unless otherwise indicated)

	2007	2008	2009	2010
GDP Growth	6.3	6.1	-1.4	0.5
Agricultural Production Growth	3.4	4.8	3.0	3.2
Industrial Production Growth	5.6	2.9	-3.9	0.4
Unemployment	9.1	8.5	10.7	11.4
Inflation	6.3	10.1	4.2	3.7
Exports (U.S. $B)	118.0	139.3	101.3	103.9
Imports (U.S. $B)	84.9	116	81.6	84.8

Source: Economist Intelligence Unit, "Indonesia, Country Report," April 2009. Figures for 2009 and 2010 are EIU forecasts.

The tsunami that devastated the province of Aceh with huge loss of life in December 2004 was an even greater challenge to the Indonesian government. Foreign aid poured into the stricken province and was managed reasonably well by President Yudhoyono and Vice President Kalla, who seized the opportunity to negotiate peace with separatist forces that had been fighting Jakarta's forces for years. Improved stability attracted badly needed foreign investment, and improved relations with the United States and many other countries resulted from what might have been a crippling disaster.

As Table 8.3 shows, the Indonesian economy registered strong economic growth of 6.1 percent in 2008, based on a sharp increase in exports to Asian countries in spite of the recession in the West. However, an economic contraction of 1.4 percent was forecast for Indonesia in 2009 as the global recession deepened in some regions. 2009 was a presidential election year in Indonesia, and the Yudhoyono government responded to the recession by enacting an economic stimulus package as well as some protectionist measures. Like the Philippines, Indonesia has very high unemployment, and a large percentage of the people live in poverty. Maintaining high economic growth is the only way to reduce these problems.

Foreign Relations

Since Suharto came to power 1967, ASEAN has been the cornerstone of Indonesia's foreign policy, and asserting a leadership role in ASEAN has been the goal of Indonesian leaders. In 2003, President Megawati Sukarnoputri hosted an ASEAN summit at which she and her colleagues signed the Bali Concord II, expressing the goal of creating an ASEAN Security Community, an ASEAN Economic Community, and an ASEAN Social and Cultural Community as three "pillars" of a more closely integrated ASEAN organization. Indonesia took the lead in promoting the concept of an ASEAN Security Community (ASC) to address regional conflicts through consultation and diplomacy.

The ASC is neither a military alliance nor a defense pact. It is not even a "security community" as the term is usually understood.[37] But Indonesia served notice through this initiative that the Yudhoyono administration intended to assert a leading role in regional security affairs. In 2005, Indonesia supported the idea of inviting the leaders of India, Australia, and New Zealand to the annual ASEAN summits, which since 1997 have included China, Japan, and South Korea.

Indonesia and Australia

Both governments regard this as one of their key relationships and one that is also highly sensitive. When Australia led the UN peacekeeping force that intervened in the East Timor crisis in 1999, Indonesia renounced its security agreement with Australia. But a broad new security treaty was signed by the two governments in November 2006. It covers defense, law enforcement, counter-terrorism, intelligence, maritime security, aviation safety, and emergency response to disasters. Australian Foreign Minister Downer, who negotiated the treaty with his Indonesian counterpart, praised Indonesia's approach to the problem of Islamic terrorism as firm but moderate rather than repressive.[38]

Indonesia and China

During Sukarno's Guided Democracy period, relations were close between the two countries and their respective communist parties. But Suharto froze relations with China after he became President in 1967. His New Order regime denied the Chinese minority cultural freedom and strongly encouraged them to become Indonesians. Although the Indonesian military regarded China as an expansionist power, Suharto restored trade relations in the late 1980s and full diplomatic relations in 1990. The serious anti–Chinese riots in 1998 led to strong protests by the Chinese government. After Habibie became president, he relaxed the cultural restrictions against ethnic Chinese, and relations with China continued to improve under his successors.[39]

Indonesia and the United States

Relations with the U.S. were badly strained during Sukarno's reign, but they improved after Suharto took over because he wanted U.S. aid and investment. Relations remained cordial throughout the cold war years, but during the 1990s the U.S. cut off military aid because of human rights violations by the Indonesian military.

Polls showed the Indonesian people strongly opposed the U.S. invasion of Iraq in 2003, and Indonesian leaders expressed their views forcefully to the Bush administration.

However, the Indonesian government has taken a strong stand against Islamic terrorism and is working closely with its ASEAN partners and the Western powers on counter-terrorism measures. U.S.-Indonesian relations warmed in 2005 when the U.S. sent a hospital ship and substantial aid to Aceh after it was destroyed by a tsunami, and the U.S. also restored its program of military aid to Indonesia.[40]

Conclusions

The 1997–98 financial crisis revealed major weaknesses in Indonesian state institutions and produced the most profound political changes in the region. The political reforms enacted by Suharto's successors have made Indonesia one of the most democratic countries in Southeast Asia. The first free elections in 44 years produced a huge turnout and were remarkably orderly. In spite of the devastating tsunami that wrecked the province of Aceh in 2004 (and to some degree because of it), the separatist war was ended, and international investors have begun to return to Indonesia.

Since recovering from the 1997–98 financial crisis, the Indonesian economy has been gathering strength and performing better than the ASEAN average of 5 percent annual growth. The country is better governed now than at any time since independence, but deeply rooted problems remain — including poverty, unemployment, inflation, and corruption. Progress is being made in each of these areas, but it is unrealistic to expect any of these problems to disappear overnight. Indonesia has become an important stabilizing force in the region, and its role as the first among equals in ASEAN is undisputed.

Further Reading

Bourchier, David, and Vedi R. Hadiz. *Indonesian Politics and Society: A Reader.* London and New York: Routledge, 2003.

Bresnan, John, ed. *Indonesia, The Great Transition.* Lanham, MD: Rowman & Littlefield, 2005.

Crouch, Harold. *The Army and Politics in Indonesia.* Ithaca: Cornell University Press, 1988.

Eldridge, Philip J. *Non-Government Organizations and Democratic Participation in Indonesia.* Kuala Lumpur: Oxford University Press, 1995.

Emmerson, Donald K., ed. *Indonesia Beyond Suharto: Polity, Economy, Society, Transition.* Armonk, NY: M.E. Sharpe, 1999.

Feith, Herbert. *The Decline of Constitutional Democracy in Indonesia.* Ithaca: Cornell University Press, 1962.

Hill, Hal. *The Indonesian Economy.* 2d ed. Cambridge: Cambridge University Press, 2000.

Houseman, Gerald L. *Researching Indonesia: A Guide to Political Analysis.* Lewiston, NY: Edwin Mellen Press, 2004.

Kahin, George McT. *Nationalism and Revolution in Indonesia.* Ithaca: Cornell University Press, 1952.

Suryadinata, Leo. *Interpreting Indonesia Politics.* Singapore: Times Academic Press, 1998.

Vatikiotis, Michael. *Indonesian Politics Under Suharto: The Rise and Fall of the New Order.* 3d ed. London and New York: Routledge, 1998.

— 9 —

BRUNEI DARUSSALAM
A Classic Rentier State

The word *rentier* is French and it means "one who has a fixed income from owning land or other assets." A *rentier state* typically allows foreign or multinational firms to exploit its natural resources (e.g. oil or natural gas) in return for royalties ("rents") that pay for most of what the *rentier* state needs to consume. Brunei is the prime example of such a country in Southeast Asia, although most of its neighbors have oil and some of the characteristics of a *rentier* state. Theoretically, receiving "rents" (royalties) without doing anything in return should make the ruling elite corrupt.[1] And if they give their people a lot of tax-free benefits, the people are likely to become lazy, and the economy will be largely undeveloped. Worse still, if the ruling elite squanders most of the money they receive as royalties on a large army for their own protection, the country may drift into war and chaos.

A closer look at Brunei offers a chance to explore the implications of this theory for Southeast Asia as a whole. The Sultan of Brunei is an absolute monarch who controls his country's oil and gas resources which account for 96 percent of its exports that produce two thirds of the gross domestic product. The government provides most Bruneians with free education, health care, and other benefits, and it does not levy an income tax. This is probably the main reason why the people acquiesce in a system that allows them little or no say in how they are governed. But Sultan Hassanal Bolkiah is popular with his subjects, because he clearly cares about their well-being. Brunei has generally been free of social unrest.

However, most of the food consumed in Brunei is imported, and there is very little in the way of entrepreneurship. Planning has barely begun for the time (estimated 15 to 30 years off) when the country's oil and gas reserves will give out.[2] The sultan's plans for diversifying the Bruneian economy resemble those of the kingdom of Bahrain on the Persian Gulf.[3] But Bahrain began several years ago to open its political system and diversify its economy to prepare for the day when it can no longer rely on oil and gas exports and its citizens will have to pay taxes.

Sultan Bolkiah of Brunei has said he favors a gradual opening of Brunei's political system, but he has not set a timetable for doing so. He has convened a largely appointed Legislative Council for a few brief sessions, but at the same time he has deregistered two of the country's three political parties.[4] Although he has been more specific about how he wants to diversify the economy, very few of his plans have been implemented, and that is the major challenge the country faces.[5] A growing list of social ills—including crime, drug use, and unemployment — will only get worse as long as political reform and economic diversification are delayed.[6]

People and Cultures

As Table 9.1 shows, Malays make up two thirds of Brunei's population, while 11 percent are Chinese, and 19 percent are foreign workers (from Europe, Asia, and the Middle East). The Malays are mostly Sunni Muslims. Ethnic Chinese play an important role in the (non-oil) private economy, especially retail trade. Tribal groups such as the Ibans and Dayaks make up about 3 percent of the population.

Table 9.1
Brunei Darussalam: Demographic Overview

Population (2007 estimate): 397,000 (includes foreign workers)
Annual Growth Rate of Population (2007 estimate): 1.8%
Ethnic Groups (2007 estimate): Malay 67%; Chinese 11%; foreign workers 19%; indigenous tribal groups 3%
Religious Affiliations (2007 estimate): Islam 67%, Christian 10%
Literacy (2006 estimate): 94.7%
Personal Computers (2001 estimate): 25,000
Internet Users (2001 estimate): 35,000
Students in Primary Schools (2004): 56,903
Students in Secondary Schools (2004): 32,435
Students in Higher Education (2001): 3,885 in Brunei's three institutions; most Bruneian college students study abroad
Life Expectancy (2006 estimate): females 77.4 years, males 74.4 years
Infant Mortality Rate (2007 estimate): 7.6 per 1,000 live births
Income per Capita (2000): $24,100 ($24,910 purchasing power parity)

Sources: Europa World Year Book; Economist Intelligence Unit; Government of Brunei statistics.

Citizens of Brunei of all ethnic groups are called "Bruneians," but the members of the politically and socially dominant Malay ethnic group are known as "Bruneis." They are related to the Malays in Indonesia and Malaysia. But Bruneis have their own distinct culture, including a dialect of the Malay language called "Standard Brunei Malay," which is used in schools, government communications, and the media. However, English is used to teach the sciences in schools, and it is widely understood, especially by younger generation Bruneians. As in most Southeast Asian countries, the population is very young. Forty percent of the people are under the age of twenty.

Social Problems

Brunei is not free of the social ills often associated with a rentier state, including crime, drug abuse, and juvenile delinquency. Truancy and lack of discipline among young Bruneians are worrisome problems, much as they are in Malaysia. The rate of car accidents is high and growing, perhaps reflecting a culture in which there are few amusements available for middle class Bruneians.

Lack of employment opportunities for university and secondary school graduates is probably Brunei's most serious social problem. The government, which employs 60 percent of the work force, can no longer absorb all who are qualified for bureaucratic positions. There are only about 7,300 registered job-seekers in the country which employs 75,000 foreign workers, but there are believed to be many more unemployed Bruneians who have not registered at employment offices. The Sultan has urged his people to seek jobs in the private sector, and the government operates training programs for would-be entrepreneurs, but Bruneians naturally prefer the high pay, benefits, and security of government jobs. Unless the government speeds up the implementation of its plans to diversify the economy, unemployment could lead to more serious tensions between Bruneians and foreign workers.[7]

Ethnic Groups

CHINESE

Ethnic Chinese dominate Brunei's non-oil private economy mainly as shop-keepers and small businessmen. This causes some resentment on the part of Bruneis. For their part, the ethnic Chinese find dealing with the slow-moving Bruneian bureaucracy frustrating. Many ethnic Chinese in Brunei have family or business ties to Chinese in Malaysia, and ethnic Chinese in both countries tend to feel like second class citizens because they are not Muslims. But Chinese born in Brunei now qualify for Bruneian citizenship, which confers important benefits, including free education and health services, subsidized housing, and no income tax.

The Middle Class

Brunei bureaucrats and ethnic Chinese businessmen comprise the Brunein middle class. Both groups are concentrated in Bandar Seri Begawan, the capital and largest town which has a population of about 60,000. Government officials are barred from participating in any form of political activity, and ethnic Chinese businessmen are strongly discouraged from any political activity outside their ethnic community groups. Businessmen and other professionals can have their licenses or government contracts withdrawn if they engage in political activity. Those who find these conditions unacceptable can and often do leave the country. Those who stay and openly contest the political restrictions risk being imprisoned under the Internal Security Act.[8]

Status of Women

The government has taken important steps toward giving women equal rights in government employment. In 2009, it announced that the employment status for married women in the civil service would be the same as for unmarried women. Both Muslim and non–Muslim women in Brunei have more freedom and more opportunities for professional advancement than women in the Middle East. The political rights of Bruneian women are very limited, but the same holds true for Bruneian men. Women are not represented in the cabinet, but the Chief Magistrate of the lower courts is a woman, and so is the Solicitor-General. Women occupy most of the top positions in the state broadcasting and publishing companies and in several large banks and insurance companies. Overall, women make up about a third of the active work force. Female students outnumber males in Brunei's secondary schools and in its post-secondary colleges and institutes, but this reflects a preference by Bruneian families for educating their daughters in Brunei and sending their sons to be educated abroad.[9]

Historical Background

During the fifteenth and early sixteenth centuries, the sultanate of Brunei controlled the coastal areas of northwest Borneo (Kalimantan) and the southern Philippines. But European colonial expansion marked the start of Brunei's decline. In 1888, the Sultan of Brunei accepted British government protection to save his country from being absorbed by Sarawak, a territory controlled by the British "white rajah" Sir James Brooke. Under a 1906 treaty, executive power was transferred from the Sultan to a British Resident, whose advice the Sultan was obliged to accept on all matters except religion and local customs.

In 1929, oil was discovered near the town of Seria, and it has transformed Brunei from a loss-making colony into one of the richest states in the region on a per capita basis.[10] The British granted Brunei internal self-rule in 1959, but they thought it was incapable of surviving on its own and wanted it to join the Federation of Malaysia.

Table 9.2
Events in Bruneian History

Late 15th century	Brunei dominates much of Borneo, but European colonialism steadily reduces Bruneian influence.
1888	British protectorate saves Brunei from extinction.
1929	Oil reserves discovered in Belait district of Brunei.
1941–45	Japanese occupation during World War II.
1950	Sultan Omar Ali Saifuddin III succeeds to throne.
1959	Constitution gives Sultan supreme power, but provides for a Chief Minister and an elected Legislative Council.
1962	Brunei People's Party (PRB) wins election, and its military wing revolts to block joining Malaysia. British crush rebellion with a Gurkha unit flown in from Singapore.
1963	Brunei stays out of the federation to keep control of its oil.
1965	First and last direct election for Legislative Council.
1966	Sultan Hassanal Bolkiah succeeds his father on throne.
1970	Elections for Legislative Council abolished.
1984	Brunei gains full independence; joins UN and ASEAN.
1997	Accused of embezzlement, Prince Jefri leaves cabinet.
1998	Sultan Bolkiah's eldest son proclaimed as Crown Prince.
2000	Civil suit against Prince Jefri to recover funds.
2004	Sultan briefly convenes an appointed Legislative Council (Legco), sketches vague plan to open political system and more specific plans to broaden the economy. The Legco was convened again for a few days in 2005 and 2006 to discuss the budget.

Sultan Omar Ali Saifuddin III, who ascended the throne in 1950, initially agreed that this was desirable. In 1962, the Brunei People's Party (Parti Rakyat Brunei, PRB) swept Brunei's first election for a Legislative Council. The PRB was against joining Malaysia because it would mean the Malaysian government would control Brunei's oil revenue. But the Sultan delayed convening the Legislative Council, possibly to prevent them from passing a resolution against joining Malaysia. In December 1962, the military arm of the PRB staged a rebellion, which was quickly suppressed by a Gurkha unit of the British army that was flown in from Singapore.

Sultan Omar then changed his mind and decided not to join Malaysia. In 1967, he abdicated in favor of his son, Hassanal Bolkiah, who was twenty-one-years old at the time. Under a state of emergency declared by his father during the 1962 revolt, Sultan Hassanal Bolkiah has ruled by decree ever since. Sultan Omar took the title of Seri Begawan Sultan and remained active in political affairs (usually opposing political and social liberalization) until his death 18 years later.[11]

In 1984, Brunei became a fully independent state and joined the United Nations, the Association of Southeast Asian Nations, the British Commonwealth, and the Organization of Islamic Conference. Basically, Sultan Hassanal Bolkiah continued his father's policy of using the country's mineral wealth to create a welfare state while resisting any movement toward democracy. After his father's death in 1986, he made some changes aimed at modernizing the state, although he did not resist the trend toward Islamic conservatism in the 1990s.

However, by 2005, Bruneians were beginning to be concerned about the rise of Islamic extremism. In that year, the Sultan replaced the ultra-conservative Education Minister, Abdul Aziz, with Ahmat Jumat, who had been serving as Minister of Development. This was expected to lead to more emphasis on science and technology in the educational curriculum and less emphasis on religious education. Two leading business executives were also brought into the cabinet to serve as Minister of Industry and Deputy Minister of Development. An ethnic Chinese, Lim Jock Seng, became Deputy Foreign Minister and the first non–Muslim to reach cabinet rank.[12] The stage seemed to be set for further political reform.

Political System

Britain returned limited sovereignty to Brunei in the 1959 constitution, which assigned "supreme executive power" to the sultan. But under the constitution the sultan was to have been advised and assisted by a Chief Minister, a State Financial Officer, and a partially elected Legislative Council. Instead, Sultan Bolkiah suspended the Legislative Council in 1984 and appointed himself prime minister, finance minister, defense minister, minister of Islamic affairs, and commander-in-chief of the armed forces.

Elections (except for village headmen) were abolished in 1970. In 1994, a Constitutional Committee was appointed by the government with Prince Mohamad Bolkiah, the Sultan's brother, as chairman. The Constitutional Committee recommended that the constitution be amended to provide for an elected legislature.

Ten years later, in 2004, it was announced that the Sultan had decided to reconvene the Legislative Council (usually known as Legco). An entirely appointed Legco was convened in 2004, but a new Legco with 5 indirectly elected members was convened for a few days in 2005, 2007 and 2008 to hear government presentations on the budget. In the 2007 session, the government was asked by Legco for more details on government investment funds. However, two of the country's three political parties were deregistered (meaning they could not take part in elections), and at time of writing no date had been set for direct Legco elections.[13]

The Monarchy

Sultan Hassanal Bolkiah has ruled Brunei since 1967. He is an exceptionally hardworking monarch who attempts to carry out the duties of his many offices while also making frequent trips abroad to represent Brunei at meetings of the UN, ASEAN and other organizations.

His popularity is attested by the large crowds that attend royal events, and he likes to sample public opinion by meeting informally with people in their homes.[14]

The Sultan, who was sixty-three-years old in 2008, has made his eldest son, Crown Prince Al-Muhtadee Billah Bolkiah, the heir to the throne. Although the crown prince's education was academic rather than military, he was made a general in the Brunei armed forces and deputy inspector-general of police in 2005. He was also appointed senior minister in the Prime Minister's office. Lee Kuan Yew used much the same grooming process to prepare his son to be Prime Minister of Singapore.

Political Parties

As of 2008, there was only one political party that was legally registered (i.e., authorized) by the Sultan.[15] The National Development Party (PP) was approved in 2005 with Muhamad Yasin as its leader. (Yasin was leader of the winning party in the last election in 1962, but the parliament was not allowed to convene.) Two other political parties were deregistered in 2007 and early 2008. Any public statement by a political leader that can be construed as anti-monarchy is likely to lead to his party being dissolved and could result in a prison sentence under the Internal Security Act.[16]

The Judiciary

The judiciary is Brunei's most independent state institution even though judges are appointed by the sultan. The government and lower-ranking relatives of the royal family are willing to be cited as defendants in foreign courts and to accept foreign arbitration in commercial disputes. But Bruneian citizens can not sue their own government.

In 2000, a civil case was brought against the sultan's younger brother, Prince Jefri, who was accused of stealing a huge but undisclosed sum (estimates go as high as U.S. $35 billion) while serving as Minister of Finance and director of the Brunei Investment Agency (BIA). The case was settled out of court, and the terms of the settlement were not announced.

In 2007, Prince Jefri embarrassed the sultan by appealing the out-of-court settlement to the Privy Council in Britain, which ruled that the settlement was to be enforced, meaning that Prince Jefri must hand back to the sultanate cash and property worth billions of dollars.[17] Civil cases can be appealed to the Privy Council in London if all parties agree to this before the appeal is heard in the Brunei Court of Appeal. Malay judges have been gradually replacing British judges in the Brunei judicial system as they gain experience in the lower and intermediate courts.

Ideology

In 1990, the Brunei government began to promote a state ideology aimed at reinforcing support for the monarchy by linking it to Islamic values which were undergoing a conservative revival at the time. Brunei's ideology, *Malayu Islam Beraja* (Malay Islamic Monarchy, MIB) places strong emphasis on the Muslim religion. Although the MIB ideology has been accepted by Bruneians who are Muslim (e.g., Bruneis and Kedayans), the main message to non–Muslim tribal groups is that they are strongly encouraged to convert to Islam in order to be fully integrated into Bruneian society. Likewise, the ideology seems to exclude the Chinese minority, who have shown little interest in converting to Islam.

Two of the main proponents of the MIB ideology, Pehin Abdul Aziz bin Umar and Pehin Badaruddin Bin Othman, have been leaders of the more conservative Islamic group within the small circle of political leaders. A major thrust of MIB ideology in the 1990s was to counter the trend toward a materialistic, consumer-oriented society. However, the recent rise of Islamic terrorist groups in Southeast Asia, particularly Jemaah Islamiyah, has made Brunei and other states more cautious about allowing conservative Islamic movements to gain a political foothold. As noted earlier, Pehin Aziz lost his position as Education Minister in 2005 amid criticism that he had stifled economic development by emphasizing religious studies rather than science and technology in the school curriculum.[18]

Civil Society

In Brunei, all nongovernmental organizations (NGOs) and clubs, even ones of a purely social nature, must be approved by the police Special Branch and the Ministry of Home Affairs. Their approval is likely to be withheld if the organization adopts a controversial positions on social issues, such as the plight of foreign domestic servants and construction workers in Brunei.

Political parties, even those that profess loyalty to the monarchy, are allowed very little "democratic space" in which to operate. The Brunei National Democratic Party (PKDB) was dissolved by the government in 1988 when it called for the Sultan to resign his position as prime minister and hold democratic elections. The leaders of the PKDB were arrested under the Internal Security Act (ISA) and held in prison without trial for two years.

Although Brunei clearly lacks the political freedom that now exists in Indonesia and Malaysia, it is well ahead of many Middle Eastern kingdoms in terms of religious freedom and gender equality. For the most part, people are free to practice their religion. Non-Muslim tribal groups are urged (though not required) to embrace Islam. As in Malaysia, however, non–Muslims who marry Muslims have to convert to Islam.

Human rights violations certainly occur in Brunei, especially arbitrary imprisonment under the Internal Security Act. But there have been no serious race riots for many decades and no massacres like the ones that have taken place in Cambodia, Indonesia, and Myanmar. The government's attitude toward political and social liberalization resembles that of the PAP leadership in Singapore. They seem to be loosening social controls very cautiously in order to attract foreign investors and tourists, rather than because they believe it is the right thing to do. Neither in Brunei nor in Singapore is the government under any real pressure from its own people to reform. Those citizens who feel strongly about the need for reform can leave, and considerable numbers do. But many people in both countries seem willing to accept tight state controls as the price for a relatively high standard of living.

The Media

Brunei's first newspaper, *The Borneo Bulletin,* was launched in 1953 and sold to the Singapore *Straits Times* group in 1959. In 1990, the *Bulletin* was acquired by a holding company owned by the Brunei royal family. The paper was then relaunched as an English-language daily still called *Borneo Bulletin* but with no editorials or analysis, and only one or two pages of local news. The letters to the editor column was one of its liveliest feature.[19]

In October 2001, a royal decree gave the government the right to close newspapers and ban foreign publications that it deemed detrimental to public morals or domestic security. The English-language *News Express* (which began publishing in 1999) had to cease operations in 2002 because it could no longer meet financial requirements set forth in the decree. Malaysian and Singaporean newspapers are available in Brunei's capital city, as are some foreign news magazines such as *Time, Newsweek,* and *Asiaweek.*

Radio and television broadcasting in Brunei is controlled by Radio Televisyen Brunei (RTB), which is under the Prime Minister's Office. An Islamic radio channel was added in 1997. Radio Brunei also broadcasts on the internet (www.rtb.gov.bn). The British Forces Broadcasting Service (military) broadcasts a 24-hour radio service from the town of Seria. Radio Televisyen Brunei broadcasting in Malay and English was the only television operator until 1999, when Brunei's first commercial cable TV channel, Kristal, began broadcasting.

Economic Development

Oil and natural gas make up 96 percent of Brunei's exports, as Table 9.3 shows, and these exports produce two thirds of the country's gross domestic product. A small percentage of the country's mineral resources are refined at Seria for local use. The rest is exported, mainly to Japan and South Korea under longterm contracts.[20] There is almost nothing in the way of "downstream" industries in Brunei (i.e., additional industries based on mineral resources). Public information about Brunei's mineral reserves is incomplete, partly because of government secrecy but also because exploration is ongoing and the technology for extraction is constantly improving. Brunei may also be able to share in exploiting areas in the South China Sea which are believed to contain large mineral resources.

In Table 9.3, the estimates for GDP growth in 2008 and 2009 are based on the following assumptions: the government is deliberately limiting exploitation of the country's oil and gas reserves to make them last as long as possible, and the government can afford to provide benefits to Bruneian citizens to help them weather the major worldwide recession that began in 2008.

Table 9.3
Brunei Darussalam's Economy, 2006–09
(figures are percentages unless otherwise indicated)

	2006	2007	2008	2009
GDP Growth (%)	5.1	0.6	1.0	1.0
Crude Oil Production (thousands of barrels per day)	220.0	205.0	205.0	205.0
Inflation (%)	0.2	0.3	2.7	n/a
Exports (Bruneian $ millions)	10397	12119	11000	11000

Sources: Economist Intelligence Unit, London, "Brunei, Country Report," March 2009, p.4. Note: Bruneian government statistics tend to be incomplete and not very timely. The above figures for 2008 and 2009 are estimated based on EIU data and press reports.

The government has long professed to be concerned about diversifying the economy to prepare for the day when income from mineral exports diminishes. But until recently, very little was being done to prepare for the transition. As noted earlier, the sultan has begun instituting some political reforms to prepare for a time when it will no longer be possible to operate the government without an income tax, apparently reasoning that his people will only accept taxes if they have some say in instituting them.

Economic Diversification

Two areas of economic diversification, banking and tourism, appear to offer considerable potential, even though the results so far have been limited. In 2000, the Brunei Darussalam Economic Council (BDEC) issued a report that warned that Brunei's oil and gas-based economy was becoming unsustainable. The Sultan endorsed the report and appointed his brother, Prince Mohamad, to oversee the implementation of BDEC's recommendations.

This led to the launching of the Islamic Development Bank of Brunei later the same year as the first step toward making Brunei a center of Islamic banking. But because of the Asian financial crisis, the total assets and liabilities of commercial banks in Brunei contracted in the three years to 2002. They rose 22 percent in 2003, and were still growing in 2007 but not yet making a major contribution to GDP.[21]

Tourism

Brunei receives about a million foreign visitors a year, but although it has built a large modern airport, the vast majority of tourists arrive from Malaysia via land-entry points. Only about 100,000 are business or leisure tourists from more distant countries who stay an average of three days. The major tourist attractions are the mosques and traditional Malay water villages of Bandar Seri Begawan, and the flora and fauna of the rain forest and national parks. Brunei hopes to specialize in ecotourism, which will require considerable investment in roads and hotels. A slight loosening of social controls has been aimed at attracting foreign tourists.[22]

Agriculture

Brunei's agriculture sector declined sharply in the 1960s and 1970s as the government instituted its "Shellfare state" (thanks to Shell Oil). Agriculture now accounts for less than 2 percent of gross domestic product, and Brunei imports 80 percent of its food, but rice production tripled between 2001 and 2006.[23] Total agricultural output expanded 9 percent in 2003 and 10 percent in 2004. Brunei farmers now supply 60 percent of local demand for vegetables, and fish-farming and fish-processing are among the country's fastest-growing industries. The government has targeted the food industry for development, particularly *halal* foods which meet certain Islamic standards.[24]

Manufacturing

A whole range of obstacles restrict the growth of manufacturing: bureaucratic delays, high labor costs, a shortage of skilled labor, the small domestic market, and the ban on foreigners owning land. Brunei's garment industry benefited from a quota agreement with the U.S., but when that expired in 2005 sales plunged 16 percent. Not surprisingly, Malaysian and Singaporean firms are among the most active investors in Brunei, but few Bruneians are willing to work in low wage manufacturing jobs.

Foreign Relations

When Brunei achieved full independence in 1984, it joined the United Nations, ASEAN, the Organization of the Islamic Conference (OIC), the British Commonwealth, and the non-aligned movement. ASEAN membership is particularly important to Brunei, a micro-state that might have found it hard to survive on its own without the added leverage that ASEAN provides in dealing with East Asian nations and the West.

As noted earlier, much of Brunei's trade is with its ASEAN partners. The organization has provided a useful framework for improving Brunei's relations with Indonesia and Malaysia. Brunei has sent some of its armed forces to the Philippines to help keep the peace between the government and the Moro Islamic Liberation Front (MILF). It has also sent military observers to Aceh province to help monitor the implementation of the autonomy agreement in that province.[25]

Armed Forces

In 2003, the Royal Brunei Armed Forces (RBAF) numbered 7000 with 4,900 in the army, 1000 in the navy, and 1100 in the air force. Brunei has bought small naval vessels, fighter aircraft, and other military hardware from Britain. The RBAF is considered loyal to the government, but the Sultan entrusts his personal security and the arsenal of the

RBAF to a Gurkha Reserve Unit numbering more than 2500. The unit is led by retired British officers. Another 800 Gurkhas and 200 British support forces are based at Seria to protect the oil facilities. The British use jungle-training facilities in Brunei and participate in joint military exercises with the RBAF. Singapore, Indonesia, Japan, and the United States also conduct joint military exercises with the RBAF.[26]

Relations with Singapore

Brunei has very close economic and political ties with Singapore. The armed forces of the little city-state are allowed to train on Brunei's territory, and most of Brunei's petroleum exports are shipped through Singapore. The leaders of these two small countries are skeptical about the merits of Western-style democracy, and they have adopted social and political controls that are in some ways similar despite their very different cultures.

Relations with Malaysia

In 2007, the leaders of Brunei and Malaysia reportedly made progress on resolving their longstanding territorial issues, a task made more urgent because of the discovery of additional mineral reserves in the disputed areas.[27] As noted earlier, Brunei and Malaysia are closely linked culturally and economically. Brunei nearly joined Malaysia when the federation was formed in the 1960s, but the reigning sultan decided to keep Brunei's oil revenues for his country's use.

Relations with China

In 2005, the President Hu Jintao paid the first official visit to Brunei by a Chinese head of state.[28]

Trade relations between the two countries are increasing from a very low base, and China is obviously interested in gaining access to Brunei's oil and gas. Brunei is one of several Southeast Asian states that dispute China's claim to the resources of the South China Sea.[29]

Conclusions

Brunei has just begun to prepare for the time when oil and gas revenue can no longer provide a comfortable, tax-free existence for Bruneian citizens, but the people seem willing to leave most of the initiative for change to the sultan. He has been more specific about his plans for economic diversification than for broadening political participation. The people of Brunei seem unprepared to meet the challenges they will face when oil and gas revenues can no longer support their present lifestyle.

Brunei's social problems include an increase in crime, drug use, juvenile delinquency, and unemployment. The relatively large number of unemployed or underemployed Bruneians could lead to serious conflict between them and the large force of foreign workers in Brunei in the years ahead. The bureaucracy can no longer absorb all of the country's university and secondary school graduates, but the government has it within its power to solve the unemployment problem by speeding up the implementation of its plans to diversify the economy.

Further Reading

Cleary, Mark, and Wong Shuang Yann. *Oil, Economic Development and Diversification in Brunei Darussalam*. London and New York: St. Martin's Press, 1994.

Gunn, Geoffrey C. *Language, Power and Ideology in Brunei Darussalam*. Athens: Ohio University Center for International Studies, 1997.

Hewison, Kevin, Richard Robison, and Garry Rodan, eds. *Southeast Asia in the 1990's: Authoritarianism, Democracy & Capitalism*. St. Leonards, Australia: Allen & Unwin, 1993.

Hussainmiya, B.A. *Sultan Omar Ali Saifuddin III and Britain: The Making of Brunei Darussalam*. Kuala Lumpur: Oxford University Press, 1995.

Kershaw, Roger. *Monarchy in South-East Asia: the Faces of Tradition in Transition*. London: Routledge, 2000.

– 10 –

THE PHILIPPINES

People Power Fatigue

Gloria Macapagal Arroyo was the second female president of the Philippines to be put in office by a "People Power" revolt led by middle class activists against a corrupt "crony capitalist" regime. In each case, the revolt was supported by the army and the Catholic Church, but the wealthy families that have long dominated Philippine politics and society retained their hold on power. Their priorities clearly did not include doing anything that would undermine their own class interests. This led to increasing cynicism among middle and lower class Filipinos about the likelihood of reducing poverty — the Philippines' most urgent problem — through the existing political system.[1]

President Arroyo's administration, which began in 2001, achieved some important economic reforms leading to the highest growth rates in many years. Also, a ceasefire was agreed with Muslim separatists in the south, and two top Islamic terrorist leaders were killed by the Philippine army. In 2004, Arroyo became the first Philippine president in three decades to seek and win a second term in office. Her term ends in 2010, and the constitution does not allow her to seek another term as president.

But just when the situation seemed to be stabilizing, Arroyo's voter approval ratings sank because of public perceptions of electoral fraud and widespread corruption. In 2007, she lost control of the Philippine Senate and was pressured by the Catholic Bishops Conference to give up her power to prevent government officials from testifying before Congress. Her main political goal was to replace the country's presidential system of government with a parliamentary one. But analysts tended to see this as irrelevant to the main issue of reducing poverty since the same self-seeking politicians would be running the system.[2]

People and Cultures

With a population of 92.2 million people in 2009, the Philippines is the second largest country in Southeast Asia, and it adds about 1.5 million people a year. This rapid growth rate makes it difficult to reduce the amount of poverty in the Philippines. The World Bank estimates that 38 percent of the population live on $2 a day or less. Malnutrition is all too common, and the 2008 increase in the world price of rice caused severe suffering.

156

Table 10.1
The Philippines: Demographic Overview

Population (2009 estimate): 92.2 million
Annual Growth Rate of Population (2007 estimate): 2.04%
Ethnic Groups (2000): Malay 95.5%, indigenous groups 3%, Chinese 1.5%
Religious Affiliations (2000): Catholic 80.9%, other Christian denominations 11.6%, Muslim 5%, Buddhist and others 2%
Literacy (2003): 93.4%
Personal Computers (2001): 1.7 million
Percentage of Students in Primary Schools (2008): 85%
Percentage of Students in Secondary Schools (2008): 62%
Life Expectancy (2005): females 72.5 years, males 67.8 years
Infant Mortality Rate (2006): 24 per 1,000 live births
Income per Capita (2008): $1,624
Percentage of People Living on $2 a Day or Less (2007): 38%

Source: Embassy of the Philippines, Washington, D.C.; The World Bank, *East Asia Update*; Asian Development Bank, *Key Indicators of Developing Asian and Pacific Countries*; U.S. Department of State, "Background Notes: Philippines," April 2008.

Food Shortages

According to a recent poll, 15 percent of Philippine households have too little food to eat. The problem was most severe on the island of Mindanao, where 23 percent of households were experiencing hunger. The Philippines is the world's biggest importer of rice and is highly vulnerable to falling global rice stocks and rising prices. In early 2008, the price of rice rose 75 percent, and many producing countries blocked rice exports to secure their own needs. But Japan agreed to sell 200,000 tons of rice to the Philippines, and Cambodia lifted its ban on exports, causing world rice markets to ease.[3]

Status of Women

The idea of gender equality is rooted in the Philippines' early, pre–Spanish history when women could own and inherit property, engage in trade, and succeed to a chieftainship in the absence of a male heir.[4] While Philippine women are expected to be submissive to their husbands, especially in public, they run their households with an iron hand, and they are active in the upper levels of business, the media, and academia. Two of the last four presidents have been women. Like their male counterparts, women who rise to the top ranks of the Philippine government are mostly from elite political families.

Religion

CHRISTIANITY

With Catholics comprising 81 percent of the population, the Church has been very active in the social and political life of the Philippines. Catholic groups span the political spectrum from far right to far left. Other Christian denominations comprise 11.6 percent of the population. The largest of these groups are the Aglipayans (members of the Philippine Independent Church).[5]

Figure 10.1. Philippines.

ISLAM

Filipino Muslims live mostly on the island of Mindanao and the Sulu archipelago. The Spanish called them "Moros" because they reminded them of the North African Moors who had occupied Spain. Farming and fishing are the Muslims' main occupations, but the southern provinces are the poorest in the country because fishing stocks have been badly depleted and the region's infrastructure lags behind the rest of the Philippines. For several decades, an armed separatist movement discouraged local and foreign investors, but in 1996 a peace agreement was signed by the government and the Moro National Liberation Front (MNLF), leading to the establishment of an Autonomous Region in Muslim Mindanao (ARMM).

Although a breakaway group called the Moro Islamic Liberation Front (MILF) continued the struggle for several more years, they agreed to a cessation of hostilities in 2003 and began negotiating with the Philippine government (with Malaysia serving as mediator). Philippine forces with U.S. support pursued a Muslim terrorist group called Abu Sayyaf which was believed to have connections with Al Qaeda.[6]

Ethnic Groups

CHINESE

Ethnic Chinese first began to play a commercial role in the Phillippines over a thousand years ago. Today, those who identify themselves as pure Chinese number somewhat over a million, but many more have been assimilated through intermarriage with Filipinos of Malay stock. This is a common practice, because the families of both marriage partners gain increased economic or political status through the union.[7] Thus, it is likely that most middle and upper class Filipino families have some Chinese blood. The offspring of Philippine-Chinese marriages are usually raised as Catholics and regarded as Filipinos.

INDIGENOUS PEOPLE

Living in remote mountainous regions of Luzon and on the island of Mindanao are approximately fifty indigenous ethno-linguistic groups that were not westernized during the colonial period and generally remain outside the mainstream of Philippine culture. Under the 1987 Constitution, the government assumed responsibility for protecting the rights of these people, but scarce resources and a host of other priorities have limited what the government can or will do.[8]

Languages

In the Philippines, there are some eighty-eight local languages, but more than half of them are spoken by very small ethno-linguistic groups. The five most widely used regional languages are Tagalog, Cebuano, Ilocano, Ilongo, and Bicol. Pilipino, the official national language, is taught in all schools and is gaining wide acceptance, especially as a means of communication between people who speak different regional languages. Pilipino is based on Tagalog, the dialect of Manila and parts of central and southern Luzon. English has been taught in Philippine public schools for the past hundred years and is often used in business and government circles. Spanish is spoken by a small number of families who were part of the elite in the Spanish period. Most members of the Chinese minority speak Cantonese or Fukienese.[9]

Historical Background

The Philippines, like Malaysia and Indonesia, owes its original political unification to colonial rule. When the Spanish occupied the Philippines in the 1500s, the largest political unit they found was the *barangay,* a village-size kinship group ruled by a *datu* (chief).[10] In the fourteenth century, Islamic influence began to spread from Malaya and Borneo into the southern Philippines, reaching as far north as Manila by the time the Spanish arrived there. If the Spanish had come a hundred years later, they might have found all of the Philippine islands converted to Islam. But they made it one of their priorities, along with commercial exploitation, to convert the Philippine people to Christianity. Spanish friars were the main link between the colonial administration and the country's largest ethnic group, people of Malay stock who lived on the lowland plains. The Spanish had much less contact with the hill tribes in northern Luzon, and they never fully conquered the Muslim minority in the south.

Besides building a centralized administration and converting large numbers of Filipinos to Christianity, the Spanish also created a semi-feudal society in which wealthy landowning families lorded it over a large class of very poor tenant farmers. By the middle of the nineteenth century, upper class Filipinos were able to travel to Europe to gain an education. They returned with exciting new ideas about democracy and nationalism which appealed to their fellow countrymen.

Foremost among the European-educated scholars was Jose Rizal, a physician, novelist, and poet who was falsely accused of leading an armed uprising. His execution by a Spanish firing squad in 1896 helped to ignite the Philippine Revolution, and in July 1898 the Philippines became the first European colony in Asia to declare its independence. In the same year, the United States launched a war against Spain, and Filipinos hoped that America would support their revolution. Instead, the United States annexed the Philippines despite strong doubts on the part of Americans that their "manifest destiny" required a colonial empire.[11]

Table 10.2
The Philippines: Key Historical Events

1521	Ferdinand Magellan claims the Philippines for Spain.
1896	Philippine patriot Jose Rizal is executed, and armed revolution against Spanish rule begins.
April 1898	U.S. launches war against Spain.
June 1898	Philippine nationalists declare independence.
December 1898	Spain cedes the Philippines to the U.S.
1935	Filipinos gain domestic self-rule.
1942–45	Japan occupies the Philippines.
1946	The U.S. grants independence to the Philippines.
1972	Ferdinand Marcos declares martial law.
1983	Senator Benigno Aquino murdered at Manila airport.
1986	"People Power" revolt supported by army and Church ousts Marcos; Corazon Aquino is inaugurated as President.
1992	Fidel Ramos is elected President.
1998	Actor Joseph Estrada succeeds Ramos.
2001	Estrada ousted by another People Power revolution; Vice President Gloria Macapagal Arroyo becomes President.
2004	Arroyo wins election against Actor Fernando Poe, Jr.
2005	Tape of Arroyo phone conversation with election official creates political crisis.

Once the Philippines had been pacified by military force, U.S. administrators set about trying to institute key features of the American political system, including political parties, elections, and a U.S.-style legislature. The Philippine landowning aristocracy was ready and willing to take part in these new institutions, but this did not lead to a more egalitarian society. Instead, it legitimized the landowners' dominant position and enabled them to resist U.S. land reform schemes. However, the United States also created a public education system, which proved to be the most positive contribution America would make to Philippine society.[12]

In 1935, the Philippines gained Commonwealth status, and elected Filipino officials took charge of domestic affairs. The United States also provided free access for Philippine exports and promised the country full independence in ten years. When Japan invaded the Philippines in World War II, Philippine and American soldiers fought together at Bataan and Corregidor, delaying the Japanese conquest by four months at enormous cost in lives. During the war, resistance to the Japanese occupation was much more broadly based in the Philippines than in the rest of Southeast Asia, but some of the political elite supported the pro–Japanese puppet regime led by Jose Laurel.

Despite enormous damage to the country's infrastructure during the war, the Philippines gained its independence on July 4, 1946.[13] Under a separate but linked agreement, free trade with the United States was extended for eight years, and Americans were given the right to exploit Philippine natural resources until 1974. A 1947 agreement allowed the United States to maintain its air and naval bases until 1991.[14]

The Nacionalista Party, which had dominated Philippine politics before the war, broke into two factions, one called the Liberal Party and the other retaining the old Nacionalista name. From 1946 to 1972, they fought for control of the legislative and executive branches in elections that were marred by considerable violence and corruption, but there was no ideological difference between the two parties. When Ferdinand Marcos failed to get the Liberal Party nomination for president in 1965, he switched to the Nacionalista Party and won the election.[15]

Marcos and Martial Law

During Marcos's second term (1969–72), he declared martial law as a means of extending his administration beyond the two-term limit. Warning of an imminent communist takeover, he arrested thousands of people and imposed strict censorship on the previously free press. Although he appointed some able technocrats to the National Economic Development Authority (NEDA), he often ignored their advice and ran up huge debts with a patronage system that resembled Suharto's in Indonesia. Because of Marcos's economic mismanagement and the oil price shocks of the 1970s, the average Philippine worker lost ground economically during the decade, and the economy began to unravel completely.[16]

In 1983, Senator Benigno Aquino, Marcos's main opponent, was murdered when he returned from exile in the United States. The circumstances of his death clearly pointed to the government's responsibility for the murder, and it crystalized the Philippine people's anger at Marcos and his administration.[17]

First People Power Revolution

Marcos called an election in early 1986 to try and shore up his regime, but a coalition of opposition parties quickly formed to support the candidacy of Corazon Aquino, widow of the murdered senator. Marcos claimed victory in the election, but he was widely believed to have engaged in massive fraud. Fidel Ramos, deputy chief of the armed forces, and Defense Secretary Juan Ponce Enrile defected to Aquino's side. (Ramos was Marcos's cousin and had served him loyally until 1986.) Cardinal Sin, head of the Catholic hierarchy, called on the people of Manila to join the rebellion. When huge numbers of people responded, Marcos resigned, and he fled to Hawaii where he died three years later.[18]

Aquino's presidency restored many of the political institutions that existed before Marcos's reign, but in doing so it preserved the dominant position of the landowning elite. In 1987, a new constitution restored civil rights and a free press and recognized the rights of ethnic and religious minorities. It also legitimized the role of nongovernmental organizations and called for a devolution of government powers to the local level. Aquino also began to implement much-needed economic reforms to attract investors, but she failed to enact any significant land reform measures. A major land-owner herself, she admitted that she could not bring herself to harm the interests of her own class.[19]

Economic growth resumed on a modest level, but communist and Muslim insurgents gained the initiative in many provinces, and rogue bands of vigilantes supported by the army added to the security problem. Aquino's presidency survived frequent coup attempts mainly because General Ramos was at her side to protect her.[20] With Aquino's support, Ramos won the 1992 presidential election, and his was one of the most productive administrations in the nation's history. Internal security was restored by a policy of reconciliation with dissident forces. Foreign investment increased, and the economy grew at a steady pace until the 1997 financial crisis. Much also was done to repair the country's infrastructure and improve funding for education and other long-neglected social programs.[21]

Joseph Estrada, a movie actor and Marcos loyalist, won the 1998 election by a landslide, creating a new vogue for actors and media stars in politics. Estrada's short-lived administration accomplished some useful economic reforms, but he presided over a return to patronage politics, and he was linked to major corruption scandals. In 2001, he was forced out of office by street demonstrations in Manila ("People Power II"), which were again supported by the Catholic Church and the military. In January 2001, the Supreme Court declared the presidency vacant, and Vice President Gloria Macapagal Arroyo was sworn in as Estrada's replacement.

President Arroyo, like her father President Diosdado Macapagal, was a trained economist. During her first four years in office, she persuaded Congress to enact reforms to reduce the national debt and annual budget deficits. In 2004, she won a hard-fought election against a popular movie star named Fernando Poe, Jr. Her coalition of parties also won majorities in both houses of Congress.[22]

But in 2005, tapes surfaced of alleged telephone conversations between President Arroyo and a member of the Election Commission after the 2004 election. Arroyo found herself fighting to survive in the face of opposition charges of vote-rigging. She lost the support of her cabinet when she delayed implementing a new tax on corporate profits in order to keep business leaders on her side.[23]

Former President Aquino went on television and urged her to resign, and her opponents tried to organize a massive demonstration in Manila. But middle class Filipinos failed to turn out in significant numbers because they were suffering from "People Power fatigue," a pervasive feeling that nothing would be gained by replacing Arroyo with her political opponents. Leaders of the Church and armed forces also pledged to remain neutral during the political crisis.[24] So the charges against President Arroyo were dismissed by the lower house of Congress. But she lost her majority in the Senate two years later, and it became more and more difficult for her to implement a reform agenda.

Political System

The "People's Constitution" that was adopted in 1987 with President Aquino's support called for the restoration of civil liberties that were often abused during the Marcos years. Even so, President Aquino's administration (1986–1992) was a time of frequent violations of human rights, often committed by or sanctioned by the armed forces, police, and local officials.[25]

In 1991, the Philippine Congress approved a Local Government Code which transferred powers, personnel, and revenue from the central government down to local government units. As noted in chapter 8, a similar experiment is underway in Indonesia, and in both countries the effectiveness of newly empowered local officials has varied greatly from one area to another. In the Philippines, thousands of NGO's became involved in the program, but they made slow progress in developing effective relationships with local government units.

The 1987 constitution also provided for the creation of autonomous regions to protect the interests of ethnic and religious minorities. An autonomous region for indigenous people was created in northern Luzon, and another was established on Mindanao for Muslims.[26]

Executive Branch

Under the Philippine constitution, the powers of the Philippine president are analogous to those of the U.S. president, but the Philippine president is limited to one six-year term in office. (Because President Arroyo was appointed by the Supreme Court to replace President Estrada in 2001 and then went on to win the 2004 election, she may serve until 2010.) The Philippine vice president is elected separately from the president but may serve in the president's cabinet.

Legislative Branch

The Philippine Congress has a lower house with 274 members and an upper house (Senate) with 24 members. The lower house controls the purse strings through the annual General Appropriations Act. House members may serve no more than three consecutive three-year terms but they can run again after sitting out for one term. About 60 percent of the seats in the lower house are held by elite political families that have held the same seats for generations.[27]

Change to a Parliamentary System?

A move to change from a presidential to a parliamentary form of government is supported by those Filipinos (including most members of the lower house) who believe the president has too much power. Members of the lower house would keep their seats if a unicameral parliamentary system was adopted, but Senators would lose their seats under such a system, so they generally opposed the change. Some people, including former president Aquino, also opposed moving to a parliamentary system, because they feared this might lead to the complete unraveling of the 1987 constitution.[28] President Arroyo argued that moving to a parliamentary system would make it easier to enact bold economic reforms, but she only favored the change on condition that she be allowed to serve out her term to 2010.[29]

Constitutional Commissions

In an effort to provide checks and balances between the branches of government, the 1987 constitution provides for a number of commissions. The president must submit most nominations for senior appointments to the Commission on Appointments, which is composed of twelve Senators and twelve members of the House of Representatives. If the commission rejects a nominee twice, the president must nominate someone else.

The Commission on Elections (COMELEC), the Civil Service Commission, and the Commission on Audit are all appointed by the president with the approval of the Commission on Appointments, so they tend to be composed of the president's friends and supporters. COMELEC is responsible for running the Philippine elections, and it has not succeeded in reducing the amount of violence and corruption that has traditionally marred the process.[30]

The Civil Service Commission is responsible for managing well over a million civil servants. Studies by the World Bank and other organizations have shown that there is much duplication of effort in the bureaucracy. Corruption has been estimated to reduce gross national product by 10 percent.[31]

Political Parties and Elections

The Philippine political system has been called a stable but low quality democracy.[32] Members of the political elite compete aggressively among themselves to win elections, and they tacitly cooperate among themselves to preserve a social order in which they occupy a very privileged position. Thus, from 1946 to 1972, the Nacionalista and Liberal parties won most of the elections and ran the country. Their failure to produce a more equitable society caused thousands of peasants and even some middle class Filipinos to back the communist insurgency. Marcos exploited these tensions by declaring martial law so he could remain in office beyond the constitutional limit, which at that time was eight years.[33]

From 1972 to 1986, Marcos ruled mainly by decree. He banned political parties (except ones that he had approved), and he tried to destroy those members of the elite whom he could not co-opt. But because of the weakness of state institutions and the poor performance of the economy, opposition parties began to reemerge around 1979 as Marcos's supporters deserted him.

Salvador Laurel, a former Marcos supporter, organized the United Democratic Party (UNIDO). Senator Benigno Aquino formed Lakas ng Bayan (LABAN) while he was in prison, and the Mindanao Alliance became the Pilipino Democratic Party (PDP). These three parties united to form a coalition that backed Corazon Aquino in the 1986 election, and Salvador Laurel became her vice president. He expected her to let him run the government, and when she did not, he joined the opposition but remained vice president.[34]

President Aquino later added the Liberal Party (Salonga faction) and the National Union of Christian Democrats to her coalition, which became known as LAKAS. Although critics faulted her for not making full use of her popularity while it lasted, she supported Ramos in his successful bid for the presidency in 1992. One of Ramos's major achievements was to promote national reconciliation by legalizing the communist party, making peace with the Muslim separatist organization, and encouraging a more disciplined and professional attitude in the military.

In the 1998 election, Joseph Estrada, a former actor in Grade B movies, was supported by his own Partido ng Masang Pilipino (PMP), plus LABAN and the Nationalist People's Coalition (NPC). The NPC was run by Corazon Aquino's cousin and political foe, Edwardo Cojuanco, one of Marcos's richest cronies, and the election set new records for political expenditure.

President Arroyo won the bitterly contested 2004 presidential election by a margin of 1.12 million votes, according to the official tally. Her main opponent, the movie actor Fernando Poe, Jr. was backed by Marcos crony Eduardo Cojuangco and a broad coalition of parties.[35]

In the 2004 Congressional elections, candidates nominated by President Arroyo's coalition preserved their majorities in both houses.[36] But in the 2007 elections, she lost her majority in the Senate.

Armed Forces of the Philippines (AFP)

During the Marcos martial law period (1972–86), the armed forces numbered 200,000 and played an active political role. By 2003, the number of people in the military had been reduced to about 106,000, and the army had only 66,000 troops.[37] They were sometimes outnumbered by insurgent forces, and they were also responsible for civic action and disaster relief programs. Since 1986, the main impact of the military on the political system has been through attempted coups by disaffected younger officers and the support (or lack of same) for People Power movements by the leaders of the AFP.

General Ramos, who supported Marcos (his cousin) during his administration, helped lead the People Power revolt that brought Cory Aquino to power in 1986. She supported Ramos in the closely fought 1992 election, and he tried hard to reform the military during his term as president, particularly by redirecting them toward civic action programs to counter the communist and Islamic insurgencies. Despite his efforts, the Philippines remains one of the most violent and dangerous countries in Asia, not least because of corruption and lack of discipline in the AFP, the police and paramilitary forces.[38] In 2000, the AFP again supported the People Power II revolt against President Estrada but remained neutral in 2005 when President Arroyo's opponents tried to launch People Power III.

The Judiciary

Under the 1987 constitution, the judicial system consists of the Supreme Court and a series of lower courts, which the Supreme Court supervises. Efforts to make them independent of political pressure from the legislative and executive branches have only been marginally effective. The Congress can not reduce the budget for the judiciary below the previous year's level, and nominees to the Supreme court are chosen by the Judicial Bar Council (JBC). They prepare a short list of three nominees from which the president chooses one. President Arroyo was able to replace nine of the fifteen Supreme Court justices who had reached the mandatory retirement age of seventy. In 2004, her appointees helped her survive a major political crisis by voting to "freeze" a tax on corporations. Although this helped her retain the support of business leaders, it also raised questions about the independence of the court.

Civil Society

Of all the countries in Southeast Asia, the Philippines probably has the largest and most diverse range of nongovernmental organizations—and organizations that resemble NGOs but are openly or secretly controlled by the government. The Philippines also has the freest press in the region and a multiparty system that is in constant flux.

Marcos did his best to co-opt or suppress his opponents during his reign, but in the end they defeated him with the support of the Catholic Church and armed forces (AFP). Both the Church and the AFP have tried to use Philippine civil society to accomplish their own objectives. As in other Southeast Asian countries, a large number of Philippine NGOs have an urban, middle-class membership and a religious orientation. In particular, they reflect a wide range of Catholic viewpoints, from far right to far left.[39]

Each Philippine administration, from Cory Aquino's on, has tried to work closely with civil society. NGOs played a major role in drafting the 1987 constitution (much like the role of NGOs in shaping Thailand's 1997 constitution). They helped overthrow President Estrada in 2001, and their failure to mount another People Power revolt against Arroyo has been characterized as "People Power Fatigue," a growing belief that regime change will not produce significant reforms.

The Media

According to the Committee to Protect Journalists (based in New York) and Reporters Without Borders, which is located in Paris, the Philippines is second only to Iraq in the number of journalists killed in the line of duty. Between 1986 and 2004, 61 journalists were killed in the Philippines. The attacks intensified during Arroyo's administration and were often carried out by rogue units of the armed forces or police.[40]

Nevertheless, Filipinos probably still have the widest choice of news sources in Southeast Asia. Dozens of daily and weekly newspapers are published in Manila and other major towns and cities. The most influential newspapers include the *Daily Inquirer* (www.inquirer.net) and the *Philippine Star* (www.philstar.com). There are also a large number of privately owned TV and radio stations as well as some which are operated by the government.

Economic Development

In 2004, economists at the University of the Philippines issued a study showing how the swollen national debt and chronic budget deficit severely limited the country's economic growth. The total public sector debt was 130 percent of GDP. Interest payments on past debt were eating up a third or more of the national budget, and while the gap between rich and poor was one of the world's largest, the rich were paying almost no taxes. During President Arroyo's administration, tax collections rose, but government expenditure on health, education, and infrastructure remained well below what was needed.[41]

Economic Growth

During the past four decades, Philippine economic growth has been very uneven and has failed to keep pace with growth in the other Southeast Asian countries. In the 1960s, the Philippines had one of the more successful economies in Asia, but it fell to the bottom of the league during the martial law period (1972–86) when Marcos ran up heavy annual deficits by handing out economic monopolies to his family and friends. Philippine per capita GDP was on a par with Thailand's in the 1960s, but by 1986 it was more than 50 percent lower. The income gap between the richest and poorest Filipinos also widened steadily. By 1986, when Marcos fled the country, real wages of unskilled urban workers were far below their level in 1969 when Marcos became president. The incidence of poverty ranged from 44 percent of the population of Manila to more than 70 per cent in Bicol and the Visayas.[42]

During the Aquino administration, the Philippines achieved modest growth during 1988 and 1989, but over the next two years, growth was flat partly because of low rates of investment. Also, the first U.S. war in Iraq raised oil prices and dislocated Philippine workers in the Middle East, whose remittances were an important source of national income.

During President Ramos's administration, improved security and a more concerted effort at economic reform led to increased investment, and the economy grew by about 5 percent a year from 1993 to 1997. Private investors were invited to "build, operate, and transfer" electric power plants, toll roads, and other badly needed infrastructure. This was one of the few Philippine economic programs that could serve as a model for the rest of Southeast Asia.

But the 1997 financial crisis forced a devaluation of the peso, and the Manila stock market collapsed when foreigners pulled their money out. Many Filipinos lost their jobs or were forced to take large pay cuts, but the peso's decline against the dollar helped Philippine exports and raised the value of remittances from Philippine workers overseas.[43] Despite the political turmoil during President Arroyo's administration, economic growth returned to the 5 percent range, as Table 10.3 shows.

Table 10.3
The Philippines' Economy, 2007–10
(all figures are percentages unless otherwise indicated)

	2007	2008	2009	2010
GDP Growth	7.2	4.6	-1.9	1.4
Agricultural Production Growth	4.9	3.2	3.2	3.5
Unemployment	7.3	7.4	9.7	11.8
Inflation	2.8	9.3	1.9	3.6
Government Budget Balance	-0.2	-0.9	-2.7	-2.6
Exports (U.S. $B)	49.5	48.2	34.0	35.8
Imports (U.S. $B)	57.9	60.8	43.1	45.2

Sources: Economist Intelligence Unit, "Philippines, Country Report," April 2009. Figures for 2009 and 2010 are EIU forecasts.

After a long struggle with Congress (and some wavering in her own resolve), Arroyo succeeded in getting a value added tax on corporations passed in December 2005, adding significantly to government revenue. According to the economist Hal Hill, the main reason the Philippine economy has been so resilient is because key elements such as overseas workers' remittances, call centers, the IT sector, and medical tourism all function without much interference and "conflicts from the political elite."[44]

As Table 10.3 shows, Philippine economic growth remained fairly strong (at 4.6 percent) in 2008, but it was expected to contract by 1.9 percent in 2009 before returning to modest growth in 2010. These figures were very disappointing, because analysts had expected the Philippines to do better. With very high levels of unemployment and poverty, the country needs high economic growth as badly as any in the region. A government stimulus package was delayed for several months by political wrangling in the Philippine Congress, but it was finally passed by mid–2009. Household consumption, a key driver of economic growth in the Philippines, was down because of the large number of workers laid off or expecting to be laid off.

Foreign Relations

The Philippines became a founding member of ASEAN in 1967 mainly to emphasize its identity as a Southeast Asian country. It played an active diplomatic role in the Cambodian peace process, and later a Philippine general commanded the military component of the UN Transitional Administration in East Timor (UNTAET). In 1998, the Philippine and Thai foreign ministers spoke out in favor of "constructive intervention" in ASEAN countries' internal affairs.[45]

At the time, this seemed a bold departure from ASEAN's traditional policy of nonintervention in member states' affairs. But the need for ASEAN to set some standards for its members has gradually been accepted by other ASEAN states, particularly in regard to the Burmese junta. In 2006, the Philippines took Myanmar's place as ASEAN chair after Myanmar agreed to relinquish the role. In 2007, a senior Philippine diplomat led the committee drafting an ASEAN Charter which was expected to embrace the change.[46]

Support for Overseas Workers

A major priority of Philippine foreign policy is to support the interests of Philippine overseas workers who numbered over 8 million in 2007, and their remittances for the year totaled $14.3 billion, a major contribution to the Philippine balance of payments and domestic spending.[47] In 2002, overseas workers were given the right to vote in Philippine elections and to be represented in the Philippine Congress.

A large number of Filipinos work in the Middle East, including about 4,200 in Iraq. In 2004, a worker was kidnapped by insurgents who threatened to behead him if the Philippines did not withdraw its contingent of fifty-one soldiers and police. President Arroyo felt compelled to comply with the insurgents' demands.[48]

Hundreds of thousands of Filipino workers are employed in Malaysia, Singapore, and Brunei in a variety of occupations. The Malaysian government's effort to deport undocumented Filipino workers has been a continuing source of friction between the two neighboring countries.[49]

U.S.-Philippine Relations

More than a million Filipinos live and work in the United States, and the U.S. is the Philippines' leading trade partner and source of direct investment. The U.S. economic aid and Peace Corps programs are also among the largest in the region.[50]

Until 1992, the United States retained the right to use major air and naval bases in the Philippines. In 1991, Clark Air Base was buried in ash after an eruption of Mount Pinatubu. When the Philippine Senate decided not to extend the U.S. Navy's access to the Subic Bay facilities, the United States turned to other countries including Singapore for alternate arrangements. In 1999, the Philippine Senate approved a Visiting Forces Agreement under which the U.S. Navy resumed visits to Philippine ports, and U.S. forces conducted combined training exercises with Philippine forces. The United States also operates one of its largest military aid and training programs with the Philippines.[51]

Philippine Relations with China and Taiwan

The Philippines established diplomatic relations with China in 1975 and recognized that Taiwan was an integral part of China's territory. But Philippine relations with Taiwan remained close, because many members of the Sino-Philippine elite have family and business ties with Taiwan.

Some or all of the Spratly islands in the South China Sea are claimed by the Philippines, China, Vietnam, Malaysia, Brunei, and Indonesia. The disputed area is believed to contain rich oil reserves, and the overlapping claims have led to naval clashes between these countries. In August 1995, China finally agreed to settle disputes in the South China Sea according to international law rather than insisting that its historical claim to the entire area should take precedence. Over the next few years, several additional clashes took place between Chinese and Philippine naval forces, and in 1999 ASEAN leaders approved a Philippine draft for a voluntary code of conduct aimed at preventing future conflicts in the South China Sea. The Philippines and China agreed not to occupy any more islands or build new structures on them, but China did not sign the code of conduct.[52]

Conclusions

The Philippine people suffered political and economic setbacks during the Marcos martial law years from which they have not fully recovered. The People Power revolts in 1986 and 2000 did not lead to basic social reforms, and the political system has failed to achieve a significant reduction in the level of poverty.[53]

Many of the same land-owning families and corporate billionaires that have dominated the Philippines for generations are as powerful today as they ever were. This static social situation has been partially offset by the development of new economic sectors that are not greatly affected by government interference — information technology and call centers, for example. Even more important are the billions of dollars pouring into the country from overseas Filipino workers, making domestic consumption an important source of economic growth. Although the economy is still performing far below its potential, the cumulative effect of reforms undertaken since the Marcos years has gradually made the government a more positive force for social and economic change.

Further Reading

Clarke, Gerard. *The Politics of NGOs in Southeast Asia.* London and New York: Routledge, 1998.

Coronel, Sheila, ed. *Pork and Other Perks: Corruption and Governance in the Philippines.* Manila: Philippine Center for Investigative Journalism, 1998.

De Guzman, Raul P., and Mila A. Reforma, eds. *Government and Politics of the Philippines.* Singapore: Oxford University Press, 1988.

Karnow, Stanley. *In Our Image: America's Empire in the Philippines.* New York: Random House, 1989.

Nadeau, Kathleen M. *Liberation Theology in the Philippines: Faith in a Revolution.* Westport, CT: Praeger, 2002.

Steinberg, David J. *The Philippines: A Singular and Plural Place.* Boulder, CO: Westview Press, 1982.

Wurfel, David. *Filipino Politics: Development and Decay.* Ithaca, NY: Cornell University Press, 1991.

– 11 –

LOOKING AHEAD

To a More Closely Integrated Region

When the U.S. financial crisis began in 2008, some analysts thought the Southeast Asian states might be spared because their economic ties were increasingly with the rest of Asia. Also, domestic consumption was becoming an important engine of growth in the region. So in early 2008, the International Monetary Fund and the Economist Intelligence Unit issued relatively optimistic forecasts for Southeast Asia's economic growth in the remainder of 2008 and 2009, as Table 11.1 shows, but these forecasts were revised downward in April 2009.

Table 11.1
Forecasts of Southeast Asian Growth,
April 2008 and April 2009
(all figures are percentages unless otherwise indicated)

	April 2008 EIU Forecast		April 2009 EIU Forecast	
	2008	2009	2009	2010
Thailand	5.3	5.6	-4.4	1.4
Vietnam	7.3	7.3	1.6	2.0
Cambodia	6.8	6.4	-3.0	2.2
Laos	6.5	6.5	3.0	5.0
Myanmar	3.4	3.6	0.3	1.2
Malaysia	5.0	5.2	-3.0	1.1
Singapore	4.0	4.5	-8.8	0.9
Indonesia	6.1	6.3	-1.4	0.5
Brunei	2.0	2.0	0.2	0.3
Philippines	5.8	5.8	-1.9	1.4

Source: Economist Intelligence Unit (EIU), April 2008 and April 2009; the International Monetary Fund, "World Economic Outlook Update," January 28, 2009, provided a somewhat more optimistic forecast for the five original ASEAN members (Thailand, Malaysia, Indonesia, Singapore, and the Philippines): their combined GDP growth for 2009 would be 2.7 percent, and for 2010 it would be 4.1 percent. However, by mid–2009, IMF and World Bank forecasts for Southeast Asia's economic growth were at least as pessimistic as those of the Economist Intelligence Unit.

However, the April 2009 forecasts may turn out to have been too pessimistic, because Southeast Asian countries strengthened their defenses against global market fluctuations in the decade following the 1997 Asian financial crisis. They reformed their financial institutions, adopted more conservative macroeconomic policies, and increased their trade with neighboring states.

Some progress in Asian regional integration was also made in the 1990's and in the decade following the 1997–98 crisis. The 1990s saw the enlargement of ASEAN to include the Indochina states and Burma and the creation of the ASEAN Free Trade Area. This led to a substantial increase in economic ties between the ten Southeast Asian countries, because the new ASEAN members are less developed than the founding members, and they rely heavily on the founding members of ASEAN as trade partners and for investment capital, technology, and economic expertise. Before the enlargement, the five original ASEAN members mainly produced the same commodities and competed with each other for shares of the same foreign markets. Their relations with the Indochina states were often hostile. So the chances for economic integration of the region were minimal.

Since the end of the cold war, ASEAN leaders have not been shy about offering their organization as the core institution around which an Asian political, economic, and cultural community might be built. In response to the Asian financial crisis that began in 1997, currency swap agreements were concluded, ASEAN leaders began to hold annual summits, and leaders of the more powerful Asia-Pacific nations began to meet on the margins of these summit meetings as well as the annual ASEAN ministerials. The idea of creating an Asian currency unit and an Asian monetary fund (to eliminate the need for dealing with the International Monetary Fund) was discussed but not implemented. ASEAN is negotiating or planning to negotiate free trade agreements with Japan, China, India, and Australia. Also, the ASEAN Regional Forum is the first organization to be created for the purpose of discussing Asia's most sensitive security issues.[1]

The prominent role that ASEAN currently plays in promoting Asian regional integration raises some interesting questions about what the future holds for ASEAN and its members. For example, is ASEAN becoming less vulnerable to recessions in the West than it was in the past? How will Southeast Asia be affected by continued high world wide prices for food and oil? Will demographic trends help Southeast Asia become more competitive with China and India? Or will the ASEAN countries slip further behind their rapidly growing Asian neighbors? What role will Asian migrant workers play in the regional economy? Which countries can best attract managerial talent?

Will the trend toward more democratic government in Southeast Asia continue? And will the ASEAN states strengthen their organization by requiring their members to meet certain minimum standards of governance?

Will the integration of Asian markets eventually lead to some form of Asian union designed to compete with North America and the European Union? If so, what role will the ASEAN members play in this new Asian regional organization?

Finally, as noted in the country chapters, China has succeeded in strengthening its ties with Southeast Asian states by the use of "soft power," including trade agreements and economic aid, visits to the region by top level Chinese officials, and resolving territorial disputes through negotiation. Will Chinese leaders continue to use this low-key approach to relations with Southeast Asia, or will China become more domineering as its power increases along with its need for the resources which Southeast Asia can supply?

Is ASEAN becoming more or less vulnerable to recessions in the West than it was in the past?

According to the International Monetary Fund, the U.S. recession in the early 1990s had a relatively modest impact on Asian economic output — averaging a quarter to a half percentage point slowdown in developing Asian countries for every full point drop in U.S. economic output. But the U.S. recession in 2001 had a larger impact on Asia, with 1.75 percent drop in U.S. economic output causing a 1.25 percent drop in Asia's output. The IMF predicted the 2008 U.S. slowdown would provide more of a challenge to Asia, because of the turbulence it caused in international banking and because Europe's economic output would be affected as well.[2] Nevertheless, the IMF predicted that most Asian countries had enough economic momentum to withstand the shock caused by the U.S. slowdown. The Asian countries that were already experiencing weaker growth than the regional average would be hardest hit by the 2008–9 U.S. slowdown.[3]

How will Southeast Asia be affected by the sharp increase in world prices for food and oil which began in 2007?

The large increases in world prices for food and oil caused a sudden return to double-digit inflation in several Southeast Asian countries, including Vietnam and Indonesia, where food and fuel absorb a large portion of the average person's budget. Increased inflation threatened to sharply reduce economic growth in a number of developing Asian countries. Vietnam, India, and several non–Asian governments such as Egypt reacted to the crisis by imposing a ban on rice exports which threatened to increase food shortages and malnutrition in the Philippines, the world's largest rice importer, and other countries. The Thai government announced it would try to organize a system to control the rice price in ASEAN countries, but analysts predicted the Southeast Asian states would be unable to affect a price that was governed by global supply and demand.[4]

Japan responded to the Philippines' plight by offering to sell the country 200,000 tons of stockpiled rice, and Cambodia (the world's eighth largest rice exporter) announced it would resume rice exports that had been temporarily blocked. These measures helped to stabilize the world price of rice and other food grains, but analysts expected the price to remain high for an extended period of time. To help poor countries cope with the problem, the World Bank announced a $1.2 billion fast-track funding facility to help governments combat the impact of rising food prices on the poor.[5]

By mid–2008, analysts believed that the world price of oil might also stabilize for several years at the exceptionally high level it had reached. More than half of the Southeast Asian countries produce some oil, but Indonesia and most of the rest are net importers of oil. These countries faced a choice of maintaining subsidies to reduce the impact on their people (leading to large budget deficits) or reducing subsidies, which carried a risk of creating serious domestic unrest and high inflation.

Indonesian leaders chose to cut subsidies, as they did once before in 2005, to avoid a major budget deficit. They reportedly believed the danger of domestic unrest was not great and that inflation would subside in a short period of time, as it did in 2005. The Indonesian government also withdrew from OPEC which was in large part responsible for the price increase.[6]

Will demographic trends help the Southeast Asian states become more competitive? Or will they slip further behind their East Asian neighbors?

Table 11.2 provides an estimate of the amount of population growth that will take place in selected Asian countries by 2025. Long-range forecasting of population growth is subject to many variables, but the figures in the right hand column at least give a rough idea of how much the population of some countries (e.g., India) may increase compared to other countries, such as China, which has one of the slowest population growth rates in Asia.

Table 11.2
Estimated Population of Asian Countries in 2008 and 2025

	Population (2008) (Million unless otherwise indicated)	*Growth Rate (2008) (%)*	*Population (2025) (Million unless otherwise indicated)*
ASEAN			
Indonesia	245	1.1	290
Philippines	90.5	2	125
Vietnam	85.2	1	110
Thailand	67.0	0.3	71
Myanmar	57.6	0.8	68
Malaysia	27.0	1.8	70
Cambodia	15.0	1.72	20
Laos	6.5	1.5	12
Singapore	4.6	1.6	4.3
Brunei	0.4	2.8	0.6
Total ASEAN	598.8		770.9
China	1.32 billion	0.606	1.5 billion
India	1.12 billion	1.3	1.6 billion
Japan	127.5	-0.088	120
South Korea	48.9	0.42	46
Taiwan	23	0.36	21
Australia	21	1.3	28
New Zealand	4.3	0.7	3.9

Sources: 2008 population adn growth rates are based on estimates by the UN Development Program. The 2025 figures are based on a 2006 ILO study cited below and on estimates in Milton Osborne's *Exploring Southeast Asia* (New South Wales, Australia: Allen & Unwin, 2002), p. 10.

According to a 2006 study by the International Labor Organization (ILO), the rate of increase in the work force of China and several other Asian countries is expected to slow down over the next few years, in some cases with serious negative consequences. During the decade ending 2015, China will add less than 5 percent to its work force, and about the same small increase will take place in Thailand, Singapore and Vietnam.[7] In all four countries, labor shortages will probably force manufacturers to raise wages. This may help to reduce poverty in some countries, but it will also make their exports less competitive on world markets.

By contrast, India is likely to suffer problems related to rapid population growth. It will have the largest population in the world by 2016, and by that date the number of working age people will grow by over 70 million. Partly because of India's weak education system, there will be a large increase in the number of unemployed and part-time workers.[8]

The ILO also predicts there are likely to be substantial increases in the work force of Indonesia, Malaysia, the Philippines, Cambodia, and Laos, which may help some of these countries increase the productivity of their economies. Malaysia is sparsely populated, and the government hopes to more than double its population over the next few decades in order to reduce its dependence on foreign workers.[9] But Indonesia and the Philippines, which have serious unemployment and export large numbers of workers abroad, may find that having more mouths to feed will make it even harder to reduce the level of poverty in their countries.

What role will a more mobile work force play in the Asian regional economy? Which countries will win the competition to attract highly qualified managers?

Asian workers increasingly travel from one Asian country to another in search of short-term or long-term employment instead of going mainly to Western countries and the Middle East as they once did.[10] Highly qualified immigrants are welcomed by all the Southeast Asian countries, because their skills are needed to develop the modern sectors of these economies. But Thailand, Malaysia, and Singapore have large numbers of unskilled (and often undocumented) migrant workers. These people are sometimes viewed as potential criminals by the native-born population, and the host governments try to enforce very strict rules about how long they can remain in their countries.[11]

Japan has also had very restrictive policies concerning foreign workers even though the native Japanese population is aging and shrinking, and Japan's economy has lost much of its economic dynamism since the early 1990s.[12] Within a few decades at most, China and many other countries in Asia will experience the same demographic problems that Japan already faces. But while the Japanese people still have a comfortable middle class lifestyle, China and some Southeast Asian countries are in danger of "growing old before they become rich."[13]

Will the trend toward more democratic government in Southeast Asia continue? And qill the ASEAN states strengthen their organization by requiring each of their members to meet certain minimum standards of governance?

The five original ASEAN states have developed stronger democratic institutions than the five newer ASEAN members. But the region's political and social systems also have much in common, and they may become more alike in the future. For example, Malaysia's political system has been described as "semi-democratic" because opposition parties can take part in state and national elections but the ruling coalition makes it all but impossible for the opposition to win control of the national government. This system appeals to many Southeast Asian elites because it allows some airing of public concerns during state and national elections while maintaining the "stability" of one-party dominance.[14] But this form of government invites corruption and fails to provide equal opportunities for all citizens.

The leaders of the newer ASEAN member states are under varying degrees of pressure from their foreign trading partners, aid donors, foreign and domestic NGO's, and multinational firms to broaden political participation in their countries. They may see advantages in following Malaysia's example (or Singapore's somewhat more authoritarian approach). Unfortunately, some leaders of the more democratic countries (Thailand,

Philippines, and Indonesia) may also feel tempted to regress toward the "semi-democratic" model.[15]

The Malaysian government's record of protecting the rights of its citizens is far from perfect. Former prime minister Mahathir and other Malaysian leaders have imprisoned their political opponents without trial under laws which were supposedly designed to deal with social unrest. But in some ways Malaysia's political system could serve as a model for political reform in neighboring states. Malaysia's armed forces have generally stayed out of politics, and they have not committed human rights violations on the same scale as the armies of Burma, Indonesia, the Philippines, or the Indochina states.[16]

ASEAN members' reluctance to intervene in member states' affairs has not been greatly changed by the addition of five new members with autocratic rulers.[17] Malaysian and Philippine leaders have been more outspoken than others in the region when it comes to criticizing the Burmese junta's human rights record and trying to persuade the Burmese generals to raise their standards.[18]

In 2007, ASEAN celebrated its fortieth anniversary by adopting an ASEAN Charter and creating a Human Rights Commission. But the Commission will have no enforcement powers, and when the heads of government met in Singapore to sign the Charter, they failed to take action in support of the Burmese people, who risked their lives a few weeks earlier to demonstrate against the Burmese junta. Philippine President Arroyo offered the most vigorous criticism of her colleagues' failure to publicly criticize the Burmese junta.[20] India's decision to end its arms sales to Myanmar provided an example to the ASEAN states that have been reluctant to apply such overt pressure.[21]

Will Asia's economic integration lead to some form of Asian union designed to compete with North America and the European Union? If so, what role will the ASEAN members play in this new Asian regional organization?

Until the Asian countries recover from the 2008 recession, their political leaders will almost certainly focus on national interests rather than new schemes for regional integration. Even in the best of times, Asian leaders find it difficult to agree on basic questions regarding a regional economic and/or political union. Which countries will be invited to join? Will it be ASEAN's ten members plus Japan, China, South Korea, India, Australia, and New Zealand (the group now known as ASEAN+6)? Some Asian leaders might insist on excluding "non–Asian" countries (e.g., Australia and New Zealand) as well as those that are most closely aligned with the West.[22]

What economic or political role would an Asian union be expected to perform? An Asian common market providing free movement of goods, services, and labor within the region would have many advantages over the existing "noodle bowl" of free trade agreements. But agreeing on such an innovation would be very difficult. Asian economists have also expressed interest in creating an Asian Monetary Fund and an Asian currency unit to help the region survive another financial crisis. But which country's currency would form an anchor for the system as the deutsche mark did in Europe? Would China and Korea be willing to accept such a role for the Japanese yen?[23]

The ASEAN states have tried to place their organization at the center of Asian regional organizations such as the ASEAN Regional Forum and the Asia-Pacific Economic Cooperation organization.[24] There are several reasons why these initiatives have met with little opposition from the larger and more powerful Asian countries. The ASEAN states do not threaten the major powers' interests. They can (and do) provide support for Japan's quest for a permanent seat on the UN Security Council. Also, the number of middle class consumers is growing rapidly in Southeast Asia, making it an attractive market for China, Japan, Korea, and other Asian countries. Finally, the ASEAN states have helped to reduce tensions between other Asian countries by providing opportunities for their leaders to meet informally at ASEAN summit meetings. So the major Asian powers may continue to encourage ASEAN's efforts to promote Asian regional integration.

China has succeeded in strengthening its ties with southeast Asia by pursuing "soft" policies, but is regional dominance Beijing's ultimate strategic goal?

Chinese leaders have developed good working relations with the ASEAN countries by using trade, aid, and high-level visits to persuade many Southeast Asian leaders that Beijing's goal is simply to create a mutually advantageous situation.[25] One example of this has been cited several times in this study. Southeast Asian manufacturers of electronic and other goods have lost market share in the West because of competition with China, but they have found niche markets in China for component parts of goods that are assembled in China and sold abroad.

Southeast Asian countries have also been losing out to China in the competition to attract foreign direct investment from outside the Asian region. But this loss has been partially compensated by Chinese investment in and aid to Southeast Asia, particularly the mainland states (Cambodia, Laos, Myanmar, Vietnam, and Thailand). Large numbers of students from Southeast Asia have gone to China to study.[26] More Chinese tourists visit the region than tourists from the United States, while many ethnic Chinese from Southeast Asia visit China to renew ties with their ancestral villages.

The improvement in relations between China and its southern neighbors has been a "win-win" situation for both sides, to use a favorite cliché of Chinese and Western diplomats. It has also served the interests of Japan and the West by helping to make Southeast Asia more prosperous and politically stable. So far, China's growing influence in Southeast Asia has not proved to be an obstacle to the political aims of the West, which include supporting the spread of democratic values in the region and assisting Southeast Asian countries' efforts to cope with transnational crime, terrorism, trafficking in persons, and degradation of the ennvironment.

Beijing's emphasis on "soft power" in dealing with Southeast Asia has clearly been motivated by self-interest, and it has produced tangible gains for China, including improved access to the region's raw materials. But there is no guarantee that such a low key approach will serve China's needs indefinitely.

China is much more actively involved in developing projects in the mainland Southeast Asian Countries than in the island countries of the region. Thus, there is more opportunity for a clash of interests between China and its mainland neighbors. For example, Chinese dam building on the upper Mekong River threatens the vital interests of other riparian states by reducing the flow of water and the supply of fish. China also has a close economic and security relationship with Myanmar's military government, which limits ASEAN's ability to influence the Burmese junta. Some Southeast Asian leaders also question the value of Chinese aid projects and have expressed doubts about whether China's promised aid will be forthcoming.[27]

Given the uncertainties about China's future relationship with its neighbors, most

Southeast Asian governments seek continued close ties with Japan, Europe, and the United States to balance China's influence in their region. Southeast Asian political elites, particularly in Malaysia and Indonesia, have been critical of the U.S. role in the Middle East, and they have been offended by the Bush administration's tendency to focus exclusively on its "war on terrorism" rather than the much broader range of political and economic interests that link the U.S. and Southeast Asia.[28] President Obama's African-American heritage and the fact that he lived in Indonesia as a child has made him a popular figure in Southeast Asia.

We began this book by noting that the goal of most Southeast Asian governments is to join the ranks of the economically advanced countries as soon as possible. The ILO demographic study cited above suggests their best window of opportunity to achieve their goal may be the years before 2025. After that, the work force in Thailand, Singapore, and Vietnam may begin to shrink as Japan's already has. Countries with a very young population like Cambodia may have more time in which to raise their peoples' living standards, but even those countries will eventually have a declining population.

Good governance is essential for economic growth. The countries with the best chance of reaching advanced economic status will be those that succeed in raising their standards of government, reducing corruption, and protecting their citizens' rights and the rule of law. If the ASEAN states can require all their members to meet certain minimum standards of governance, they will be able to maximize their influence in the Asian region and beyond.

Further Reading

Acharya, Amitav. *The Quest for Identity: International Relations in Southeast Asia.* Singapore: Oxford University Press, 2000.

Beeson, Mark, ed. *Reconfiguring East Asia: Regional Institutions and Organizations After the Crisis.* London: RoutledgeCurzon, 2003.

Callahan, William B. *Contingent States: Greater China and Transnational Relations.* Minneapolis: University of Minnesota Press, 2004.

Eisenman, Joshua, Eric Heginbotham, and Derek Mitchell, eds. *China and the Developing World: Beijing's Strategy for the Twenty-first Century.* Armonk, NY: M.E. Sharpe, 2007.

Ho, K.C., Randolph Kluver, and Kenneth C.C. Yang, eds. *Asia.com: Asia Encounters the Internet.* London and New York: RoutledgeCurzon, 2003.

Huntington, Samuel P. *The Clash of Civilizations and the Remaking of the World Order.* New York: Touchstone Books, 1997.

Lincoln, Edward J. *East Asian Economic Regionalism.* New York: Council on Foreign Relations; Washington, D.C.: Brookings Institution Press, 2004.

Tan, See Seng, and Amitav Acharya, eds. *Asia-Pacific Security Cooperation.* Armonk, NY: M.E. Sharpe, 2004.

Weatherbee, Donald E. *The International Relations of Southeast Asia.* Lanham, MD: Rowman & Littlefield, 2005.

GLOSSARY

Country Abbreviations

All—all Southeast Asia	M—Malaysia	T—Thailand
B—Brunei	My—Myanmar	V—Vietnam
C—Cambodia	P—Philippines	
I—Indonesia	S—Singapore	

Abangan — Indonesian Muslims whose faith includes elements of Hinduism or native animism. (I)

adat — Malay customary law. (B, I, M, S)

Angkor — capital of Khmer empire from A.D. 802 to 1431. (C)

animism — the belief that natural objects such as trees and water possess a soul.

the "ASEAN way" — a preference for addressing political problems through informal consultation and consensus-building rather than through political, military, or economic coercion.

Asian Values — Neoconfucianist system of political and social values favored by Lee Kuan Yew and other autocratic leaders in preference to western-style democracy.

Baba-Nyonya — descendants of Chinese settlers in the Straits Settlements (Melaka, Singapore, and Penang) who intermarried with Malays and adopted many Malay customs. Also known as *Peranankan* or *Straits Chinese*. (M, S, I)

Bahasa Malaysia — Malaysia's national language, which is closely related to Indonesian.

Bamar — new English-language name for the Burman ethnic group. (My)

barangay — a community, usually with a local government. (P)

Barisan Nasional — coalition of Malaysian political parties that has run the Malaysian national government (and most state governments) since it was formed in 1974.

Borobudur — in Indonesia, an enormous Buddhist temple complex built in the ninth century A.D. in Central Java. (I)

Buddha — enlightened being. The historical Buddha was an Indian prince of the sixth century B.C. who renounced his royal life and attained the highest stage of enlightenment by meditation.

Buddhism — religion based on the teachings of Buddha.

Bumiputera — literally means "Sons of the Soil" but theoretically applies to all indigenous peoples of Malaysia. In a political context, it usually refers to Malays and to the native peoples of Sabah and Sarawak, all of whom are eligible for affirmative action programs. (M)

Cao Dai — an indigenous Vietnamese religious sect. (V)

chettiar — money lender from southern India.

CLMV states — Cambodia, Laos, Myanmar, and Vietnam, the four newest and poorest members of ASEAN, which are trying to raise their living standards to the ASEAN level.

179

civil society	nongovernmental organizations concerned with social and political affairs, including the media, and religious, professional, and economic organizations.
Corvee	manual labor service required by the state. (V, L, C, My)
dato	traditionally refers to a village chief in the Philippines. It is now a title bestowed by the Malaysian federal or state governments to recognize outstanding public service. (P, M)
doi moi	Vietnam's renovation of its economic and foreign policies, promulgated in 1986 at the Sixth Party Congress. (V)
entrepot	a port where goods are assembled, traded and stored for transhipment.
Farang	Western; a westerner. (T) In Cambodian, the term is *barang*.
Five Power Defense Arrangement	links Australia, Britain, Malaysia, New Zealand, and Singapore.
Gestapu coup	the 1965 murder of six top Indonesian generals, apparently by disaffected elements of the military. Led to a massive pogrom in which perhaps half a million people were killed and Suharto replaced Sukarno as Indonesia's president. (I)
Greater East Asian Co-prosperity Sphere	Japan's World War II area of conquest, which included all of Southeast Asia.
Guided Democracy	authoritarian system of government instituted by President Sukarno in Indonesia in 1959. By cutting all foreign economic ties, he plunged the country into a deep recession. (I)
hajj	the pilgrimage to Mecca, one of the duties of Muslims who can afford the journey.
Hinduism	Indian religion with many gods and local cults. Shares a number of gods and concepts with Buddhism.
Hmong	Tribal group in Laos and neighboring states. They were recruited by the U.S. to fight on the anti-communist side during the second Indochina war. Many were resettled in the U.S. (L, V)
Ho Chi Minh City	commercial capital of Vietnam and largest city in South Vietnam, still often referred to as Saigon.
Islam	the religious system of the Almighty Allah according to the Prophet Mohammed. Also refers to the whole body of believers in Islam, their civilization, and their lands.
istana	palace (B, I, M, S)
Jamaah Islamiah	major terrorist movement in Southeast Asia, which is concentrated in Indonesia and Malaysia and believed to have links to al-Qaeda.
Javanese	Indonesia's politically dominant ethnolinguistic group, who are numerically dominant in East and Central Java. (I)
kampung	village; also spelled *kampong*. In urban context, it can mean a neighborhood or suburb. (B, I, M, S)
Karen	a major non–Buddhist minority group in Myanmar, many of whom are Christian.
Khmer	a Southeast Asian linguistic and ethnic group in Cambodia, Vietnam, and Thailand. Pronounced *Khmae* in the Cambodian language. (C)
Khmer Rouge	name given by Prince Sihanouk to Khmer leftists, especially Pol Pot's communist forces. (C)
madrasah	Islamic schools which offer a combination of religious and secular subjects. (I, M, B, S)
Majapahit	Hindu empire that arose in East Java and reached its peak in the 1400s before being displaced by the arrival of Islam.
Malay	In Malaysia, any inhabitant of the country is a Malay if he or she meets the constitutional definition of speaking the Malay language, professing Islam, and following Malay customs. In Indonesia, Singapore, Brunei,

	Thailand, and Cambodia, Malays are mainly identified by the fact that they speak a form of the Malay language.
mestizo	person of mixed blood or a Philippine native with Chinese blood. (P)
montagnards	hill tribes, mountain people. (C, L, V)
Mon	a Southeast Asian linguistic group in Myanmar, Thailand, and Cambodia. (My, T, C)
Moro	the Muslim minority in southern Philippines.
Muhammadiyah	modernist Muslim movement founded in Yogyakarta in 1912. Muhammadiyah has largely eschewed formal politics and concentrated on aiding people in need. Its schools provide religious education but also teach science, mathematics, and history. Strongly supported by the urban middle class. (I)
Nahdlatul Ulama	traditionalist Muslim movement founded in East Java in 1926. Unlike Muhammadiyah, NU emphasizes the privileged role of Muslim scholars as interpreters of Islamic law. NU has been active in Indonesian politics. Supported mainly by rural Indonesians. (I)
New Economic Policy	Malaysia's system of affirmative action for Malays from 1970 to 1990. Designed to equalize the economic status of Malays with that of Chinese Malaysians. Although the NEP was officially terminated in 1990, Malays continued to receive preferential treatment in business and education. (M)
New Order	Indonesian President Suharto's authoritarian form of government with heavy involvement of the military and no political opposition allowed. (I)
nongovernmental organization	organization that functions outside the direct control of government but performs social services or researches and promotes solutions to problems. May be entirely independent of government support and direction or work closely with government and receive some public funds.
orang asli	literally "original peoples," who live in the interior of the Malay peninsula and theoretically are entitled to affirmative action because they are "indigenous." (M)
Overseas Chinese	ethnic Chinese who migrated into Southeast Asia by sea mainly during the last two centuries (as distinct from those people who migrated overland from China during much earlier centuries). In many cases, the overseas Chinese were initially recruited as laborers by the European colonial regimes, but they now play a major economic role in the economies of most Southeast Asian countries. (All)
Pagan	capital of a Buddhist empire from 1044 to 1207 in what is now Myanmar. Spelled "Bagan" by the current Burmese regime. (My)
Pancasila	secular Indonesian ideology favored by Presidents Sukarno, Suharto and now Yudhoyono, who have opposed making Indonesia an Islamic state. The five principles of Pancasila are monotheism, humanitarianism, national unity, democracy by consensus, and social justice. (I)
pasar	market (I, M). In Cambodian, the word is *psar.*
patron-client relations	system of supposedly mutual obligations between an influential member of the community (patron) and his followers. The patron is expected to provide protection and other favors in return for political support and possibly other services by his followers. System functions to varying degrees throughout Southeast Asia. (All)
people power revolutions	Philippine popular uprisings in Manila, supported by the Catholic Church and the army, which overthrew President Marcos in 1986 and President Estrada in 2001. (P)
Peranankan	see *Baba-Nyonga.*
Pribumi	literally "Sons of the Soil." Also refers to the indigenous peoples of Indonesia, but ethnic Chinese are usually excluded from this category no matter how long their families have lived in Indonesia. (I)

priyayi	Javanese aristocrats with a rigid code of personal behavior, which involves never showing anger or other strong emotions. (I)
Ramayana	the Indian epic story of Rama's battle with the demons, which forms the theme of much Southeast Asian drama and dance. The Thai version is called *Ramakian*.
Reformasi	primarily political reform movement that caused the fall of Indonesian President Suharto in 1998.
Straits Settlements	Penang, Singapore, and Melaka (formerly spelled Malacca), which were brought together for administrative purposes in 1826, with Singapore becoming the administrative center in 1832.
Sukhothai	city in north-central Thailand that was a major Buddhist center. From 1257 to 1379, it was the first major capital of what is now Thailand. (T)
Sangha	Buddhist clergy in Myanmar, Thailand and other primarily Buddhist countries.
Santri	Indonesian Muslims who have studied their religion and are observant of Islamic rules and restrictions. (I)
security community	a regional grouping of nations in which the possibility of one member attacking another has been virtually eliminated.
semi-democracy	a system in which a dominant political party rules a country but allows some leeway for the expression of opposition viewpoints in the media and by opposition parties in election campaigns. Opposition parties exist at the pleasure of the ruling party, but the electoral laws are stacked against them.
Shari'ah	Islamic law (also spelled Syariah).
Siam	the name for the Siamese-Thai kingdom until 1939, when it was changed to Thailand. (T)
Srivijaya	Buddhist empire that ruled southern Sumatra and much of the Malay peninsula from the 7th to the 12th centuries A.D. (M, I)
Sudanese	second largest ethnolinguistic group in Indonesia, concentrated in West Java. (I)
swidden	method of preparing land for agriculture by felling trees and brush and burning them before planting seeds. (All)
Tai or T'ai	A large linguistic group of people who have settled in Thailand, Laos, China, Vietnam, Cambodia, Myanmar, and Malaysia.
Tatmadaw	armed forces in Myanmar who have governed the country since 1962. Literally the "royal military." (My)
Thai	a citizen of Thailand. Also the national language of Thailand. (T)
Totok	unassimilated Chinese in Indonesia. (I)
Tunku	Malay title for male, non-reigning royalty, roughly equivalent to "prince." (M)
Viet Minh	Launched in 1941 by the Indochina Communist Party to unite all strata of Vietnamese society behind a national liberation policy. (V)
Visiting Forces Agreement	approved by the Philippine Congress in 1999, the VFA includes joint military training and exercises. It also provides a framework for U.S. aid to modernize and strengthen the Philippine military forces.
Wat	Buddhist temple-monastery. (C, L, T)
Yangon	official English-language name for Myanmar's capital city, although the old name, Rangoon, is still widely used. (My)

ABBREVIATIONS
AND ACRONYMS

ABRI	Armed Forces of Indonesia (former name)
ADB	Asian Development Bank
AEC	ASEAN Economic Community
AEMM	ASEAN-EU Ministerial Meeting
AFP	Armed Forces of the Philippines
AFTA	ASEAN Free Trade Area
AMM	ASEAN Ministerial Meeting
APEC	Asia Pacific Economic Cooperation
ARF	ASEAN Regional Forum
ASC	ASEAN Security Community
ASCC	ASEAN Social and Cultural Community
ASEAN	Association of Southeast Asian Nations
ASEAN ISIS	ASEAN Institutes of Strategic and International Study
ASEM	Asia-Europe Meeting (ASEAN and the EU)
BIMP-EAGA	Brunei, Indonesia, Malaysia, Philippines, East ASEAN Growth Area
BN	Barisan Nasional (Malaysia)
BSPP	Burmese Socialist Program Party
CGI	Concultative Group on Indonesia
CLMV	Cambodia, Laos, Myanmar, and Vietnam (development grouping)
CPP	Communist Party of the Philippines; also, Cambodian People's Party
EAEC	East Asia Economic Caucus
EEZ	Exclusive economic zone
FDI	foreign direct investment
FPDA	Five Power Defense Arrangement (Australia, Great Britain, Malaysia, New Zealand, Singapore)
FRETILIN	Frente Revolutionaria do Timor Leste Independente
FTA	Free Trade Agreement
FUNCINPEC	United National Front for an Independent, Peaceful, and Cooperative Cambodia
GAM	Free Aceh Movement (Indonesia)
GATS	General Agreement on Trade in Services
GDP	Gross Domestic Product
GNP	Gross National Product
IBRD	International Bank for Reconstruction and Development (World Bank)
ICJ	International Court of Justice (World Court)
ILO	International Labor Organization
INGO	international non-governmental organization
INTERFET	International Force for East Timor

IMF	International Monetary Fund
JI	Jem'aah Islamiyah (terrorist organization)
KPRP	Khmer People's Revolutionary Party
KR	Khmer Rouge (Cambodia)
LPDR	Lao People's Democratic Republic
LPRP	Lao People's Revolutionary Party
MCA	Malayan Chinese Association
MIC	Malayan Indian Congress
MILF	Moro Islamic Liberation Front (Philippines)
MNLF	Moro National Liberation Front (Philippines)
MP	Member of Parliament
MPR	Indonesian Parliament, which includes: the DPD — Council of Provincial Representatives (upper house); and DPR — Council of People's Representatives (lower house)
MRC	Mekong River Commission
NAM	Nonaligned Movement
NDF	National Democratic Front (Philippines)
NEP	New Economic Policy (Malaysia)
NGO	nongovernmental organization
NIC	newly industrialized country
NLD	National League for Democracy (Myanmar)
NPA	New People's Army (Philippines)
NU	Nahdlatul Ulama (Indonesian traditional Muslim organization)
NUP	National Unity Party (Myanmar)
ODA	official development assistance
OIC	Organization of Islamic Countries
OPM	Free Papua Organization (Indonesia)
PAP	People's Action Party (Singapore)
PAS	Partai Islam Se-Malaysia — the Islamic Party of Malaysia
PAVN	People's Army of Vietnam
PDI-P	Indonesian Democratic Party-Struggle
PKI	Communist Party of Indonesia
PNG	Papua New Guinea
PRC	People's Republic of China
PRK	People's Republic of Kampuchea
PULO	Pattani United Liberation Organization (Thailand)
SLORC	State Law and Order Restoration Council (Myanmar)
SOM	Senior Officials Meeting (ASEAN)
SPDC	State Peace and Development Council (Myanmar)
TAC	Treaty of Amity and Cooperation in Southeast Asia
TNI	Indonesian armed forces (current name)
UMNO	United Malay Nationalist Organization (Malaysia)
UNDP	United Nations Development Program
UNHCHR	United Nations High Commissioner for Human Rights
UNHCR	United Nations High Commissioner for Refugees
UNTAC	United Nations Transitional Authority in Cambodia
UNTAET	United Nations Transitional Authority for East Timor
VCP	Vietnamese Communist Party
VFA	Visiting Forces Agreement (U.S.–Philippines)
WTO	World Trade Organization
ZOPFAN	Zone of Peace, Freedom, and Neutrality (ASEAN)

CHAPTER NOTES

Introduction

1. World Bank, "East Asia & Pacific Update," April 2007, pp. 25–31. Thailand, Malaysia, Indonesia, and the Philippines meet the World Bank's definition of "middle-income" countries. Vietnam may join this group in a few years. Singapore and Brunei are wealthier than the middle income states, but their tightly-controlled political and social systems limit the creativity of their citizens.

2. Because of demographic factors, the best window for achieving this goal may be the years before 2025. After that, the working age population in many Asian countries (including China) will begin to shrink. Andrew Taylor, "Asian Economies Near 'Demographic Cliff,'" *Financial Times*, August 13, 2007.

3. Howard Crouch, *Government and Society in Malaysia*, pp. 95–97.

4. Former Prime Minister Thaksin of Thailand made no secret of his aim to make his party the permanent majority party.

5. The Burmese military junta developed a constitution that would allow them to retain control of the government.

6. Amy Kazmin, "Calling the Shots, Thais Vote on a Military-Backed Constitution," *Financial Times*, August 16, 2007.

7. The heads of these governments were mainly absorbed with domestic issues, and they tended to leave the management of ASEAN to their foreign ministers until the 1980s.

8. John H. Miller, *Modern East Asia, An Introductory History*, pp. 177–79.

9. Ironically, this placed them squarely in the middle of the major power struggle for control of Indochina.

10. Miller, *Modern East Asia*, p. 179.

11. Donald E. Weatherbee, *International Relations in Southeast Asia*, pp. 69–79.

12. World Bank, "The East Asian Miracle: Economic Growth and Public Policy."

Chapter 1

1. "Thailand's Prime Minister, a 'Caretaker' on a Roll," *Washington Post*, September 16, 2006. The article, published three days before the coup, quoted Anand Panyarachun, a highly respected diplomat who was close to the king, as saying the country under Thaksin's rule was in danger of becoming a "failed state." For background on tensions between Thaksin and the military, see Duncan McCargo and Ukrist Pathmanand, *The Thaksinization of Thailand* (Copenhagen: Nordic Institute of Asian Studies, 2005), pp. 248–53.

2. "Thailand in Grip of Economic Nationalism," *Financial Times*, February 27, 2007.

3. Seth Mydans, "Thais to Vote on a Constitution That Would Restore Civilian Rule in Diluted Form," *New York Times*, August 18, 2007. Economics Professor Pasuk Pongpaichit, who briefly served as an advisor to the interim government, was quoted by Mydans as saying the constitution would lead to a form of "managed democracy" with military oversight of political activity at all levels. See also Seth Mydans, "New Thai Constitution Paves Way for Vote," *New York Times*, August 20, 2007.

4. Since 2005, the Democrat Party has regained some of the support it lost to Thaksin in Bangkok and the central region. It won 164 seats in the December 2007 election, while the governing coalition won 316 seats.

5. Supang Chantavanich, "From Siamese-Chinese to Chinese-Thai," in Suryadinata, ed., *Ethnic Chinese as Southeast Asians*, pp. 254–57.

6. David Brown, *State and Ethnic Politics in Southeast Asia*, 1994, pp. 170–73.

7. Seth Mydans, "Thai Vote Shows Divisions Among Classes Is Simmering," *New York Times*, August 21, 2007.

8. Peter A. Poole, *The Vietnamese in Thailand*, pp. 97–127.

9. "Thailand: Insurgency's High Toll in 2007," *Washington Post*, January 8, 2008. The research group's tally was compiled from news media and police and army reports.

10. "Thaksin Backers Suspected in Arson Attacks," *Financial Times*, September. 28, 2006, and "Thai Islamic Insurgency Escalates," *Financial Times*, July 27, 2007.

11. Frank M. Lebar, Gerald C. Hickey, and John K. Musgrave, *Ethnic Groups of Mainland Southeast Asia* pp. 202–03.

12. Ruth McVey, ed., *Money and Power in Provincial Thailand* (Honolulu: University of Hawai'i Press, 2000), describes a free-wheeling culture in provincial towns.

13. James Ockey, in *Making Democracy* (Honolulu: University of Hawai'i Press, 2004), pp. 151–71, argues that middle-class Thais do not always support democracy.

14. See Peter A. Jackson, *Buddhadasa: A Buddhist Thinker for the Modern World* (Bangkok: Siam Society, 1988).

15. Walter F. Vella, *The Impact of the West on Government in Thailand*, p. 349.

16. For background on the period, see Kenneth P. Landon, *Siam in Transition*, 2d ed. (Westport, CT: Greenwood Press, 1969). (First published in 1939 by Kelly and Walsh in Shanghai.)

17. Fred W. Riggs, *Thailand: Modernization of a Bureaucratic Polity*, pp. 91–119.

18. Sarit, who was highly autocratic and corrupt, amassed a huge fortune while in office, but he also laid the groundwork for the country's economic transformation. King Bhumibol developed the modern institution of monarchy during Sarit's administration.

19. John L.S. Girling, *Thailand, Society and Politics*, p. 215.

20. Prem was widely viewed as one of the main instigators of the 2006 coup. Some critics of the king's support for the 2006 coup took the safer course of demonstrating against Prem's role and criticizing him on the Internet.

21. Pasuk Phongpaichit and Chris Baker, *Thailand, Economy and Politics*, pp. 373–80.

22. Ibid., pp. 427–31.

23. Ibid., pp. 445–49.

24. "New Prime Minister Says Sorry to Muslims in South," *Financial Times*, November 3, 2006.

25. McCargo and Pathmanand, *The Thaksinization of Thailand*, pp. 130–31.

26. "Thais Face New Poll as Election Result is Quashed," *Financial Times*, May 9, 2006.

27. Amy Kazmin, "Calling the Shots, Thais Vote on a Military-backed Constitution," *Financial Times*, August 16, 2007.

28. The degree requirement made most Thais ineligible to run for parliament.

29. With his huge fortune, Thaksin began bribing people to switch parties long before the election, but he stopped in time to comply with the letter of the law.

30. Pasuk Phongpaichit and Chris Baker, *Thaksin and the Business of Politics in Thailand*, pp. 173–76.

31. McCargo and Pathmanand, *Thaksinization*, p. 213.

32. Ibid., pp. 134–57.

33. Ibid., pp. 121–57.

34. Pasuk Phongpaichit and Sungsidh Piriyarangsan, *Corruption and Democracy in Thailand*, pp. 99–120.

35. The Democrats, who ruled during most of the 1990s, won only half as many seats as Thaksin's party.

36. Pasuk and Baker, *Thaksin and the Business of Politics in Thailand*, pp. 173–76.

37. "Thailand's Turmoil," *Financial Times*, May 24, 2006.

38. "Thaksin Looms Large as Referendum Clears Way for Poll," *Financial Times*, August 21, 2007, and "New Thai Premier Seen as Thaksin's Proxy," *Financial Times*, January 29, 2008.

39. David Brown, *State and Ethnic Politics in Southeast Asia*, p. 199, says the Isan became pro-military in the 1980s because of aid provided by the military, and they later switched their allegiance to Thaksin because he was more generous.

40. The Democrat Party is Thailand's oldest political party, and it has generally been on the side of limiting the army's involvement in politics. The Democrats played a major role in drafting the 1997 reform constitution.

41. Economist Intelligence Unit, "Thailand, Country Report," February 2008, p. 5. See also Amy Kazmin, "Thais 'to End Chaos with Fiscal Policy,'" *Financial Times*, April 16, 2007, regarding the economic problems caused by the interim government.

42. Pasuk and Baker, *Thailand, Economy and Politics*, pp. 385–416. For background on Dr. Puey Ungphakorn, see his article "Violence and the Military Coup in Thailand," *Bulletin of Concerned Asian Scholars* 9 (5), 1977.

43. Pasuk and Baker, *Thailand, Economy and Politics*, pp. 293–97.

44. Over 600,000 Thais live with HIV or AIDS, according to the U.S. State Department, "Background Notes, Thailand," Washington, D.C., 2007.

45. "Disgruntled Media Baron is Bad News for Thai Premier," *Financial Times*, November 28, 2005.

46. "Chat Room Opens after Ban," *Financial Times*, April 12, 2007.

47. Growth averaged 5 percent in the first 6 years of the new century, somewhat below the ASEAN average of 5.5 percent.

48. Thaksin's critics said the credit card forgiveness scheme would only encourage people to run up more debt.

49. The new airport seemed likely to make Bangkok a strong competitor with Singapore for the role of regional transport hub.

50. "Rural Thais Urged Toward Greater Self-sufficiency," *Financial Times*, May 4, 2007.

51. See "Self-sufficiency in Rice Put in Question After Delta Destroyed," *Financial Times*, May 8, 2008.

52. Weatherbee, *International Relations in Southeast Asia*, pp. 77–83.

53. Ibid., pp. 91–92, 97, and 227–32.

54. "Thai-Singapore Axis Set to Unravel," *Financial Times*, September 21, 2006.

55. In May 1975, U.S. forces based in Thailand rescued the crew of a ship called the *Mayaguez*. The Thai government protested the failure of the U.S. to consult with them before mounting the operation. This may have reflected Thai pique at the hasty departure of U.S. forces from the region. Peter A. Poole, *Eight Presidents and Indochina*, 2d ed. (New York, Kreiger 1988), pp. 235–36.

56. U.S. Department of State, "Background Notes, Thailand," October 2007.

57. "ASEAN Nears Pact on Anti-terrorism," *Financial Times*, November 7, 2006.

58. "Free Trade with China Sparks Anxiety in North," *The Nations*, Bangkok, March 8, 2004. For a discussion of the implications of an ASEAN-China Free Trade Agreement, see Weatherbee, *International Relations in Southeast Asia*, pp. 209–11.

Chapter 2

1. From 1993 to 2003, Vietnam's growth rate averaged 7.4 percent a year, and the number of people living in poverty was reduced from 58 percent of the population in 1993 to 28 percent in 2003. By 2007, the percentage of people living at or below the $2 per day level (the World Bank's measure of poverty) was lower in Vietnam than in Indonesia or the Philippines. World Bank, *East Asia and Pacific Update*, April 2007, pp. 57–59.

2. Brian Van Arkadie and Raymond Mallon, *Vietnam: A Transition Tiger?*, pp. 252–66.

3. Ta Huu Phuong, "Comments on 'Ethnic Chinese in Vietnam,'" in Suryadinata, ed., *Ethnic Chinese as Southeast Asians*, pp. 293–95.

4. Dang Nghiem Van, Chu Tai Son, and Luu Hung, *Ethnic Minorities in Vietnam* (Hanoi: The Gioi Press, 2000), pp. 266–75, provides figures from a 1994 survey.

5. Sophie Quinn-Judge, "Rethinking the History," in McCargo ed., *Rethinking Vietnam*, p. 37; Abuza, *Renovating Politics in Contemporary Vietnam*, p. 156, note 17.

6. Carlyle Thayer, "Vietnam in 2001," *Asian Survey*, January-February 2002, pp. 81–89.

7. Interviews with Vietnamese and Cambodian officials.

8. Greg Fealy, "Islam in Southeast Asia," in Beeson, ed., *Contemporary Southeast Asia*. See also Lebar, Hickey and Musgrave, *Ethnic Groups of Mainland Southeast Asia*, pp. 245–48.

9. Hy V. Luong, "Vietnam in 2005," *Asian Survey*, January-February 2006, pp. 148–53. In 2005, the government approved spending 62 trillion dong (U.S. $4 million) on village healthcare and education in the poorest provinces where many of the hill tribes are located.

10. Jonathan London, "Rethinking Vietnam's Mass Education and Health Systems," in McCargo, ed., *Rethinking Vietnam*, pp. 140–41.

11. Alan Riding, "Vietnamese Writer Won't Be Silenced," *New York Times*, July 11, 2005, and Seth Mydans, "Shunned, Women With HIV Join Forces in Vietnam," *New York Times*, May 28, 2006.

12. Phuong An Nguyen, "Pursuing Success in Contemporary Vietnam," in McCargo, ed., *Rethinking Vietnam*, pp. 165–76, and Economist Intelligence Unit, "Vietnam, Country Report," April 2006, p. 19.

13. Zachary Abuza, *Renovating Politics in Contemporary Vietnam*, pp. 183–206.

14. Ibid., pp. 203–4.

15. Gerald Hickey, *Village in Vietnam*, pp. 276–85.

16. Joseph Buttinger, *Vietnam: A Political History*, pp. 176–85.

17. Hoang Van Chi, *From Colonialism to Communism, A Case History of North Vietnam*, pp. 33–34.

18. Bernard Fall, *Viet-Nam Witness*, pp. 160–89.

19. Peter A. Poole, *Eight Presidents and Indochina*, 2d ed, pp. 175–83.

20. Nayan Chanda, *Brother Enemy*, pp. 341–62. Prince Norodom Sihanouk, Cambodia's leader in the 1960s, gave the Cambodian communist guerrillas the name "Khmer Rouge."

21. Lewis Stern, *Renovating the Vietnamese Communist Party, Nguyen Van Linh and the Programme for Organizational Reform, 1987–91*, pp. 5–26.

22. Foreign Minister Nguyen Co Thach, who strongly favored joining ASEAN and normalizing relations with the U.S., was forced out of the Politburo and government by conservative rivals in 1991 when his efforts failed to bring quick results.

23. For a useful discussion of governance issues raised at the Tenth Party Congress in 2006, see, Hy V. Luong, "Vietnam in 2006," *Asian Survey*, January-February 2007, pp. 168–74.

24. Nong Duc Manh's official biography is provided at the web site of the Vietnamese embassy in Washington, D.C., www.vietnamembassy-usa.org.

25. *Europa World Year Book 2006*, p. 4,826.

26. Between 2000 and 2005, trade between Vietnam and China quadrupled to $8 billion.

27. Carlyle Thayer, "Vietnam in 2001," *Asian Survey*, January-February 2002, pp. 84–86.

28. Sophie Quinn-Judge, "History of the Vietnamese Communist Party," in McCargo, ed., *Rethinking Vietnam*, pp. 27–37.

29. See William Duiker's biography *Ho Chi Minh* (St. Leonards, Australia: Allen & Unwin, 2000).

30. *Europa World Year Book 2006*, p. 4,832.

31. Ibid., p. 4,827.

32. For example, in 2002, fifty police officers were put on trial for accepting bribes to protect organized crime gangs, and the deputy minister of Public Security was dismissed for his involvement in the matter.

33. Ibid., p. 4,828.

34. Ibid., p. 4,827.

35. Secretary-General Nguyen Van Linh threw his weight behind Do Muoi, ensuring his victory.

36. *Europa World Year Book 2006*, p. 4,828.

37. Ibid., p. 4,825. The judge was sentenced to two years in prison.

38. Abuza, *Renovating Politics in Contemporary Vietnam*, p. 206.

39. Joerg Wischermann, "Vietnam in the Era of *Doi Moi*," *Asian Survey*, November-December 2003, pp. 867–89.

40. The dissident United Buddhist Church of Vietnam angered the VCP by organizing a relief effort to help victims of a major flood along the Mekong River in 1994.

41. Wischermann, "Vietnam in the Era of *Doi Moi*," *Asian Survey*, pp. 885–87.

42. Alan Sipress, "Vietnam's Freer Press Sharpens Its Teeth on Bird Flu Story," *Washington Post*, November 20, 2005, p. A27.

43. *Europa World Year Book 2006*, p. 4,827 and 4,828.

44. International Telecommunications Union statistics.

45. Tran Thi Thu Trang, "Vietnam's Rural Transformation: Information, Knowledge and Diversification," in McCargo, ed., *Rethinking Vietnam*, pp. 120–21.

46. In 2004, just under one million workers were classified as unemployed out of a total work force of 43.2 million.

47. Van Arkadie and Mallon, *Vietnam: A Transition Tiger?*, pp. 252–66.

48. Vietnam's Economy: The Good Pupil," *Economist*, May 8, 2004, pp. 39–40.

49. Amy Kazmin, "Meat Off the Menu as Vietnamese Workers Feel Economic Strains," *Financial Times*, April 24, 2008.

50. Economist Intelligence Unit, "Vietnam, Country Report," April 2006, p. 14. Because local universities are not free to raise their academic standards, the minister planned to send 400 students to foreign universities between 2006 and 2010.

51. ASEAN's middle-income countries (Thailand, Malaysia, Indonesia, and the Philippines) all have similar problems.

52. Economist Intelligence Unit, "Vietnam, Country Report," April 2007, p. 19. In 2005, industrial output in non-state industries financed locally rose 24.1 percent, compared with 8.7 percent in state industries, and 20.9 percent in foreign-invested firms.

53. Carlyle A. Thayer and Ramses Amer, *Vietnamese Foreign Policy in Transition*, p. 19.

54. Vietnam was elected to the UN Security Council in October 2007 and began a two-year term on the Council in January 2008.

55. Weatherbee, *International Relations in Southeast Asia*, pp. 80–83.

56. From 2001 to 2005, the Vietnamese and Cambodian governments engaged in difficult negotiations over the status of more than a thousand hill tribesmen who were given temporary refuge in Cambodia. The U.S. government and the UN High Commissioner for Refugees sometimes participated in the negotiations, which eventually led to the repatriation of many of the tribesmen to Vietnam and the settlement of others in the U.S., Finland, and Canada. *Europa World Year Book 2006*, p. 4,829.

57. Economist Intelligence Unit, "Vietnam, Country Report," April 2006, p. 15. Laos publicly honored Vietnamese cryptographers for "helping ensure the supply of clandestine ... information."

58. Jorn Dosch and Ta Minh Tuan, "Recent Changes in Vietnamese Foreign Policy," in McCargo, ed., *Rethinking Vietnam*, pp. 197–213.

59. U.S. Department of State, "Background Notes, Vietnam," Washington, D.C., December 2007.

Chapter 3

1. Sorpong Peou, *Intervention and Change in Cambodia, Towards Democracy?*, pp. 409–29.

2. Ben Kiernan, *The Pol Pot Regime*, pp. 456–63.

3. Seth Mydans, "Big Oil in Tiny Cambodia: The Burden of New Wealth," *New York Times*, May 5, 2007. The "semi-democratic" freedoms include limited press freedom, tolerance for NGOs, and the right of opposition parties to take part in elections.

4. Economist Intelligence Unit, "Cambodia, Country Report," August 2009, p. 10.

5. Ian Brown, *Cambodia: An Oxfam Country Profile*, pp. 49–53.

6. Baldas Goshal and Jae H. Ku, *Minorities in Cambodia*, pp. 26–29.

7. Ben Kiernan, *The Pol Pot Regime*, p. 458.

8. Despite the pogroms and expulsions of Vietnamese during the Lon Nol years, Kiernan's estimate of only 20,000 Vietnamese remaining in Cambodia when the KR took over in 1975 may be too low. By my calculations, there were about 165,000 Vietnamese in Cambodia as late as 1973. During a visit to Cambodia in 1973, I spoke with a variety of sources about the Vietnamese minority in Cambodia, and we estimated there were more than 100,000 Vietnamese in the country at that time. See P.A. Poole, "Communism and Ethnic Conflict in Cambodia, 1960–1975," in Zasloff and Brown, eds., *Communism in Indochina*, pp. 249–55.

9. Evan Gottesman, *Cambodia After the Khmer Rouge*, pp. 143 and 316–35.

10. Ramses Amer, "The Ethnic Vietnamese in Cambodia: A Minority at Risk?," in Peou, ed., pp. 447–75.

11. Gottesman, *Cambodia After the Khmer Rouge*, pp. 170–87.

12. Lebar, Hickey, and Musgrave, *Ethnic Groups of Mainland Southeast Asia*, pp. 248–49.

13. Baldas Goshal and Joe H. Ku, *Minorities in China*, pp. 10–11.

14. Ibid., pp. 12–13.

15. Kyoko Kusakabe, Wang Yunxian and Govind Kelkar, "Women and Land Rights in Cambodia," pp. 425–30.

16. Judy Ledgerwood, "Politics and Gender," in Ledgerwood, ed., pp. 411–24.

17. David P. Chandler, *A History of Cambodia*, 2d ed., pp. 97–98.

18. Milton Osborne, *The French Presence in Cochinchina and Cambodia*, pp. 211–14.

19. Milton Osborne, *Sihanouk, Prince of Light, Prince of Darkness*, pp. 72–78.

20. Chandler, *A History of Cambodia*, p. 198.

21. Poole, *Eight Presidents and Indochina*, pp. 206–16.

22. Ibid., pp. 231–32. Lon Nol was evacuated, but members of his regime who stayed behind were executed by the KR.

23. Among the first-hand accounts by Cambodian survivors of this nightmarish period, Haing Ngor's *Survival in the Killing Fields* is one of the most vivid.

24. Nayan Chanda's *Brother Enemy: The War After the War* (New York: Harcourt Brace Jovanovich, 1986) provides the most complete record of the wars and diplomacy in the decade after the fall of Saigon.

25. Gottesman, *Cambodia After the Khmer Rouge*, pp. 316–35. After the Vietnamese withdrew their forces in 1989, the PRK changed its name to the State of Cambodia and (following Hanoi's example) adopted some free market practices which increased economic growth. It also enabled Hun Sen and other leaders to enrich themselves because they controlled the awarding of contracts and business licenses.

26. Erika Kinetz, "In Cambodia, a Clash Over History of the Khmer Rouge," *New York Times*, May 8, 2007.

27. Curtis, *Cambodia Reborn?*, pp. 7–14.

28. FUNCINPEC officials were barred from many provincial offices and had to work from hotel rooms, but being part of the coalition gave them some opportunities to strengthen their party's electoral position.

29. MacAlister Brown and Joseph J. Zasloff, *Cambodia Confounds the Peacemakers*, pp. 211–15 and 262–68.

30. During the 1980s, the Vietnamese occupation helped Hun Sen's PRK regime establish tight political control down to the village level. Their control was not relaxed in the 1990s, so Hun Sen's government could afford to conduct the 1998 elections in a manner that foreign observers certified as fair.

31. According to Brown and Zasloff, *Cambodia Confounds the Peacemakers*, pp. 201–04, Sihanouk was rumored at one time to have prostate cancer and leukemia, but he was believed to be in remission by 1996.

32. King Sihamoni is the son of Monique, Sihanouk's principal wife, who reportedly urged that he become king.

33. Brown and Zasloff, *Cambodia Confounds the Peacemakers*, pp. 247–48.

34. In 2006, Ranariddh resigned from his National Assembly position; Chea Sim was regarded as one of the two most powerful men in Cambodia (along with Hun Sen), but he was much older than Hun Sen and in poor health.

35. Brown and Zasloff, *Cambodia Confounds the Peacemakers*, pp. 218–19.

36. Ibid., pp. 240–44. In 1997, a political demonstration by Rainsy's party was attacked by hooligans

who tossed hand grenades into the crowd, killing sixteen people and wounding about a hundred. Sam Rainsy accused Hun Sen of ordering the attack.

37. Sam Rainsy has strong support among young, educated Cambodians, and he is admired by foreign diplomats and aid workers for his reformist views and courage in expressing them.

38. Gottesman, *Cambodia After Khmer Rouge*, p. 345.

39. Economist Intelligence Unit, "Cambodia, Country Report," November 2006, p. 1.

40. Brown and Zasloff, *Cambodia Confounds the Peacemakers*, pp. 219–20.

41. See David P. Chandler, *Brother Number One: Biography of Pol Pot*. A useful source of information about the tribunal is the Document Center in Phnom Penh that is partly funded by the United States. Its web site is www.dccam.org.

42. John Marston, "Cambodian New Media in the UNTAC Period and After," pp. 239–41.

43. Their web sites were www.phnompenhdaily.com.kh and www.phnompenhpost.com.

44. Curtis, *Cambodia Reborn?*, pp. 110–45.

45. World Bank, "Asia & Pacific Update," April 2007, p. 57. See also Melanie Beresford, "Cambodia in 2004, an Artificial Democratization," *Asian Survey*, January-February 2005, pp. 134–39.

46. Economist Intelligence Unit, "Cambodia, Country Report," November 2006, notes that Cambodia's garment exports rose 27.5 percent in the first half of 2006 but grew much more slowly in the second half of the year.

47. See note 3 above. In other oil and gas producing states (e.g., Malaysia, Indonesia, Myanmar, and Brunei), the revenue has sometimes been a mixed blessing, as discussed in those country chapters.

48. Amy Kazmin, "A Land Where Stealing Food from the Poor is Big Business," *Financial Times*, September 10, 2004.

49. Economist Intelligence Unit, "Cambodia, Country Report," August 2007, pp. 4–5.

50. Weatherbee, *International Relations in Southeast Asia*, p. 28.

51. Ibid., p. 233.

52. See note 8.

53. Interviews with Japanese and Western diplomats.

54. In March 2006, Rainsy was pardoned and his colleague released as part of a series of actions by Hun Sen apparently aimed at impressing Western aid donors. "Cambodia Moves Toward Openess," *Washington Post*, March 10, 2006.

55. Brown and Zasloff, *Cambodia Confounds the Peacemakers*, p. 268.

56. Ibid., pp. 247–48.

57. U.S. Department of State, "Background Notes, Cambodia," December 2007.

Chapter 4

1. Economist Intelligence Unit, "Laos, Country Report," July 2007, pp. 12–13 and EIU, "Laos, Country Report," January 2008, pp. 7 and 12.

2. For example, both governments increased their controls over religious groups in 2007. EIU, July 2007, p. 14.

3. World Bank, "Asia and Pacific Update," April 2007, p. 57.

4. Vatthana Pholsena, "Laos in 2004. Towards Subregional Integration: 10 Years On," in *Southeast Asian Affairs 2005*, pp. 173–88.

5. W. Courtland Robinson, "Laotian Refugees in Thailand: The Thai and US Response, 1975–1988," in Zasloff and Unger, eds., pp. 215–40.

6. Economist Intelligence Unit, "Laos, Country Report," 2006, p. 6.

7. Ng Shui Meng, "Social Development in the People's Democratic Republic," in Zasloff and Unger, eds., pp. 173–79.

8. Interviews with Laotian and U.S. officials.

9. Between 1975 and 1988, 206,660 Lao sought refuge in Thailand, according to Robinson, "Laotian Refugees in Thailand," in Zasloff and Unger, eds., pp. 236–37.

10. Arthur J. Dommen, *Laos, Keystone of Indochina*, pp. 26–27.

11. Ibid., pp. 28–39. The Vietnamese numbered 40,000 by 1949, but in the final years of the first Indochina war, they began to leave, some settling in Thailand and some in Vietnam.

12. MacAlister Brown, "Communists in Coalition Governments: Lessons from Laos," in Zasloff and Unger, eds., pp. 41–63.

13. In 2007, ten people were arrested in the United States on charges of violating the U.S. Neutrality Act by plotting to overthrow the government of Laos. Among those arrested was Vang Pao, who had led Hmong troops in alliance with the United States during the Indochina war.

14. According to the Economist Intelligence Unit, "Laos, Country Report," 2006, p. 8, Choummaly's involvement in expanding the army's economic activities has given him a stake in the reform process.

15. Ibid, p. 7.

16. *Europa World Year Book 2005*, p. 2,623.

17. Interviews with U.S. and World Bank officials.

18. Economist Intelligence Unit, "Laos, Country Report," 2006, p. 8.

19. *Europa World Year Book 2005*, pp. 2,630–31.

20. Ibid., pp. 2,631–32. The website of the *Vientiane Times* is www.vientianetimes.org.la.

21. *Europa World Year Book 2005*, p. 2,632.

22. Jose L. Tongzon, *The Economies of Southeast Asia*, 2d ed., pp. 163 and 207.

23. Geoffrey C. Gunn, "Laos in 2006, Changing the Guard," pp. 185–86.

24. Economist Intelligence Unit, "Laos, Country Report," 2006, p. 22. These problems have not changed much over the years. See Joseph J. Zasloff, "Political Constraints on Development in Laos," pp. 3–40.

25. Pholsena, "Laos in 2004. Toward Subregional Integration: 10 Years On," in *Southeast Asian Affairs 2005*, p. 177.

26. Ibid., pp. 177–79. According to Geoffrey C. Gunn, "Laos in 2006," pp. 185–86, the Nam Theun 2 dam project would require moving some 100,000 people off their land.

27. Economist Intelligent Unit, "Laos, Country Report," 2006, pp. 26–27.

28. Martin Stuart-Fox, "Laos: Toward Subregional Integration," in *Southeast Asian Affairs 1995*, pp. 179–86.

29. Economist Intelligence Unit, "Laos, Country Report," April 2006, p. 13.

30. U.S. Department of State, "Background Notes, Laos," August 2007 and interviews with U.S. officials.

Chapter 5

1. After seizing power in 1988, the military junta known as SLORC (State Law and Order Restoraton Council) changed the English-language name of Burma to Myanmar, and the names of Rangoon and other towns and rivers were also changed. Except for Myanmar, the traditional names are used in this book.

2. Thant Myint-U, *The River of Lost Footsteps, Histories of Burma*, pp. 342–48.

3. "Revolt Presents ASEAN with its Greatest Challenge," *Financial Times*, September 29, 2007. Singapore's Goh Chok Tong said Suu Kyi must be allowed to take part in the election.

4. "UN Sends Top Official to Burma Amid Fears of Humanitarian Crisis," *Financial Times*, May 18, 2006.

5. Michael A. Aung-Thwin, *The Mists of Ramanna, The Legend That Was Lower Burma*, pp. 1–12.

6. Thant Myint-U, *River of Lost Footsteps*, p. 231.

7. Christina Fink, *Living Silence*, p. 118.

8. Josef Silverstein, *Burmese Politics: The Dilemma of National Unity*, pp. 115, 130–31, and 141.

9. David I. Steinberg, *Burma: The State of Myanmar*, pp. 227–28.

10. Mya Than, "The Ethnic Chinese in Myanmar and Their Identity," in Suryadinata, ed., pp. 122–30.

11. Michael Fredholm, *Burma: Ethnicity and Insurgency*, pp. 188–203.

12. Ibid., pp. 50–51.

13. Kyaw Yin Hlaing, "Myanmar in 2004: Why Military Rule Continues," in *Southeast Asian Affairs 2005*, pp. 231–55.

14. Steinberg, *Burma: The State of Myanmar*, pp. 198–99, 213–15.

15. Fink, *Silence*, p. 215. The junta has also used a TV satire to attack Aung San Suu Kyi by showing a toothless old crone haranguing people who pass her ramshackle cottage.

16. Myint-U, *The River of Lost Footsteps*, pp. 328–42.

17. Silverstein, *Burmese Politics: The Dilemma of National Unity*, pp. 26–39.

18. Ibid., pp. 406–49.

19. Myint-U, *River*, pp. 180–97.

20. Winston Churchill, who was then leader of the opposition in Parliament, argued for establishing law and order first before granting independence. *Times*, London, December 21, 1946, p. 4.

21. U Saw, the assassin, had been a minister in Myanmar's prewar government. Aung San was thirty-two when he was killed, and his daughter Aung San Suu Kyi was two.

22. Silverstein, *Burmese Politics*, pp. 150–51.

23. Ibid., pp. 152–54.

24. Maureen Aung-Thwin, "Burmese Days," *Foreign Affairs*, Spring 1989, pp. 143–61. The Burmese were offended by having their country designated an LDC, but Ne Win sought the designation in order to have access to cheaper loans.

25. Steinberg, *Burma: The State of Myanmar*, pp. 128–33.

26. Fink, *Living Silence*, pp. 50–62.

27. The students received some military training from the ethnic minority insurgent groups, but they proved no match for the battle-hardened Burmese army. Most of the students either returned to their homes or went abroad where many joined pro-democracy groups.

28. Fink, *Living Silence*, pp. 63–72.

29. Steinberg, *Burma: The State of Myanmar*, pp. 77–78, and interviews.

30. Fink, *Living Silence*, pp. 155 and 263 note 11.

31. The junta's announced plan to begin implementing its "road map to democracy" may have been prompted by Chinese and ASEAN urging. Singapore described the announcement as a step forward, but the Indonesian foreign minister said the junta's constitution would have to be amended before elections are held.

32. The junta's "basic constitutional principles" are outlined in various issues of the official news organ *New Light of Myanmar*.

33. Helen James, "Myanmar in 2005: In a Holding Pattern," *Asian Survey*, January-February 2006, p. 164.

34. Steinberg, *Burma: The State of Myanmar*, pp. 164–65.

35. Kyaw Yin Hlaing, "Myanmar in 2004," in *Southeast Asian Affairs 2005*, pp. 237–38.

36. Ibid., pp. 232–38.

37. Ibid., pp. 250–54, and "Impoverished Burmese Willing to Settle for Small Change," *Financial Times*, October 2, 2006.

38. James, "Myanmar in 2005," p. 163.

39. *Europa World Year Book 2006*, p. 3,116, provides a list of all the parties that won any percentage of the vote.

40. "Burma Moves Ministries From Capital," *Financial Times*, November 8, 2005, and "Burma Defends Move Out of Rangoon," *Financial Times*, November 15, 2005.

41. In previous military governments in Indonesia and Thailand, large numbers of military officers were appointed to serve in the legislature.

42. Steinberg, *Burma: The State of Myanmar*, pp. 80–83.

43. For example, "Protest in Burma Is Largest Since '88," *Washington Post*, September 24, 2007, and "Monks' Action Upholds Long Tradition," *Financial Times*, September 27, 2007.

44. U.S. Department of State, "Background Notes, Burma," September 2006.

45. James, "Myanmar in 2005," p. 165. Cancellation of the U.S. contribution adversely affected 46,000 critically ill HIV/AIDS patients in Myanmar.

46. *Europa World Year Book 2006*, p. 3,114. In October 2007, the junta cut Myanmar's Internet connections with the outside world to stop the flow of images of their crackdown on the pro-democracy movement.

47. Tongzon, *The Economies of Southeast Asia*, 2d ed., pp. 159–63.

48. Steinberg, *Burma: The State of Myanmar*, p. 297.

49. Ibid., pp. 83, 89, 250 note 45.

50. Jim Hoagland, "In Burma, a Price for 'Stability,'" *Washington Post*, May 18, 2008, p. B7. Hoagland notes that in 2005 the United Nations "formally acknowledged its 'responsibility to protect' civilians from the crimes and human rights abuses of their own governments," but after the 2008 cyclone it was "having little luck in pressuring the junta to let UN experts help the country's 1.6 to 2.6 million 'severely affected' cyclone victims." In the same op-ed piece, Hoagland quotes Prime Minister Fukuda of Japan as questioning whether it would really be "humanitarian" for the UN or member states to "push" their way into Myanmar to help its people without the Burmese government's permission.

51. Economist Intelligence Unit, "Burma, Country Report," September 2007, p. 6.

52. Ibid., pp. 4–6.

53. James, "Myanmar in 2005," p. 165.

54. After stalling for several months, the junta agreed to the visit by Foreign Minister Syed of Malaysia, but he cut short his stay in Rangoon after the junta refused to let him meet with Aung San Suu Kyi.

55. Glenn Kessler, "Neighbors to Press Burma on Response," *Washington Post*, May 17, 2008, p. A9.

56. Desmond Ball, *Burma's Military Secrets: Signals Intelligence from the Second World War to Civil War and Cyber Warfare*, pp. 219–29.

57. "U.S. Wants China to Push for Reforms in Burma," *Financial Times*, February 12, 2007.

58. Soe, *Burma File*, pp. 1–33.

59. Weatherbee, *International Relations in Southeast Asia*, p. 176, and U.S. Department of State, "Background Notes, Burma," September 2006.

60. Although the U.S. ban on imports of Burmese products resulted in thousands of Burmese garment workers losing their jobs, the National League for Democracy supported the imposition of economic sanctions against the junta. "Crisis Revives the Sanctions Conundrum," *Financial Times*, September 27, 2007.

61. "Burma accuses Foreigners of Bomb Attacks," *Financial Times*, May 17, 2005.

62. "U.S. Wants China to Push for Reforms in Burma," *Financial Times*, February 12, 2007.

63. The junta reportedly barred Aung San Suu Kyi from taking part in an election on the grounds that she had been married to a foreigner. When her English husband was dying of cancer, the junta denied her the right to speak to him by telephone and ruled that if she went to England to be with him she could not return to Myanmar.

Chapter 6

1. As Prime Minister, Mahathir altered the language policy (which he had enforced when he was Education Minister) and let the Chinese use Mandarin in their schools. He also allowed much greater use of English in the government, schools, and universities to increase Malaysia's economic competitiveness.

2. "Malaysia Kicks off Election Campaign," *The China Post*, Malaysia (AP dispatch), February 24, 2008, and "Abdullah Calls Snap Election," *Financial Times*, February 14, 2008.

3. Economist Intelligence Unit, "Country Report, Malaysia," August 2009, pp. 3–5 and 10–14.

4. In December 2007, Malaysia's highest court rejected a plea by a Hindu woman to prevent her Muslim-convert husband from changing their son's religion to Islam. Many non–Muslim Malaysians protested that this proved they were second-class citizens.

5. Crouch, *Government and Society in Malaysia*, pp. 13–31. However, in Indonesia and the Philippines, ethnic Malays are not necessarily Muslim.

6. Heng Pek Koon, *Chinese Politics in Malaysia*, pp. 1–33.

7. John Clammer, *Straits Chinese Society*, pp. 1–11.

8. Virginia Matheson Hooker, *A Short History of Malaysia*, pp. 152–54.

9. Lee Hock Guan, "Affirmative Action in Malaysia," in *Southeast Asian Affairs 2005*, p. 221.

10. Malays' control of corporate shares rose from 4.3 percent of the total in 1971 to 20.6 percent in 1995 but declined to 18.7 percent by 2002, causing opposition members to accuse the government of neglecting Malay interests.

11. Lee Hock Guan, "Affirmative Action in Malaysia," pp. 213–15.

12. Ibid., pp. 221–23.

13. Crouch, *Government and Society*, pp. 177–218.

14. Fealey, "Islam in Southeast Asia," in Beeson, ed., *Southeast Asia: Regional Dynamics*, pp. 136–55.

15. Anwar founded the Islamic youth movement ABIM in 1971.

16. Cheah Boon Kheng, *Malaysia, the Making of a Nation*, pp. 212–15, and John Hilley, *Malaysia: Mahathirism, Hegemony and the New Opposition*, pp. 15 and 221.

17. Many members of the Straits Chinese community in Melaka moved to Singapore after the British acquired it. Clammer, *Straits Chinese Society*, pp. 122–41.

18. The federal government gained control of their oil revenue and provided relatively little development aid in return, but plans were being drafted in 2007 for the development of Sabah and Sarawak.

19. Crouch, *Government and Society*, pp. 16–17.

20. Ibid., pp. 22–24.

21. Ibid., p. 23.

22. In his book, *Malay Dilemma*, Mahathir claimed the 1957 constitution was a "worthless scrap of paper" because it had been amended so often. Yet as prime minister he sponsored numerous constitutional amendments. *Malay Dilemma* was banned in Malaysia from 1970 until Mahathir's election as prime minister in 1981.

23. Boo Teik Khoo, *Beyond Mahathir: Malaysia Politics and Its Discontents*, pp. 71–96.

24. Crouch, *Government and Society*, p. 96.

25. "Police Raid Malaysia Rights Rally," *Washington Post*, January 6, 2008, p. A15.

26. Abdullah's timing of the March 8, 2008, election reflected the fact that opposition leader Anwar Ibrahim was legally barred from politics until April 2008.

27. John Burton, "Abdullah Vows Not to Quit as Premier," *Financial Times*, March 10, 2008.

28. PAS leader Nik Aziz is from Kelantan, which had a PAS government before the 2008 election.

29. Crouch, *Government and Society*, pp. 146–47.

30. Ibid., pp. 139–42.

31. Ibid., pp. 134–37.

32. Bridget Welsh, "Tears and Fears: Tun Mahathir's Last Hurrah," in Southeast *Asian Affairs 2005*, p. 151.

33. Crouch, *Government*, pp. 131–34, and Lee Hock Guan, "Affirmative Action in Malaysia," p. 216.

34. Jane Perlez, "Within Islam's Embrace, a Voice for Malaysia's Women," *New York Times*, February 19, 2006, described the work of the Sisters in Islam, a women's group that advocated dialogue between Muslims and non–Muslims. Prime Minister Abdullah's daughter was a member.

35. Khoo, *Beyond Mahathir*, pp. 101–06.

36. "Mahathir Steps up Feud with Successor," *Financial Times*, October 24, 2007. Mahathir was quoted as saying, "I consider this a police state. I also consider my civic rights have been taken away."

37. Khoo, *Beyond Mahathir*, pp. 124–26.

38. In his speech at the 2006 UMNO party congress, Abdullah warned that affirmative action was producing racial tensions, but he did not press for an end to

affirmative action. "Malaysia PM Predicts Race Tension," *Financial Times*, November 16, 2006.

39. Tongzon, *The Economies of Southeast Asia*, pp. 160, 168, 171–75.

40. By contrast, Indonesia had 15 percent negative growth in 1998 and only achieved 0.3 positive growth in 1999. Thailand had 8 percent negative growth in 1998 and 4.8 percent positive growth in 1999.

41. In 2005, Malaysia expelled 400,000 illegal workers, mainly from Indonesia. But shortly afterward Malaysia recruited 100,000 Pakistanis. "Malaysia to Recruit Overseas Workers to Ease Labour Shortage," *Financial Times*, March 19, 2005. See also Economist Intelligence Unit, "Country Report, Malaysia," February 2008, pp. 2 and 12–13.

42. Conversations with U.S. officials and "Protest Vote Shifts Political Landscape," *Financial Times*, March 10, 2008.

43. See "Chairman's Statement of the 11th ASEAN Summit," Kuala Lumpur, December 13, 2005.

44. Tongzon, *The Economies of Southeast Asia*, pp. 170–78.

45. Bridget Welsh, "Tears and Fears," *Asian Survey*, January-February 2006, pp. 140–41.

46. Ralf Emmers and Leonard C. Sebastian, "Terrorism," in Weatherbee, *International Relations in Southeast Asia*, pp. 156–84.

47. "Fight Roots of Terror, Not the Symptoms," *Financial Times*, January 29, 2007.

48. "ASEAN's Record on Burma Defended," *Financial Times*, July 27, 2006.

49. "Thai Premier Pledges New Approach to Rebels," *Washington Post*, October 19, 2006.

50. Patricia A. Martinez, "Malaysia in 2004," in *Southeast Asian Affairs 2005*, pp. 191–92.

Chapter 7

1. Lee Kuan Yew's memoir, *The Singapore Story*, was published in 1998. He remains a senior advisor to the government with the title of Minister Mentor.

2. Garry Rodan, "Singapore in 2005: 'Vibrant and Cosmopolitan' without Political Pluralism," *Asian Survey*, January-February 2006, pp. 180–86.

3. John Burton, "Singapore Goes Back to Its Roots for Skilled Staff," *Financial Times*, August 1, 2007.

4. Clammer, *Race and State in Independent Singapore*, pp. 37–38.

5. Chiew Seen Kong, "From Overseas Chinese to Chinese Singaporeans," in Suryadinata, ed., *Ethnic Chinese as Southeast Asians*, pp. 211–26.

6. Clammer, *Race and State in Independent Singapore*, pp. 29, 52, and 220.

7. Chiew Seen Kong, "From Overseas Chinese to Chinese Singaporeans," pp. 224–25.

8. "Straits Under Strain: Why Inequality Is Centre Stage in Singapore's Election," *Financial Times*, May 4, 2006.

9. Clammer, *Race and State in Independent Singapore*, pp. 126–53.

10. Hooker, *A Short History of Malaysia*, p. 60.

11. Clammer, *Straits Chinese Society*, pp. 50–51.

12. Michael Leifer, *Singapore's Foreign Policy*, p. 8.

13. "Singapore Voters Get a Choice: Slums or the Ruling Party," *New York Times*, December 31, 1996.

14. Economist Intelligence Unit, "Country Report," Singapore, July 2009, p. 4.

15. Among other reforms, Goh Chok Tong created a Speakers' Corner, where Singaporeans could express their views, but they needed a police permit to use the forum, and there were restrictions on what they could say. See Michael Haas, "Mass Society," in Haas, ed., pp. 151–67 and 178–82.

16. William Case, *Politics in Southeast Asia*, pp. 85–89.

17. Ibid, pp. 86–87.

18. See "Mahathir Ploy Fails to Oust PM," *Financial Times*, May 21, 2008.

19. Case, *Politic in Southeast Asias*, pp. 85–86.

20. Ooi Can Seng notes that the way in which the Central Executive Committee is chosen (by party members whose careers they have advanced) inevitably gives rise to charges of cronyism. Ooi Can Seng, "Singapore," in Funston, ed., p. 363.

21. Jon S.T. Quah, "Controlling Corruption in City-States," pp. 394–96.

22. The extremely high pay scale for Singapore government officials is often cited as a major reason for the lack of corruption. The prime minister receives the equivalent of U.S.$2 million a year, and his cabinet ministers receive about $1.9 million. Seth Mydans, "Singapore's Highly Paid Officials Get Richer," *New York Times*, April 10, 2007.

23. In 1997, it was reported that Lee Kuan Yew and his son received discounts on two exclusive private condominiums. Lee Kuan Yew dismissed the matter with the comment, "it is an unfair world." Clark Neher, *Southeast Asia in the New International Order*, p. 164.

24. Quah, "Singapore," in Funston, ed., pp. 299–301.

25. In 2001, Prime Minister Goh and Lee Kuan Yew sued an opposition party member for claiming Singapore loaned $17 billion to the Suharto government in Indonesia.

26. In 2005, an Australian citizen who had been caught in the Changi Airport transit lounge in possession of 396 grams of heroin was hanged in spite of efforts by the Australian Prime Minister to obtain clemency.

27. Francis T. Seow, "The Judiciary," in Haas, ed., *Singapore Puzzle*, pp. 107–24.

28. Clammer, *Race and State in Independent Singapore*, pp. 139–40.

29. Derek Davies, "The Press," in Haas, ed., *Singapore Puzzle*, pp. 79–124.

30. Garry Rodan, "Class Transformations and Political Tensions," in Rodan, Hewison, and Robison, eds., p. 26.

31. U.S. Department of State, "Background Notes, Singapore," March 2008, p. 5.

32. Case, *Politics*, pp. 90–92.

33. Economist Intelligence Unit, "Singapore, Country Report," January 2006, pp. 9–12.

34. Leifer, *Singapore's Foreign Policy*, p. 50.

35. Economist Intelligence Unit, "Singapore, Country Report," August 2007, p. 2.

36. "Insurance Cost Set to Fall as Pirates Avoid Malacca Strait," *Financial Times*, August 9, 2006. See also Ralf Emmers and Leonard Sebastian, "Terrorism and Transnational Crime," in Weatherbee, pp. 156–72.

37. Kong, "From Overseas Chinese to Chinese Singaporeans," pp. 22–26.

38. Weatherbee, *International Relations in Southeast Asia*, pp. 37, 38, 207, and 284.

39. "Straits Under Strain: Why Inequality Is Centre Stage in Singapore's Election," *Financial Times*, May 4, 2006.

Chapter 8

1. The Economist Intelligence Unit, "Indonesia, Country Report," May 2008.

2. The Economist Intelligence Unit, "Country Report, Indonesia," August 2009, p. 3.

3. R. William Liddle, *Leadership and Culture in Indonesian Politics*, p. 157.

4. Robert W. Hefner, "Religion: Evolving Pluralism," pp. 225–29.

5. During World War II, the Japanese forced Nahdlatul Ulama (NU) and Muhammadiyah to merge, and Suharto attempted to do the same during the New Order period, but they have remained separate and to some degree competing organizations. NU has been more of a political organization than Muhammadiyah. Indonesia's fourth president, Abdurrahman Wahid, was head of NU for many years.

6. Ann Marie Murphy, "Indonesia and the World," in Bresnan, ed., p. 272.

7. For example, General Benny Murdani, Commander-in-Chief of the armed forces and one of Suharto's closest advisors, was a Catholic.

8. Donald K. Emmerson, "What Is Indonesia?," in Bresnan, ed., pp. 44–47.

9. Milton Osborne, *Exploring Southeast Asia,* pp. 54 and 200.

10. M.C. Ricklefs, *A History of Modern Indonesia, c. 1300 to the Present,* pp. 53–54.

11. R. William Liddle and Saiful Mujani, "Indonesia in 2005, A New Multiparty Presidential Democracy," *Asian Survey,* January-Feburary 2006, pp. 135–36.

12. A. Dahana, "Comments on 'The Ethnic Chinese in Indonesia: Issues of Identity," pp. 66–71.

13. Khoon Choy Lee, *A Fragile Nation: The Indonesian Crisis,* pp. 230–55.

14. Ibid., pp. 30, 233 and 241. Ambassador Lee estimates that 100,000 Chinese left Indonesia between 1949 and 1966.

15. Ricklefs, *A History of Modern Indonesia,* pp. 114–18.

16. Ibid., pp. 164–71.

17. George McT. Kahin's *Nationalism and Revolution in Indonesia* (Ithaca: Cornell University Press, 1952) is the most comprehensive account if Indonesia's history in the first half of the twentieth century.

18. West New Guinea was occupied by the Indonesian army in 1963 and incorporated into Indonesia in 1969. It was renamed West Irian and is now known as Papua.

19. Crouch, *The Army and Politics in Indonesia,* pp. 97–134. The term "Gestapu" signifies "30 September Movement." For an even broader treatment of the 1950s, see Herbert Feith's *Decline of Constitutional Democracy In Indonesia* (Ithaca: Cornell University Press, 1962). Benedict Anderson and Ruth McVey provided *A Preliminary Analysis of the October 1, 1965 Coup in Indonesia* (Ithaca: Modern Indonesia Project, Southeast Asia Program, Cornell University, 1971).

20. Annette Clear, "Politics: From Endurance to Evolution," in Bresnan, ed., pp. 141–45.

21. Ibid., pp. 145–47.

22. Hal Hill, *The Indonesian Economy in Crisis,* pp. 23–24.

23. Although General (now President) Yudhoyono was one of the organizers of the army's action against Megawati Sukarnoputri, she later appointed him to a senior position in her cabinet.

24. World Bank, *The East Asian Miracle: Economic Growth and Public Policy.*

25. Hill, *The Indonesian Economy in Crisis,* pp. 23–27. Hill notes that the impact of the 1997 crisis varied greatly from one sector of Indonesia's economy to another.

26. Michael Vatikiotis, *Indonesian Politics Under Suharto: The Rise and Fall of the New Order,* pp. 218–32.

27. Like her father, Megawati Sukarnoputri was essentially a secular leader and opposed to making Indonesia an Islamic state.

28. Liddle and Mujani, "Indonesia in 2005," *Asian Survey,* January-February 2006, pp. 132–36. There did not appear to be serious rivalry between Yudhoyono and Kalla, although they were both very powerful and forceful leaders.

29. Economist Intelligence Unit, "Country Report, Indonesia," November 2005, p. 19.

30. Amien Rais was the former head of Muhammadiyah, the main organization of *santri* reform Muslims.

31. As a gesture of reconciliation, Wahid included several members of Megawati's party in his cabinet, but he later dropped them.

32. Liddle and Mujani, "Indonesia in 2004, The Rise of Susilo Bambang Yudhoyono," *Asian Survey,* January-February 2005, pp. 119–126.

33. Liddle and Mujani, "Indonesia in 2005," pp. 132–36. In November 2006, Golkar reaffirmed its support for the Yudhoyono administration, despite pressure from regional branches for Vice President Kalla to withdraw from the administration and run against Yudhoyono in the 2009 presidential election.

34. Hill, *Economy in Crisis,* pp. 5 and 6.

35. Ibid., pp. 47–77.

36. "Asia Over a Barrel on Subsidies," *Financial Times,* May 23, 2008.

37. Weatherbee, *International Relations in Southeast Asia,* pp. 151–55. Karl Deutsch defined a security community as a group of countries that have virtually eliminated expectations of warlike behavior of one member against another. See Karl Deutsch et al., *Political Community in the North Atlantic Area* (Princeton: Princeton University Press, 1957).

38. "Indonesia 'Has Best Strategy on Terrorism,'" *Financial Times,* March 6, 2007.

39. This reflects the diminished role of the Indonesian military in shaping the country's China policy.

40. U.S. Department of State, "Background Notes, Indonesia," March 2008.

Chapter 9

1. Gunn, "Rentier Capitalism in Negara Brunei Darussalam," in Hewison, Robison and Rodan, eds., *Southeast Asia in the 1990s,* pp. 109–32. Gunn argues that Brunei exactly fits the paradigm of a "rentier" state in which people lose the spirit of entrepreneurship when they have a fixed income from some resource such as oil.

2. Precise information about the two countries' reserves of oil and gas are not available because full data is not released and also because the technology for extracting oil and gas is constantly changing.

3. For example, Brunei is planning to build a large Methanol plant, and it has begun developing Islamic banking facilities.

4. Economist Intelligence Unit, "Brunei, Country Report," September 2007, pp. 7–8.

5. Unlike the middle income countries of Southeast Asia (Thailand, Malaysia, Indonesia, and the Philippines), the Bruneian government is not under much pressure from its people to raise GDP. The real challenge the government faces is to manage the diversification of the economy more effectively.

6. Azman Ahmad, "Brunei Darussalam, Towards Reform and Sustainable Progress," in *Southeast Asian Affairs 2005*, pp. 99–109.

7. Pushpa Thambipillai, "Consolidating the Party," in *Southeast Asian Affairs 2006*, pp. 64–67.

8. As in Malaysia and Singapore, Brunei's Internal Security Act allows for imprisonment without trial. It has been used to silence opposition members in Brunei, but more sparingly than in Malaysia or Singapore.

9. Gunn, *Language, Power and Ideology in Brunei Darussalam*, pp. 161–68.

10. In 2005, the World Bank estimated that per capita GDP was $24,100.

11. B.A. Hussainmiya, *Sultan Omar Ali Saifuddin III and Britain: The Making of Brunei Darussalam* (Kuala Lumpur: Oxford University Press, 1995).

12. "Sultan of Brunei Abandons Architect of Islamist Policies," *Financial Times*, May 26, 2005.

13. Economist Intelligence Unit, "Country Report, Brunei," December 2007, p. 6.

14. Roger Kershaw, *Monarchy in South-East Asia* (London: Routledge, 2000).

15. Economist Intelligence Unit, "Country Report, Brunei," March 2008, p. 6.

16. Kershaw, "Brunei," p. 17. Kershaw lists the sultan's many duties and notes that among other things he has the power both to send a person to prison without trial and to pardon him.

17. Economist Intelligence Unit, "Country Report, Brunei," December 2007, p. 8. Prince Jefri was appealing that decision in various jurisdictions around the world where the property he claimed to own was located.

18. "Sultan of Brunei Abandons Architect of Islamist Policies," *Financial Times*, May 26, 2005.

19. Gunn, "Rentier Capitalism in Negra Brunei Darussalam," pp. 120 and 125–26.

20. Economist Intelligence Unit, "Country Report, Brunei," 2005, pp. 17–18.

21. Economist Intelligence Unit, "Country Report, Brunei," March 2007, p. 11, notes that financial services contributed 3 percent to GDP in 2005.

22. Interviews with government officials.

23. Economist Intelligence Unit, "Country Report, Brunei," March 2008, p. 12. But Brunei still had to import at least two thirds of the rice its people consumed as their staple food.

24. Economist Intelligence Unit, "Country Report, Brunei," December 2007, p. 11.

25. Ibid., p. 2. Brunei sent another group of peace monitors to the Philippines in 2007 and conducted joint exercises with the Philippine navy.

26. *Europa World Year Book 2004*, p. 870.

27. Economist Intelligence Unit, "Country Report, Brunei," September 2007, p. 7.

28. Eisenman et al., *China and the Developing World*, p. 163.

29. Weatherbee, *International Relations in Southeast Asia*, pp. 27 and 135.

Chapter 10

1. Jane Hutchison, "Class and state power in the Philippines," pp. 191–212.

2. Allen Hicken, "The Philippines in 2007: Ballots, Budgets, and Bribes," *Asian Survey*, January-February 2008, pp. 75–81. In February 2008, some 30,000 people demonstrated against Arroyo's administration in Makati, but this was not nearly as many as the hundreds of thousands who demonstrated against Marcos in 1986 or against Estrada in 2000–2001. The Economist Intelligence Unit concluded ("Country Report, Philippines," April 2008) that Arroyo could probably hold on as president until her term ends in 2010, but she would have increasing trouble getting her legislative agenda enacted.

3. "Philippines Poverty Creeps Upward," *Financial Times*, March 6, 2008; "Relief in Manila After Japan Agrees to Sell Rice," *Washington Post*, May 27, 2008; "Rice Market Eases as Cambodia Lifts Ban on Exports," *Financial Times*, May 27, 2008.

4. Ledivina V. Carino, "The Land and People," in De Guzman and Reforma, eds., *Government and Politics of the Philippines*, pp. 2–8.

5. Jose V. Abueva, "Philippine Ideologies and National Development," in De Guzman and Reforma, eds., *Government and the Politics of the Philippines*, p. 37. The Philippine Independent Church, formerly part of the Catholic Church, was founded by Gregorio Aglipay in 1890s during the Philippine Revolution.

6. Fealy, "Islam in Southeast Asia," in Beeson, ed., *Southeast Asia: Regional Dynamics*, pp. 147–55. In 2007, the Philippine army killed the two top leaders of Abu Sayyaf.

7. Teresita Ang See, "Ethnic Chinese as Filipinos," in Suryadinata, ed., *Ethnic Chinese as Southeast Asians*, pp. 158–98. In many Southeast Asian countries, ethnic Chinese intermarry with the politically dominant ethnic group for the same reasons.

8. Raymundo D. Rovillos and Daisy N. Morales, *Indigenous Peoples/Ethnic Minorities and Poverty Reduction*, pp. 46–48.

9. Carino, "The Land and People," p. 10.

10. Jose V. Abueva, "Philippine Ideologies and National Development," in De Guzman and Reforma, *Government and Politics of the Philippines*, pp. 23–25.

11. James H. Blount, *The American Occupation of the Philippines*. From 1899 to 1905, Blount served as an army officer and then as a district judge in the Philippines.

12. David Wurfel, "The Philippines," in Kahin, ed., *Government and Politics in Southeast Asia*, pp. 691–93.

13. However, in 1962 the Philippines' official independence day was change to June 12 to commemorate General Aguinaldo's declaration of independence in 1898.

14. Wurfel, "The Philippines," in Kahin, ed., *Government and Politics in Southeast Asia*, pp. 695–702.

15. Stanley Karnow, *In Our Image: America's Empire in the Philippines*, p. 365.

16. Peter Krinks, *The Economy of the Philippines*, pp. 56–65.

17. Fred Poole and Max Vanzi, *Revolution in the Philippines*, pp. 1–10.

18. Karnow, *In Our Image*, pp. 389–410.

19. Interviews with Philippine officials.

20. Karnow, *In Our Image*, pp. 411–27.

21. Krinks, *The Economy of the Philippines*, pp. 49, 66 and 94–95.

22. Temario C. Rivera, "The Philippines in 2004," *Asian Survey*, January-February 2005, pp. 127–33.

23. "The Philippines: Vote Fraud Inquiry Against Leader," *New York Times*, June 22, 2005. Tapes of the alleged conversations were distributed on DVD's by President Arroyo's opponents and played at political rallies.

24. Lorraine C. Salazar, "The Philippines: Crisis, Controversies, and Economic Resilience," in *Southeast Asian Affairs 2005*, pp. 227–44.

25. See Gerard Clarke, *Politics of NGO's*, p. 190, table of human rights violations during the administrations of Marcos, Aquino, and Ramos.

26. Ibid, pp. 133–36, and Krinks, *The Economy of the Philippines*, pp. 46–48.

27. Interviews with Philippine members of Congress.

28. Salazar, "The Philippines: Crisis, Controversies, and Economic Resilience," in *Southeast Asian Affairs 2005*, pp. 232–37.

29. In 2005, President Arroyo and members of the House of Representatives tried to expedite the adoption of the parliamentary system, but her opponents strongly objected to her serving out her term to 2010.

30. Rivera, "The Philippines in 2004," *Asian Survey*, January-February 2005, p. 128.

31. De Guzman and Brillantes, "The Bureaucracy," pp. 197–98.

32. Case, *Politics in Southeast Asia*, pp. 201–06.

33. Wurfel, *Filipino Politics*, pp. 103–13.

34. Interviews with Philippine congressmen.

35. A Philippine Movie Star Hopes to Land a New Role: President," *New York Times*, April 19 2004, p. A6. Poe died of a stroke in December 2004.

36. Rivera, "The Philippines in 2004," *Asian Survey*, January-February 2005, pp. 126–28.

37. *Europa World Year Book, 2004*, p. 3,420.

38. Weatherbee, *International Relations in Southeast Asia*, pp. 120–47.

39. Clarke, *Politics of NGOs*, pp. 68–93, and see Kathleen M. Nadeau, *Liberation Theology in the Philippines* (Westport, CT: Praeger, 2002).

40. "Death Toll for Journalists in Philippines Keeps Rising," *New York Times*, November 30, 2004.

41. Emmanuel de Dios et al., "The Deepening Crisis." See also Economist Intelligence Unit, "Country Report Philippines," September 2007, pp. 2, 3.

42. Krinks, *Economy*, pp. 80–84.

43. Rivera, "The Philippines in 2004," pp. 131–32, and "Remittances Are an Effective Weapon Against Poverty," *Financial Times*, November 17, 2005.

44. Hill's views are quoted in Salazar, "The Philippines," p. 244.

45. Weatherbee, *International Relations in Southeast Asia*, p. 237.

46. Ambassador Rosario Manalo has played a key role in ASEAN affairs throughout her distinguished career. (The author first met her in Manila in 1983.) For ASEAN documents and information concerning the ASEAN Charter, see the ASEAN Secretariat's website: www.aseansec.org.

47. Jason DeParle, "A Good Provider is One Who Leaves," *New York Times Magazine*, April 22, 2007, pp. 50–57.

48. Rivera, "Philippines in 2004," p. 132.

49. Salazar, "Philippines Crisis," p. 239.

50. U.S. State Department, "Background Notes, Philippines," April 2008.

51. When President Arroyo raised the possibility of U.S. forces participating in combat operations against Abu Sayyaf terrorists, a strong political reaction in the Philippines forced her to abandon the idea. Donald Weatherbee, *International Relations in Southeast Asia*, pp. 145–47.

52. Ibid., pp. 133–39.

53. According to the World Bank's "East Asia and Pacific Update," April 2007 (p. 58), there were 33.5 million Filipinos living in poverty in 1990 and 32.9 million in 2007.

Chapter 11

1. Weatherbee, *International Relations in Southeast Asia*, pp. 147–51.

2. International Monetary Fund, "World Economic Outlook Update," January 28, 2009.

3. IMF, "Regional Economic Outlook, Asia and Pacific," April 2008, pp. 27–38.

4. However, being the world's eighth largest exporter of rice, Cambodia was able to ease the global market by unblocking its exports.

5. Robert Zoellick, "A Ten-Point Plan for the Food Crisis," *Financial Times*, May 30, 2008.

6. See also "Jakarta Signs Methane Deal In Scramble for Energy," *Financial Times*, May 28, 2008.

7. Andrew Taylor, "Asian Economies Near 'Demographic Cliff,'" *Financial Times*, August 13, 2007.

8. Victor Mallet, "The Utopian Myth of India's Double Dividend," *Financial* Times, December 6, 2007.

9. As discussed in chapter 6, the Malay population of Malaysia is growing at a much faster rate than the Chinese-Malaysian minority, which is concerned about being further marginalized politically.

10. David Pilling and Kathrin Hills, "The new Melting Pot, Asia Learns to Cope with a Rise in the Flow of Migrants," *Financial Times*, July 9, 2007. The article summarizes a series of *Financial Times* articles on migrations of workers in Asia, based on data gathered by the Asian Development Bank.

11. John Burton, "Rights Groups Hit at Malaysia Crackdown on Illegal Workers," *Financial Times*, August 7, 2007, and John Burton, "Singapore Goes Back to Its Roots for Skilled Staff," *Financial Times*, August 1, 2007.

12. Blaine Harden, "For Japan, a Long, Slow Slide," *Washington Post*, February 3, 2008. Among OECD members, Japan now ranks twentieth in per capita Gross Domestic Product. In 1992, it ranked fourth.

13. Alfred Keidel, "The Limits of a Smaller, Poorer China," *Financial Times*, November 14, 2007. Keidel says the Asian Development Bank recently conducted the first comprehensive survey of the Chinese economy by an international financial institution. It showed that China's economy was 40 percent smaller than previous World Bank estimates indicated, and the number of people living below the dollar-a-day poverty line was 300 million, three times as many as previously estimated by the World Bank.

14. Crouch, *Government and Society in Malaysia*, p. 96. Crouch describes the Malaysian system as one of "incremental authoritarianism," but he notes that "democratic political structures were maintained and [they] encouraged, even forced, the government to respond to societal pressures."

15. For example, Thaksin Shinawatra openly sought

to create a party that would monopolize political power in Thailand like the PAP in Singapore or the UMNO-led coalition in Malaysia.

16. Crouch, *Government and Society in Malaysia*, pp. 134–37. Crouch has also described the role of the Indonesian military in his book, *The Army and Politics in Indonesia* (Ithaca: Cornell University Press, 1978).

17. Weatherbee, *International Relations in Southeast Asia*, pp. 91–93.

18. Prime Minister Mahathir was one of the few Southeast Asian leaders who publicly threatened Myanmar with expulsion from ASEAN.

19. Singapore is one of Myanmar's main trading partners, and the Singapore government, which hosted the 2007 ASEAN summit, was concerned that the meeting would be marked by demonstrations protesting Singapore's relationship with the junta.

20. Quentin Peel, "Suu Kyi Detention Is a Test for ASEAN, Says Macapagal," *Financial Times*, December 7, 2007.

21. Glenn Kessler, "India's Halt to Burma Arms Sales May Pressure Junta," *Washington Post*, December 30, 2007, p. A29.

22. For example, ex-prime minister Mahathir objected to his successor inviting the leaders of Australia and New Zealand to the ASEAN summit in Kuala Lumpur in 2005.

23. Wolfgang Munchau, "Asian Monetary Integration Poses Many Questions," *Financial Times*, May 7, 2007.

24. Weatherbee, *International Relations in Southeast Asia*, pp. 95–110, 147–51.

25. Michael Glosny, "Stabilizing the Back Yard: "Recent Developments in China's Policy Toward Southeast Asia," in Eisenman, et al., eds., *China and the Developing World*, pp. 150–77.

26. According to the Chinese Ministry of Foreign Affairs, 9,437 students from Southeast Asia were studying in China in 2002. This number increased to 10,376 in 2003 and 15,023 in 2004. Eisenman et al., eds., *China and the Developing World*, p. 168.

27. Evelyn Goh, "China in the Mekong River Basin," in Caballero-Anthony, Mely, Emmers, and Acharya, eds., *Non-Traditional Security in Asia: Dilemmas in Securitisation*, pp. 225–43.

28. President George Bush tended to dwell mainly on the issue of terrorism when he attended the 2003 APEC summit, and Secretary of State Rice's absence from several ASEAN ministerial meetings was criticized by Southeast Asian elites.

Bibliography

Abueva, Jose V. "Philippine Ideologies and National Development." In De Guzman and Reforma, eds., *Government and Politics of the Philippines*, pp. 18–73.

Abuza, Zachary. "The Lessons of Le Kha Phieu: Changing Rulers in Vietnamese Politics." *Contemporary Southeast Asia*, vol. 23, no. 1 (2001): pp. 121–45.

_____. *Renovating Politics in Contemporary Vietnam.* London and New York: Routledge, 2001.

Acharya, Amitav. *The Quest for Identity: International Relations in Southeast Asia.* Singapore: Oxford University Press, 2000.

Ahmad, Azman. "Brunei Darussalam: Towards Reform and Sustainable Progress." In *Southeast Asian Affairs 2005*, pp. 99–109. Singapore: ISEAS, 2005.

Alagappa, Muthiah, ed. *Civil Society and Political Change in Asia: Expanding and Contracting Democratic Space.* Stanford: Stanford University Press, 2004.

Albritton, Robert B. "Cambodia in 2003: On the Road to Democratic Consolidation." *Asian Survey*, vol. 44, no. 1 (January-February 2004): pp. 102–09.

Amer, Ramses. "The Ethnic Vietnamese in Cambodia: A Minority at Risk?" In Peou, ed., *Cambodia: Change and Continuity*, pp. 447–75.

Anderson, Benedict R. "Cacique Democracy in the Philippines: Origins and Dreams." *New Left Review*, no. 169 (1988): pp. 3–31.

_____. *Imagined Communities: Reflections on the Origin and Spread of Nationalism.* New York: Verso Press, 1996.

_____, and Ruth T. Mcvey. *A Preliminary Analysis of the October 1, 1965 Coup in Indonesia.* Ithaca: Modern Indonesia Project, Southeast Asia Program, Cornell University, 1971.

Ang See, Teresita. "Ethnic Chinese as Filipinos." In Suryadinata, ed., *Ethnic Chinese as Southeast Asians*, pp. 158–98.

Aung-Thwin, Maureen. "Burmese Days." *Foreign Affairs*, vol. 68, no. 2 (Spring 1989): pp. 144–61.

Aung-Thwin, Michael. *The Mists of Ramanna, The Legend that Was Lower Burma.* Honolulu: University of Hawai'i Press, 2005.

Balisacan, Arsenio M., and Hal Hill, eds. *The Philippine Economy: Development Policies and Challenges.* Oxford and New York: Oxford University Press, 2003.

Ball, Desmond. *Burma's Military Secrets: Signals Intelligence from the Second World War to Civil War and Cyber Warfare.* Bangkok: White Lotus Press, 1998.

Batson, Wendy. "After the Revolution: Ethnic Minorities and the New Lao State." In Zasloff and Unger, eds., *Laos: Beyond the Revolution*, pp. 133–59.

Becker, Elizabeth. *When the War Was Over: The Voices of Cambodia's Revolution and Its People.* New York and London: Simon and Schuster, 1986; second edition: *When the War Was Over: Cambodia and the Khmer Rouge Revolution.* New York: Public Affairs, 1998.

Beeson, Mark. *Southeast Asia: Regional Dynamics, National Differences.* Houndsmills, UK, and New York: Palgrave Macmillan, 2004.

_____, ed. *Reconfiguring East Asia: Regional Institutions and Organizations After the Crisis.* London: RoutledgeCurzon, 2003.

Beresford, Melanie. "Cambodia in 2004, an Artificial Democratization Process." *Asian Survey*, vol. 45, no. 1 (January-February 2005): pp. 134–39.

_____. *The Microeconomics of Poverty Reduction in Cambodia.* New York: United Nations Development Program, 2004.

Berger, Mark T. *The Battle for Asia: From Decolonization to Globalization.* London: RoutledgeCurzon, 2004.

Beyer, Chris. *War in the Blood: Sex, Politics, and AIDS in Southeast Asia.* London: Zed Books, 1998.

Blount, James H. *The American Occupation of the Phlippines.* New York and London: Putnam, 1913. Reprint: New York: Oriole, 1973.

Bourchier, David, and Vedi R. Hadiz. *Indonesian Politics and Society: A Reader.* London and New York: Routledge, 2003.

Bresnan, John. "Economic Recovery and Reform." In Bresnan, ed., *Indonesia, The Great Transition*, pp. 189–237.

_____, ed. *Indonesia, The Great Transition.* Lanham, MD: Rowman & Littlefield, 2005.

197

Brown, David. *State and Ethnic Politics in Southeast Asia*. London and New York: Routledge, 1994.

Brown, Frederick Z. *Cambodia in Crisis: The 1993 Elections and the United Nations*. New York: Asia Society, 1993.

———. *Second Chance: The United States and Indochina in the 1990s*. New York: Council on Foreign Relations Press, 1989.

Brown, Ian. *Cambodia: An Oxfam Country Profile*. Oxford: Oxfam, 2000.

Brown, MacAlister. "Communists in Coalition Governments: Lessons from Laos." In Zasloff and Unger, eds., *Laos: Beyond the Revolution*. pp. 41–63.

———, and Joseph J. Zasloff. *Apprentice Revolutionaries: The Communist Movement in Laos, 1930–1985*. Stanford: Hoover Institution Press, 1986.

———, and ———. *Cambodia Confounds the Peacemakers, 1979–1998*. Ithaca: Cornell University Press, 1998.

Brown, Michael E., and Sumit Ganguly, eds. *Fighting Words: Language Policy and Ethnic Relations in Asia*. BCSIA Studies in International Security. Cambridge: MIT Press, 2003.

Bunge, Frederica M., ed. *Burma: A Country Study*. Washington, D.C.: American University, Foreign Area Studies, 1983.

Buttinger, Joseph. *Vietnam: A Political History*. New York: Praeger, 1968.

Caballero-Anthony, Mely, Ralf Emmers, and Amitav Acharya, eds., *Non-Traditional Security in Asia: Dilemmas in Securitisation*. Aldershot, Hampshire, UK: Ashgate, 2006.

Callahan, Mary P. *Making Enemies: War and State Building in Burma*. Ithaca: Cornell University Press, 2003.

Callahan, William B. *Contingent States: Greater China and Transnational Relations*. Minneapolis: University of Minnesota Press, 2004.

Carino, Ledivina V. "The Land and People." In De Guzman and Reforma, eds., *Government and Politics of the Philippines*, pp. 3–17.

Carpenter, William M., and David G. Wiencek, eds. *Asian Security Handbook 2000*. Armonk, NY: M.E. Sharpe, 2000.

Case, William. "Democracy in Southeast Asia: How to Get It and What Does it Matter?" In Mark Beeson, ed., *Contemporary Southeast Asia*, pp. 75–97.

———. *Politics in Southeast Asia*. Richmond, UK: Curzon, 2002.

Chanda, Nayan. *Brother Enemy: The War After the War*. New York: Harcourt Brace Jovanovich, 1986.

Chandler, David P. *Brother Number One: A Political Biography of Pol Pot*. New South Wales, Australia: Allen & Unwin, 1993.

———. *A History of Cambodia*. 2d ed. Boulder, CO: Westview Press, 1992.

———. *Voices from S-21: Terror and History in Pol Pot's Secret Prison*. Berkeley: University of California Press, 1999.

Chang, Pao-Min. *Kampuchea Between China and Vietnam*. Singapore: Singapore University Press, National University of Singapore, 1985.

Chantavanich, Supang. "From Siamese-Chinese to Chinese-Thai: Political Conditions and Identity Shifts Among the Chinese in Thailand." In Leo Suryadinata, ed., *Ethnic Chinese as Southeast Asians*, pp. 232–59.

Chea, Boon Kheng. *Malaysia, the Making of a Nation*. Singapore: Institute of Southeast Asian Studies, 2002.

Chin, James. "Sabah and Sarawak: The More Things Change the More They Remain the Same." In *Southeast Asian Affairs 2004*, pp. 156–60. Singapore: ISEAS, 2004.

Chongkittavorn, Kavi. "Thailand: International Terrorism and the Muslim South." In *Southeast Asian Affairs 2004*, pp. 267–75. Singapore: Institute of Southeast Asian Studies, 2004.

Clammer, John. *Race and State in Independent Singapore, 1965–1990*. Aldershot, UK: Ashgate, 1998.

———. *Straits Chinese Society*. Singapore: Singapore University Press, 1980.

Clarke, Gerard. *The Politics of NGOs in Southeast Asia*. London and New York: Routledge, 1998.

Clear, Annette. "Politics: From Endurance to Evolution." In Bresnan, ed., *Indonesia, the Great Transition*. pp. 137–88.

Cleary, Mark, and Wong Shuang Yann. *Oil, Economic Development and Diversification in Brunei Darussalam*. London and New York: St. Martin's Press, 1994.

Coe, Michael D. *Angkor and Khmer Civilization*. New York: Thames and Hudson, 2003.

Coedes, G. *The Making of South East Asia*. Berkeley: University of California Press, 1967.

Connors, Michael Kelly. *Democracy and National Identity in Thailand*. New York and London: RoutledgeCurzon, 2003.

———. "Thailand: The Facts and F(r)ictions of Ruling." In *Southeast Asian Affairs 2005*, pp. 365–84. Singapore: Institute of Southeast Asian Studies, 2005.

Corfield, Justin, and Laura Summers. *Historical Dictionary of Cambodia*. Lanham, MD: Scarecrow Press, 2003.

Coronel, Shiela, ed. *Pork and Other Perks: Corruption and Governance in the Philippines*. Manila: Philippine Center for Investigative Journalism, 1998.

Corpus, Victor N. *Silent War*. Quezon City: VNC Enterprises, 1989.

Crew, E. C. F., and E. Lee. *A History of Singapore*. Oxford and New York: Oxford University Press, 1991.

Crouch, Harold. *The Army and Politics in Indonesia*. Ithaca: Cornell University Press, 1988.

———. *Domestic Political Structures and Regional Development*. Singapore: Institute of Southeast Asian Studies, 1984.

———. *Government and Society in Malaysia*. Ithaca: Cornell University Press, 1996.

Curtis, Grant. *Cambodia Reborn? The Transition to Democracy and Development*. Washington, D.C., and Geneva, Switzerland: The Brookings Institution and the United Nations Research Institute for Social Development, 1998.

Davies, Derek. "The Press." In Haas, ed., *Singapore Puzzle*, pp. 77–106.

de Dios, Emmanuel. "The Deepening Crisis: The Real Score on Deficits and Public Debt." Manila: School of Economics, University of the Philippines, August 2004.

De Guzman, Raul P., and Mila A. Reforma, eds. *Government and Politics of the Philippines*. Singapore: Oxford University Press, 1988.

Deutsch, Karl, et al. *Political Community in the North Atlantic Area*. Princeton: Princeton University Press, 1957.

Djiwandono, J. S., ed. *Soldiers and Stability in Southeast Asia*. Singapore: Institute of Southeast Asian Studies, 1988.

Dommen, Arthur J. *Laos, Keystone of Indochina*. Boulder, CO: Westview Press, 1985.

Dosch, Jorn, and Ta Minh Tuan. "Recent Changes in Vietnam's Foreign Policy." In McCargo, ed., *Rethinking Vietnam*, pp. 197–213.

Duiker, William J. *The Communist Road to Power in Vietnam*. Boulder, CO: Westview Press, 1981.

_____. *Ho Chi Minh*. St. Leonards, Australia: Allen & Unwin, 2000.

Ebihara, May M., Carol A. Mortland, and Judy Ledgerwood, eds. *Cambodian Culture Since 1975, Homeland and Exile*. Ithaca: Cornell University Press, 1994.

Economist Intelligence Unit, London. "Country Reports" (issued periodically on each of the Southeast Asian countries).

Eisenman, Joshua, Eric Heginbotham, and Derek Mitchell, eds. *China and the Developing World: Beijing's Strategy for the Twenty-first Century*. Armonk, NY: M.E. Sharpe, 2007.

Eldridge, Philip J. *Non-Government Organizations and Democratic Participation in Indonesia*. Kuala Lumpur: Oxford University Press, 1995.

Elliott, David W.P. *The Vietnamese War: Revolution and Social Change in the Mekong Delta, 1930–1975*. Armonk, NY: M.E. Sharpe, 2003.

Emmers, Ralf, and Leonard Sebastian. "Terrorism and Transnational Crime in Southeast Asian International Relations." In Weatherbee, et al., *International Relations in Southeast Asia*, pp. 156–86.

Emerson, Donald K. "What is Indonesia?" In Bresnan, ed., *Indonesia, The Great Transition*, pp. 7–73.

_____, ed. *Indonesia Beyond Suharto: Polity, Economy, Society, Transition*. Armonk, NY: M.E. Sharpe, 1999.

Etcheson, Craig. *After the Killing Fields: Lessons from the Cambodian Genocide*. Westport, CT: Praeger, 2005.

Europa World Year Book. Annual reference work on all countries in the world.

Evans, Grant. *Lao Peasants Under Socialism*. New Haven: Yale University Press, 1990.

_____, ed. *Laos, Culture and Society*. Chiang Mai, Thailand: Silkworm Books, 1999.

Fall, Bernard B. *Viet-Nam Witness, 1953–66*. New York: Praeger, 1966.

Fealey, Greg. "Islam in Southeast Asia: Domestic Pietism, Diplomacy and Security." In Beeson, ed., *Southeast Asia: Regional Dynamics*, pp. 136–55.

_____. "Islamic Radicalism in Indonesia: The Faltering Revival?" In *Southeast Asian Affairs 2004*, pp. 104–21. Singapore: Institute of Southeast Asian Studies, 2005.

Feith, Herbert. *The Decline of Constitutional Democracy in Indonesia*. Ithaca: Cornell University Press, 1962.

_____. "Repressive Developmentalist Regimes in Asia: Old Strengths, New Vulnerabilities." *Prisma* no. 19 (1980): pp. 39–55.

Fforde, Adam. "Vietnam in 2003: The Road to Ungovernability?" *Asian Survey*, vol. 44, no. 1 (January-February 2004): pp. 121–29.

Findlay, Robert, and Stanislaw Wellisz, eds. *Five Small Open Economies*. New York: Oxford University Press, 1993.

Findlay, Trevor. *Cambodia: The Legacy and Lessons of UNTAC*. Oxford: Oxford University Press, 1995.

Fink, Christina. *Living Silence: Burma Under Military Rule*. Bangkok, London and New York: White Lotus and Zed Books, 2001.

Fredholm, Michael. *Burma: Ethnicity and Insurgency*. Westport, CT: Praeger, 1993.

Funston, John. *Malay Politics in Malaysia, A Study of UMNO and Party Islam*. Kuala Lumpur: Heineman Educational Books, 1980.

_____, ed. *Government and Politics in Southeast Asia*. Singapore and London: Institute of Southeast Asian Studies and Zed Books, 2001.

Furnivall, John S. *Netherlands India, A Study of Plural Economy*. Cambridge: Cambridge University Press, 1939; Reprint, 1967.

Geertz, Clifford, ed. *Old Societies and New States: The Quest for Modernity in Asia and Africa*. New York: The Free Press, 1963.

Girling, John L.S. *Thailand: Society and Politics*. Ithaca: Cornell University Press, 1982.

Glosny, Michael A. "Stabilizing the Backyard: Recent Developments in China's Policy Toward Southeast Asia." In Eisenman, Heginbotham, and Mitchell, eds., *China and the Developing World*, pp. 150–86.

Goh, Evelyn. "China in the Mekong River Basin: The Regional Security Implications of Resource Development on the Lancang Jiang." In Caballero-Anthony, Emmers, and Acharya, eds., *Non-Traditional Security in Asia*, pp. 225–46.

Goshal, Baldas, and Jae H. Ku. *Minorities in Cambodia*. London: Minority Rights Group, 1995.

Gottesman, Evan. *Cambodia After the Khmer Rouge: Inside the Politics of Nation Building*. New Haven: Yale University Press, 2002.

Goudineau, Yves. *Laos and Ethnic Minority Cultures: Promoting Heritage*. Paris: UNESCO, 2003.

Guan, Lee Hock. "Affirmative Action in Malaysia," *Southeast Asian Affairs 2005*, pp. 211–28. Singapore: Institute of Southeast Asian Studies, 2005.

Gunn, Geoffrey C. *Language, Power and Ideology in*

Brunei Darussalam. Athens: Ohio University Center for International Studies, 1997.

_____. *Rebellion in Laos: Peasant and Politics in a Colonial Backwater.* Boulder, CO: Westview Press, 1990.

_____. "Rentier Capitalism in Negara Brunei Darussalam," In Hewison, Robison, and Rodan, pp 109–32.

Gunnawatra, Rohan, ed. *Terrorism in the Asia-Pacific: Threat and Response.* Singapore: Eastern Universities Press, 2003.

Haas, Michael. "A Political History." In Haas, ed., *Singapore Puzzle,* pp. 15–38.

_____, ed. *The Singapore Puzzle.* Westport, CT: Praeger, 1999.

Habito, Cielito F. "The Philippines: The Continuing Story of a Crisis-Prone Economy." In *Southeast Asian Affairs 2005,* pp. 313–27. Singapore: Institute of Southeast Asian Studies, 2005.

Hamilton-Merritt, Jane. *Tragic Mountains: The Hmong, the Americans and the Secret Wars of Laos, 1942–1992.* Bloomington: Indiana University Press, 1992.

Hamzah, B.A. *The Oil Sultanate: Political History of Oil in Brunei Darussalam.* Seremban, Malaysia: Mawaddaw Enterprise, 1991.

Heder, Steve. "Hun Sen's Consolidation: Death or Beginning of Reform?" In *Southeast Asian Affairs 2005,* pp. 113–30. Singapore: Institute of Southeast Asian Studies, 2005.

_____, and Judy Ledgerwood, eds. *Propaganda, Politics, and Violence in Cambodia: Democratic Transition under United Nations Peace-keeping.* Armonk, NY: M.E. Sharpe, 1996.

Hedman, Eva Lotta, and John R. Sidel, eds. *Philippine Politics and Society in the Twentieth Century, Colonial Legacies and Post-colonial Trajectories.* London: Routledge, 2000.

Hefner, Robert W. "Social Legacies and Possible Futures." In Bresnan, ed., *Indonesia, the Great Transition,* pp. 75–136.

Hewison, Kevin. "Vietnam in 2006." *Asian Survey,* vol. 47, no. 1 (January-February 2007): pp. 168–74.

_____, ed. *Political Change in Thailand: Democracy and Participation.* London: Routledge, 1997.

_____, Richard Robison, and Garry Rodan, eds. *Southeast Asia in the 1990's: Authoritarianism, Democracy & Capitalism.* St. Leonards, Australia: Allen & Unwin, 1993.

Hicken, Allen. "The Philippines in 2007: Ballots, Budgets, and Bribes." *Asian Survey,* vol. 48, no. 1 (January-February 2008): pp. 75–81.

Hickey, Gerald. *Village in Vietnam.* New Haven: Yale University Press, 1964.

Hill, Hal. *The Indonesian Economy in Crisis.* New York: St. Martin's Press, 1999.

_____. *The Indonesian Economy Since 1966.* Cambridge: Cambridge University Press, 1996.

_____. *The Indonesian Economy.* 2d ed. Cambridge: Cambridge University Press, 2000.

Hilley, John. *Malaysia: Mahathirism, Hegemony and the New Opposition.* London and New York: Zed Books, 2001.

Hlaing, Kyaw Yin. "Myanmar in 2004: Why Military Rule Continues." *Southeast Asian Affairs 2005,* pp. 231–55. Singapore: Institute of Southeast Asian Studies, 2005.

Ho, K.C., Randolph Kluver, and Kenneth C.C. Yang, eds. *Asia.com: Asia Encounters the Internet.* London and New York: RoutledgeCurzon, 2003.

Ho, Khai Leong. *The Politics of Policy-Making in Singapore.* Singapore: Oxford University Press, 2000.

Hodess, Robin, with Tania Inowlocki and Toby Wolfe, eds. *Global Corruption Report, Transparency International.* London: Profile Books, 2003.

Hooker, Virginia Matheson. *A Short History of Malaysia.* Crow's Nest, NSW, Australia: Allen & Unwin, 2003.

Horton, A.V.M. "Brunei in 2004: Window-Dressing an Islamizing Sultanate." *Asian Survey,* vol. 45 (January-February 2005): pp. 180–85.

Houseman, Gerald L. *Researching Indonesia: A Guide to Political Analysis.* Lewiston, NY: Edwin Mellen Press, 2004.

Hughes, Caroline. *The Political Economy of Cambodia's Transition, 1991–2001.* London and New York: RoutledgeCurzon, 2003.

Huntington, Samuel P. *The Clash of Civilizations and the Remaking of the World Order.* New York: Touchstone Books, 1997.

_____. "Will More Countries Become Democratic?" *Political Science Quarterly,* vol. 99, no. 2 (1984): pp. 193–219.

Hussainmiya, B.A. *Sultan Omar Ali Saifuddin III and Britain: The Making of Brunei Darussalam.* Kuala Lumpur: Oxford University Press, 1995.

Hutchcroft, Paul D. "Oligarchs and Cronies in the Philippine State: The Politics of Patrimonial Plunder." *World Politics,* vol. 43 (1991): pp. 414–50.

Jackson, Karl D. *Cambodia 1975–1978, Rendezvous with Death.* Princeton: Princeton University Press, 1989.

Jackson, Peter. *Buddhadasa: A Buddhist Thinker for the Modern World.* Bangkok: Siam Society, 1988.

James, Helen. "Myanmar in 2005: In a Holding Pattern." *Asian Survey,* vol. 46, no. 1 (January-February, 2006): pp. 162–67.

"Justice in Jeopardy: Malaysia 2000." A report by the International Bar Association, the International Court of Justice Centre for the Independence of Judges and Lawyers, and the Commonwealth Lawyers Association. April 5, 2000.

Kahin, George McT. *Nationalism and Revolution in Indonesia.* Ithaca: Cornell University Press, 1952.

_____, ed. *Government and Politics in Southeast Asia.* 2d ed. Ithaca: Cornell University Press, 1964.

Kamm, Henry. *Cambodia: Report from a Stricken Land.* New York: Arcade, 1998.

Karnow, Stanley. *In Our Image: America's Empire in the Philippines.* New York: Random House, 1989.

Kerkvliet, Benedict J., and Resil Mojares, eds. *From Marcos to Aquino: Local Perspectives on Political*

Transition in the Philippines. Manila: Ateneo de Manila University Press, 1991.

Kershaw, Roger. "Brunei: Malay, Monarchical, Microstate." In Funston, ed., *Government and Politics in Southeast Asia,* pp. 1–35.

_____. *Monarchy in South-East Asia: the Faces of Tradition in Transition.* London: Routledge, 2000.

Keyes, Charles F. "Buddhism and National Integration in Thailand." *Journal of Asian Studies,* vol. 30, no. 3 (1971): pp. 551–68.

_____. *Thailand: Buddhist Kingdom as Modern Nation-State.* Bangkok: Duang Kamol, 1989.

Khan, Joel S., ed. *Southeast Asian Identities.* Singapore: Institute of Southest Asian Studies, 1998.

Khanh, Tran. "Ethnic Chinese in Vietnam and their Identity." In Suryadinata, ed., *Ethnic Chinese as Southeast Asians,* pp. 267–92.

Khoo, Boo Teik. *Beyond Mahathir: Malaysian Politics and Its Discontents.* London and New York: Zed Books and Palgrave-St. Martin's Press, 2003.

_____. *Paradoxes of Mahathirism: An Intellectual Biography of Mahathir Mohamad.* Kuala Lumpur: Oxford University Press, 1995.

Kiernan, Ben. *The Pol Pot Regime: Race, Power and Genocide in Cambodia Under the Khmer Rouge, 1975–79.* New Haven: Yale University Press, 1996.

Kingsbury, Damion. "Indonesia: Accomplishments Amidst Challenges." *Asian Survey,* vol. 48, no. 1 (January-February 2008), pp. 93–110.

Kirk, Donald. *Looted, The Philippines After the Bases.* New York: St. Martin's Press, 1998.

Kong, Chiew Seen. "From Overseas Chinese to Chinese Singaporeans." In Suryadinata, ed., *Ethnic Chinese as Southeast Asians,* pp. 211–27.

Koon, Heng Pek. *Chinese Politics in Malaysia: A History of the Malaysian Chinese Association.* Singapore: Oxford University Press, 1988.

Krinks, Peter. *The Economy of the Philippines, Elites, Inequalities and Economic Restructuring.* London and New York: Routledge, 2002.

Krishner, Bernard, and Seth Meixner. *A Vision for New Asia.* Selangor Darul Ehsan, Malaysia: Pelanduk, 2003.

Kyi, Aung San Suu. *Letters from Burma.* London and New York: Penguin Books, 1997.

Leake, David, Jr. *Brunei, The Modern Southeast Asian Sultanate.* Kuala Lumpur: Forum, 1990.

Lebar, Frank M., Gerald C. Hickey, and John K. Musgrave. *Ethnic Groups of Mainland Southeast Asia.* New Haven: Human Relations Area Files Press, 1964.

Ledgerwood, Judy, and John Vijghen. "Decision-making in Rural Khmer Villages." In Judy Ledgerwood, ed., *Cambodia Emerges from the Past: Eight Essays,* pp. 109–50.

_____, ed. *Cambodia Emerges from the Past: Eight Essays.* Dekalb: Center for Southeast Asian Studies, Northern Illinois University, 2002.

Lee, Kam Hing. "Malaysian Chinese: Seeking Identity in Wawasan 2020." In Suryadinata, ed., *Ethnic Chinese as Southeast Asians,* pp. 72–114.

Lee, Khoon Choy. *A Fragile Nation: The Indonesian Crisis.* Singapore: World Scientific Publishing, 1999.

Lee, Kuan Yew. *The Singapore Story: Memoirs of Lee Kuan Yew.* Singapore: Times Editions, 1998.

Leifer, Michael. *Dictionary of the Modern Politics of South-east Asia.* London: Routledge, 1996.

_____. *Singapore's Foreign Policy, Coping with Vulnerability.* London and New York: Routledge, 2000.

Liddle, R. William. *Leadership and Culture in Indonesian Politics.* Sydney, Australia: Allen & Unwin, 1996.

_____, and Saiful Mujani. "Indonesia in 2004, The Rise of Susilo Bambang Yudhoyono." *Asian Survey,* vol. 45, no. 1 (January-February 2005): pp. 119–26.

_____, and _____. "Indonesia in 2005, A New Multiparty Presidential Democracy." *Asian Survey,* vol. 46, no. 1 (January-February 2006): pp. 132–39.

Lincoln, Edward J. *East Asian Economic Regionalism.* New York: Council on Foreign Relations; Washington, D.C.: Brookings Institution Press, 2004.

Lintner, Bertil. *Burma in Revolt: Opium and Insurgency Since 1948.* Boulder, CO: Westview Press, 1994.

Low, Linda. *The Political Economy of a City-State: Government-Made Singapore.* Singapore: Oxford University Press, 1998.

_____. *Singapore: Towards a Developed Status.* Singapore: Oxford University Press, 1999.

_____. "Singapore's Bilateral Trading Arrangements in the Context of East Asian Regionalism: State of Play, Issues, and Prospects." In *Southeast Asian Affairs 2004,* pp. 239–54. Singapore: Institute of Southeast Asian Studies, 2004.

Luong, Hy V. "Vietnam in 2005." *Asian Survey,* vol. 46, no. 1 (January-February 2006): pp. 150–51.

_____. "Vietnam in 2006." *Asian Survey,* vol. 47, no. 1 (January-February 2007): pp. 168–74.

Marsot, Alain G. *The Chinese Community in Vietnam Under the French.* San Francisco: The Edwin Mellen Press, 1993.

Martinez, Patricia A. "Malaysia in 2004: Abdullah Badawi Defines His Leadership." *Southeast Asian Affairs, 2005,* pp. 191–210. Singapore: Institute of Southeast Asian Studies, 2005.

Maung, Maung. *The 1988 Uprising in Burma.* Monograph 49. New Haven: Yale University Southeast Asia Studies, 1999.

McCargo, Duncan, and Ukrist Pathmanand. *The Thaksinization of Thailand.* Copenhagen: Nordic Institute of Asian Studies, 2005.

_____, ed. *Rethinking Vietnam.* London and New York: RoutledgeCurzon, 2004.

McHale, Shawn Frederick. *Print and Power: Confucianism, Communism and Buddhism in the Making of Modern Vietnam.* Honolulu: University of Hawai'i Press, 2004.

McVey, Ruth, ed. *Money and Power in Provincial Thailand.* Honolulu: University of Hawai'i Press, 2000.

Meng, Ng Shui. "Social Development in the Lao People's Democratic Republic." In Zasloff and Unger, eds. *Laos, Beyond the Revolution.* pp. 173–79.

Miller, John H. *Modern East Asia: An Introductory History*. Armonk, NY: M.E. Sharpe, 2007.

Milne, R.S., and Diane K. Mauzy. *Malaysian Politics Under Mahathir*. London and New York: Routledge, 1999.

_____, and _____. *Singapore: The Legacy of Lee Kuan Yew*. Boulder, CO: Westview Press, 1990.

Moffat, Abbot Low. *Mongkut, the King of Siam*. Ithaca: Cornell University Press, 1961.

Mohamad, Mahathir. *The Malay Dilemma*. Singapore: Federal Publications, 1970.

Montesano, Michael J. "Vietnam in 2004: A Country Hanging in the Balance." In *Southeast Asian Affairs 2005*, pp. 407–21. Singapore: Institute of Southeast Asian Studies, 2005.

Morell, David, and Chai-Anan Samudavanija. *Political Conflict in Thailand: Reform, Reaction, Revolution*. Cambridge, MA: Oelgeschlager, Gunn and Hain, 1981.

Muego, Benjamin N. "The Philippines in 2004, A Gathering Storm." *Southeast Asian Affairs 2005*, pp. 293–312. Singapore: Institute of Southeast Asian Studies, 2005.

Murphy, Ann Marie. "Indonesia and the World." In Bresnan, ed., *Indonesia, The Great Transition*, pp. 239–95.

Nadeau, Kathleen M. *Liberation Theology in the Philippines: Faith in a Revolution*. Westport, CT: Praeger, 2002.

Nair, S. *Islam in Malaysian Foreign Policy*. London: Routledge, 1997.

Narine, Shaun. *Explaining ASEAN: Regionalism in Southeast Asia*. Boulder, CO: Lynne Rienner, 2002.

National Economic Development Agency. *Medium-term Philippine Development Plan 2004–2010*. Manila, 2004.

Navaratnam, Ramon V. *Malaysia's Economic Sustainability*. Selangor Darul Ehsan, Malaysia: Pelanduk Publications, 2002.

Neher, Clark D. *Southeast Asia in the New International Era*. 4th ed. Boulder, CO: Westview Press, 2002.

Ngor, Haing, with Roger Warner. *Survival in the Killing Fields*. New York: Carroll & Graf, 2003.

Nguyen, Manh Hung. "Vietnam: Facing the Challenge of Integration." In *Southeast Asian Affairs 2004*, pp. 297–311. Singapore: Institute of Southeast Asian Studies, 2004.

Nguyen, Phuong An. "Pursuing Success in Present-Day Vietnam." In McCargo, ed., *Rethinking Vietnam*, pp. 165–76.

Ockey, James. *Making Democracy*. Honolulu: University of Hawai'i Press, 2004.

Osborne, Milton. *Exploring Southeast Asia: A Traveller's History of the Region*. New South Wales, Australia: Allen & Unwin, 2002.

_____. *The French Presence in Cochinchina and Cambodia*. Ithaca: Cornell University Press, 1969.

_____. *The Mekong: Turbulent Past, Uncertain Future*. New York: Grove Press, 2000.

_____. *Sihanouk, Prince of Light, Prince of Darkness*. Honolulu: University of Hawai'i Press, 1994.

Pangestu, Mari. "Southeast Asian Regional and International Cooperation." In Weatherbee, ed., *International Relations in Southeast Asia*, pp. 187–217.

Peou, Sorpong, ed. *Cambodia, Change and Continuity in Contemporary Politics*. Aldershot, UK, and Burlington, VT: Ashgate, 2001.

_____. *Intervention and Change in Cambodia, Towards Democracy?* New York, Bangkok and Singapore: St. Martin's Press, Silkworm, and Institute of Southeast Asian Studies, 2000.

Pholsena, Vatthana. "Laos in 2004. Towards Subregional Integration: 10 Years On." In *Southeast Asian Affairs 2005*, pp. 173–88. Singapore: Institute of Southeast Asian Studies, 2005.

Phongpaichit, Pasuk, and Chris Baker. *Thailand, Economy and Politics*. Oxford: Oxford University Press, 2002.

_____, and _____. *Thaksin and the Business of Politics in Thailand*. Chiang Mai: Silkworm Press, 2004.

_____, and Sungsidh Piriyarangsan. *Corruption and Democracy in Thailand*. Bangkok: Political Economy Centre, Chulalongkorn University, 1994.

Phuong, Ta Huu. "Comments on 'Ethnic Chinese in Vietnam.'" In Suryadinata, ed., *Ethnic Chinese as Southeast Asians*, pp. 293–95.

Pollack, Jonathan D. "The United States and Asia in 2003: All Quiet on the Eastern Front?" *Asian Survey*, vol. 44, no. 1 (January-February 2004): pp. 1–13.

Poole, Fred, and Max Vanzi. *Revolution in the Philippines*. New York: McGraw-Hill, 1984.

Poole, Peter A. "Communism and Ethnic Conflict in Cambodia, 1960–1975." In Brown and Zasloff, eds., *Communism in Indochina*, pp. 249–55.

_____. *Eight Presidents and Indochina*. 2d. ed. New York: Krieger, 1988.

_____. *The Vietnamese in Thailand: A Historical Perspective*. Ithaca: Cornell University Press, 1970.

_____, ed. *Indochina: Perspectives for Reconciliation*. Athens: Ohio University Center for International Studies, 1975.

Porter, Gareth. *Vietnam: The Politics of Bureaucratic Socialism*. Ithaca: Cornell University Press, 1993.

Pye, Lucien W. "Political Science and the Crisis of Authoritarianism." *American Political Science Review*, vol. 84, no. 1, pp. 3–19.

Quah, Jon S.T. "Singapore." In Funston, ed., *Government and Politics in Southeast Asia*, pp. 281–327.

Quinn-Judge, Sophie. "Rethinking the History of the Vietnamese Communist Party." In McCargo, ed., *Rethinking Vietnam*, pp. 27–39.

Ricklefs, M.C. *A History of Modern Indonesia, c. 1300 to the Present*. Bloomington: Indiana University Press, 1981.

Riggs, Fred W. *Thailand: Modernization of a Bureaucratic Polity*. Honolulu: East-West Center Press, 1966.

Rivera, Temario C. "The Philippines in 2004: New Mandate, Daunting Problems." *Asian Survey,* vol. 2005, no. 1 (January-February 2005): pp. 127–33.

Robinson, W. Courtland. "Laotian Refugees in Thailand: The Thai and U.S. Response, 1975–1988." In Zasloff and Unger, eds., *Laos: Beyond the Revolution,* pp. 215–40.

Rodan, Garry. "Class Transformations and Political Tensions." In Rodan, Hewison, and Robison, eds., *The Political Economy of South-East Asia,* pp. 25–50.

_____. "Singapore in 2004: Long-Awaited Leadership Transition." *Asian Survey,* vol. 45, no. 1 (January-February 2005): pp. 140–45.

_____. "Singapore in 2005: 'Vibrant and Cosmopolitan' without Political Pluralism." *Asian Survey,* vol. 46, no. 1 (January-February 2006): pp.180–86.

_____, Kevin Hewison, and Richard Robison, eds. *The Political Economy of South-East Asia: Markets, Power and Contestation.* 3d ed. Victoria, Australia: Oxford University Press, 2006.

Rosenberg, D. A., ed. *Marcos and Martial Law in the Philippines.* Ithaca: Cornell University Press, 1979.

Ross, Russell R., ed. *Cambodia: a Country Study.* 3d ed. Washington, D.C.: Federal Research Division, Library of Congress, 1990.

Rotberg, Robert I., ed. *Burma: Prospects for a Democratic Future.* Washington, D.C.: Brookings Institution, 1998.

Rovillos, Raymundo D., and Daisy N. Morales. *Indigenous Peoples/Ethnic Minorities and Poverty Reduction, Philippines.* Manila: Asian Development Bank, 2002.

Salazar, Lorraine. "The Philippines: Crisis, Controversies, and Economic Resilience." In *Southeast Asian Affairs 2005,* 227–44. Singapore: Institute of Southeast Asian Studies, 2006.

Sandhu, Kernial S., and Paul Wheatley, eds. *Management of Success: The Moulding of Modern Singapore.* Singapore: Institute of Southeast Asian Studies, 1989.

Saunders, G. *A History of Brunei.* London: RoutledgeCurzon, 2002.

Selth, Andrew. *Burma's Armed Forces: Power Without Glory.* Norwalk, CT: EastBridge, 2002.

Seow, Francis T. "The Judiciary." In Haas, ed., *Singapore Puzzle,* pp. 107–124.

Silverstein, Josef. *Burmese Politics: The Dilemma of National Unity.* New Brunswick: Rutgers University Press, 1980.

_____, ed. *Independent Burma at Forty Years: Six Assessments.* Ithaca: Cornell University Southeast Asia Program, 1989.

Singh, Ranjit. *Brunei, 1839–1983: The Problem of Political Survival.* Oxford and Singapore: Oxford University Press, 1994.

Skinner, William G. *Chinese Society in Thailand: An Analytical History.* Ithaca: Cornell University Press, 1957.

Smith, Daniel M. *The American Diplomatic Experience.* Boston: Houghton Mifflin, 1972.

Smith, Martin. *Burma: Insurgency and the Politics of Insurgency.* London: Zed Books, 1999.

Soe, Myint. *Burma File.* Singapore: Marshall Cavendish Academic, 2004.

Steinberg, David I. *Burma: A Socialist Nation of Southeast Asia.* Boulder, CO: Westview Press, 1982.

_____. *Burma: The State of Myanmar.* Washington, DC: Georgetown University Press, 2001.

Steinberg, David J. *The Philippines: A Singular and Plural Place.* Boulder, CO: Westview Press, 1982.

Stern, Lewis M. *Defense Relations Between the United States and Vietnam.* Jefferson, NC: McFarland, 2005.

_____. *Renovating the Vietnamese Communist Party, Nguyen Van Linh and the Programme for Organizational Reform, 1987–91.* New York and Singapore: St. Martin's Press and Institute of Southeast Asian Studies, 1993.

Stuart-Fox, Martin. *Buddhist Kingdom, Marxist State: The Making of Modern Laos.* Bangkok: White Lotus Press, 1996.

_____. *A History of Laos.* Cambridge: Cambridge University Press, 1997.

_____. *Laos: Politics, Economics and Society.* London and Boulder, CO: Francis Pinter and Lynne Rienner Publishers, 1986.

_____. "Laos: Toward Subregional Integration." In *Southeast Asian Affairs 1995,* pp. 179–86. Singapore: Institute of Southeast Asian Studies, 1995.

Suryadinata, Leo. "Indonesia: The Year of the Democratic Election." *Southeast Asian Affairs 2005,* pp. 133–49. Singapore: Institute of Southeast Asian Studies, 2005.

_____. *Indonesian Foreign Policy Under Suharto.* Singapore: Times Academic Books, 1996.

_____. *Interpreting Indonesia Politics.* Singapore: Times Academic Press, 1998.

_____, ed. *Ethnic Chinese as Southeast Asians.* Singapore and New York: Institute of Southeast Asian Studies and St. Martin's Press, 1997.

Tai, Ta Van. *The Vietnamese Tradition of Human Rights.* Berkeley: Institute of East Asian Studies, University of California, 1988.

Tan, Mely G. "The Ethnic Chinese in Indonesia: Issues of Identity." In Suryadinata, ed., *Ethnic Chinese as Southeast Asians,* pp. 33–65.

Tan, See Seng and Amitav Acharya, eds. *Asia-Pacific Security Cooperation.* Armonk, NY: M.E. Sharpe, 2004.

Taylor, Robert H. "Myanmar: Roadmap to Where?" In *Southeast Asian Affairs 2004,* pp. 171–84. Singapore: Institute of Southeast Asian Studies, 2005.

_____. *The State of Burma.* London: Hurst, 1987.

_____, ed. *Political Economy Under Military Rule.* London: Hurst; New York: St. Martin's Press, 2000.

Tellis, Ashley J., and Michael Wills, eds. *Strategic Asia 2004–2005: Confronting Terrorism in the Pursuit of Power.* Seattle: National Bureau of Asian Research, 2004.

Thambipillai, Pushpa. "Brunei Darussalam: Consolidating the Polity." In *Southeast Asian Affairs 2006,* pp. 57–70. Singapore: Institute for Southeast Asian Studies, 2006.

Than, Mya. "Ethnic Chinese in Myanmar and Their Identity." In Suryadinata, ed., *Ethnic Chinese as Southeast Asians*, pp. 115–46.

Thant Myint-U. *The River of Lost Footsteps, Histories of Burma*. New York: Farrar, Straus and Giroux, 2006.

Thayer, Carlyle A. "Vietnam in 2001, The Ninth Party Congress and After." *Asian Survey,* vol. 42, no. 1 (January-February 2002): pp. 81–89.

_____, and Ramses Amer, eds. *Vietnamese Foreign Policy in Transition*. New York and Singapore: St. Martin's Press and Institute of Southeast Asian Studies, 1999.

Tongzon, Jose L. *The Economies of Southeast Asia*, 2d ed. Cheltenham, UK, and Northampton, MA: Edward Elgar, 2002.

Tran, Thi Thu Trang. "Vietnam's Rural Transformation: Information, Knowledge and Diversification." In McCargo, ed., *Rethinking Vietnam*.

Tran, Van Hoa, ed. *Sectoral Analysis of Trade, Investment and Business in Vietnam*. New York and London: St. Martin's and Macmillan, 1999.

Trocki, Carl A. *Singapore: Wealth, Power and the Culture of Control*. New York: Routledge, 2006.

Truong, Nhu Tang, with David Chanoff and Doan Van Toai. *A Vietcong Memoir*. New York: Vintage Books, 1985.

U.S. Department of State. "Background Notes" (published at intervals on most countries). Washington, D.C.

Van, Dang Nghiem, Chu Thai Son, and Luu Hung. *Ethnic Minorities in Vietnam*. Hanoi: The Gioi Press, 2000.

Van Akadie, Brian, and Raymond Mallon. *Viet Nam: A Transition Tiger?* Canberra: Asia Pacific Press at Australian National University, 2003.

Van Chi, Hoang. *From Colonialism to Communism, A Case History of North Vietnam*. New York: Praeger, 1964.

Vatikiotis, Michael. *Indonesian Politics Under Suharto: The Rise and Fall of the New Order*. 3d ed. London and New York: Routledge, 1998.

Vella, Walter F. *The Impact of the West on Government in Thailand*. Berkeley and Los Angeles: University of California Press, 1955.

Weatherbee, Donald E. *The International Relations of Southeast Asia*. Lanham, MD: Rowman & Littlefield, 2005.

Weiner, Myron, and Samuel P. Huntington, eds. *Understanding Political Development*. Boston: Little, Brown, 1987.

Welaratna, Usha. *Beyond the Killing Fields: Voices of Nine Cambodian Survivors in America*. Stanford: Stanford University Press, 1993.

Weller, Marc, ed. *Democracy and Politics in Burma: A Collection of Documents*. Manerplaw: National Coalition Government of the Union of Burma, 1993.

Welsh, Bridget. "Malaysia in 2004, Out of Mahathir's Shadow?" *Asian Survey,* vol. 45, no.1. (January-February 2005): pp. 153–160.

_____. "Tears and Fears: Tun Mahathir's Last Hurrah," *Southeast Asian Affairs 2005,* pp. 139–55. Singapore: Institute of Southeast Asian Studies, 2005.

Wischermann, Joerg. "Vietnam in the Era of *Doi Moi,* Issue-Oriented Organizations and Their Relationship to the Government." *Asian Survey,* vol. 43, no. 6 (November-December 2003): pp. 867–889.

Worcester, Dean. *The Philippines, Past and Present*. New York: Macmillan, 1930.

World Bank. *East Asia and Pacific Update*. Washington, D.C., April 2007.

_____. *The East Asian Miracle: Economic Growth and Public Policy*. Oxford: Oxford University Press, 1993.

_____. *Philippines: From Crisis to Opportunity*. Washington, D.C., 1999.

Wurfel, David. *Filipino Politics: Development and Decay*. Ithaca, NY: Cornell University Press, 1991.

_____. "The Philippines." In Kahin, ed., *Government and Politics of Southeast Asia,* pp. 679–769.

Wyatt, David K. *Thailand, A Short History*. New Haven: Yale University Press, 1984.

Zasloff, Joseph J. "Political Constraints on Development in Laos." In Zasloff and Unger, eds. *Laos: Beyond the Revolution.* pp. 3–40.

_____, ed. *Postwar Indochina: Old Enemies and New Allies*. Washington, D.C.: Center for the Study of Foreign Affairs, U.S. Department of State, 1988.

_____, and MacAlister Brown, eds. *Communism in Indochina*. London and Lexington, MA: D.C. Heath, 1975.

_____, and Leonard Unger, eds. *Laos: Beyond the Revolution*. New York: St. Martin's Press, 1991.

INDEX

205